Steel Do[...]

by

Matthew Bracey

Matthew Bracey © 2020

This is a work of creative nonfiction. The events are portrayed to the best of my memory.
While the story in this book is true, some names and identifying details have been changed to protect the privacy of the people and places involved.
I regret any unintentional harm resulting from the publishing and marketing of Steel Dogs.

All rights reserved, including the right to reproduce this book, or portions thereof in any form. No part of this text may be reproduced, transmitted, downloaded, decompiled, reverse engineered, or stored, in any form or introduced into any information storage and retrieval system, in any form or by any means, whether electronic or mechanical without the express written permission of the author.

ISBN: 978-0-244-54400-3

To Dad

Preface

I went on an adventure, and my dad was part of that adventure. At the time it felt like a mistake, but now I realise it was life. After all, bad choices make for interesting stories.

On my dad's deathbed, we sat together looking out of the hospital window. Before us, we saw a sea of pebbles and stones. At that moment, we both felt at peace because pebbles and stones hold so many memories for us. His final words to me, spoken with the only strength he had left, were, "Matt, son. You have been a good boy. Do me one last honour." He paused for breath as I waited. My dad, a strong man in good health, was in great pain.

The words he desperately wanted to get out held great meaning. He went on. "You must tell our story because, once I'm gone, you'll be the last of us.

This story cannot be lost forever. Please promise me you will write about it, and that you won't hold back. It must be finished in full." I had questions, of course, and even reluctance. Even so, this was not the time for questions, just listening.

My dad was the wisest man I've ever been privileged to know, and his final words to me struck a chord. He finished with the most powerful answer imaginable to all my questions, as if he knew I would be in turmoil. "They will forgive us. Bad publicity is good publicity."

He paused once more, taking deep breaths, and his eyes were watering. "And, in the end, the love you take is equal to the love you make." My beloved dad closed his eyes, and later that night, he died in my mum's arms. And now, I tell our story.

{ MATTHEW BRACEY }

Chapter 1 – God's Own Junkyard

As much as it might not make sense for now (don't worry – it will), God's Own Junkyard is kind of where this story both begins and ends. Of course, this isn't a reference to some immense, heavenly junkyard in the sky where the big man himself sends all the naughty angels for a time-out session (wait, are angels ever naughty?) and discards all his unwanted bibles and broken halos. No, that's not what's meant at all. But halos are a nice little hint as to the real God's Own Junkyard. Think bright!

Anyone true East Londoner knows about this fantastic place – one that would bring light into even the darkest of souls. There's no choice really. It might literally be the brightest place any human could ever encounter, outshining any pathetic little halo. A vast collection of neons, both old and new, as well as iconic signs salvaged from a whole host of films across the years, God's Own Junkyard is a fantastic neon museum with a history that spans four generations of the renowned Bracey clan.

First established back in 1978, the museum's first home was in Walthamstow's Vallentin Road, opposite a company called Electro Signs. Spoiler alert: there's a tale behind Electro Signs, but that's all you're getting to know for now. Anyone from East London? Right, well you'll have heard a good few stories about Vallentin Road. In September 2018, *The Sun* described it as the "most dangerous street in Britain" thanks to a string of crimes over the past couple of years, including "murder, arson and sex attacks" and thanks to the fact that it has "become the bloody centre of territory controlled by a gang – running a ruthless campaign of drug dealing". Phil and Kirsty from Channel 4's *Location, Location, Location* would have an absolute field day in this stretch of road. How the hell would they put a positive spin on that? Lovely window boxes eh, Phil? Naa – I don't think that would fly, love.

Vallentin Road – which is a normal-looking, mostly residential street in East London, lined with Victorian terraced houses and blocks of flats put up in the 70s and 80s – wasn't so bad back when God's Own Junkyard set up its nest there. At first, the business was literally just a junkyard that sat right in front of the railway tracks running through Wood Street Station, along – just not quite parallel to – Vallentin Road, and towards Walthamstow Central Station.

A massive array of signs was stuffed into that junkyard, left, right and centre, little colourful snippets of ideas from all over the world and all areas of life peeking out here and there. It wouldn't be altogether unreasonable to describe it as a neon graveyard. By day, the Virgin Mary would be sitting there in the outside space in front of the United States Congress and an old cinema sign, all to the right of the Chinese symbols of a takeaway restaurant and a rusty pile of car parts. By night, the place was transformed into a veritable treasure trove of beaming fluorescence. Barber Shop, Queen of Diamonds, Find Love Upstairs, Club, Byzantium, Girls Girls Girls, Circus, Hotel, Fun & Thrills, Yeehaa – those were just some of the words that could be seen blazing from the yard, the total antithesis of the gloomy, dark and lifeless sky in the background. It was (no pun intended) electric. And the workshop was just as outlandish; a real multicoloured feast on the eyes, to say the least.

Until he died in 2014, God's Own Junkyard was run by the legendary, larger-than-life Chris Bracey. There, amongst all those signs, was exactly where he belonged. Everything about it just felt right. The place, if it had been conjured up by someone else, would have been…hmm, how to put it…a bit shit really! Alas, it turned out that the days of God's Own Junkyard at Vallentin Road were numbered. About 2013, the council, determined to build a block of flats, issued Chris an eviction notice and punted him and his beloved signs out. Fear not though as this didn't spell the end of his dream. The business just moved a few streets around the corner to its current location in Ravenswood Industrial Estate, just off Walthamstow's Shernhall Street. It was actually the best thing that could have happened because God's Own Junkyard has thrived there, nestled among a few other businesses including a couple of breweries that pump out a beautiful, hoppy scent. Pint anyone?

God's Own Junkyard was born from an idea; a dream. In the 70s Chris and his wife had grafted away tirelessly to collect signs from all over the place. They were seen as mere junk, not worthy of keeping and destined for nowhere else but some sad scrapheap. But the couple saw beyond all the rust and dilapidation, spying something in all this supposed trash. They saw a vision that would realise itself, bit by bit, over the years, the fruits of which can still be seen in Walthamstow and little hints of which can be seen all over the world in some way or another.

Chris and Linda had never comprehended how iconic these signs, as well as the ones that Chris would come to craft himself, would be in later years. At the bare bones of it, they simply loved the signs and wanted to save them. Rarely missing an opportunity to salvage some poor bugger of a sign, the pair went about their mission with zeal, and the collection grew exponentially. Yet, they didn't give much thought to the items that they were gathering up, instead stashing them away for safekeeping and rarely coming back to look at them. While these signs sat in storage, patiently waiting for their big comeback and their debut back into society, Chris and Linda were piecing together the building blocks of their vision, figuring out how they could display these beauties to the public and without charging a bomb – or anything at all – for the pleasure of doing so. As opportunities often do, one fell in front of their feet when a unit and yard became available. And so, God's Own Junkyard was born.

The name was inspired by a book written by the late Peter Blake, a German-American architect and author, called *God's Own Junkyard: The Planned Destruction of America's Landscape*. The book, supposedly written in fury, examined the collusion of commerce, government, and public indifference, all of which Blake felt to be polluting the American landscape. The link to Chris and Linda's idea might seem a little tenuous, but the author was arguing that he hated those who had spoiled America for private gain, scattering reminders of their commercialism and greed all over the country. In particular, he launched a vitriolic attack on all the signs used throughout the process, referring to cinemas, petrol stations, casinos, diners and many more types of business. Blake believed that these signs "are turning God's own country into God's Own Junkyard". When the couple read this, they immediately knew that's exactly what they had on their hands: a load of signs that belong in God's Own Junkyard. Chris said, "If God had a junkyard, then it would be full up with all this kind of stuff; these neons and icons."

Using the title of Blake's book felt almost poetic for the couple in a way. The guy had been lamenting about how all these signs were a bad thing, that they spoiled the country he lived in like they were some sort of scourge. But Chris and Linda were able to give a new lease of life to stuff that had cost a lot of money to be made. Blake might have thought they were ugly, but surely a man so against commercialism and the greed it entails would support a project that involved reclaiming discarded material objects for nothing more than public enjoyment, for their aesthetic value and not for profitable gain. He was, after all, an architect, and two of the key things with which architecture is concerned are aesthetics and enjoyment. To the couple, it felt like they were honouring the author and his ideals.

Chris hadn't just made a name for himself by creating God's Own Junkyard and filling it with salvaged signs, but one as a neon light artist. Over the years, his own signs – made for artistic rather than commercial value – became more and more well-known and celebrated. The art world was finally excited about Chris's work, and he was now recognised as the neon light artist that he was. Things were going so well that he had to find himself an agent. He went for one based in Los Angeles who helped him arrange exhibitions all over the world, including the United Kingdom, Russia, India, Singapore and the United States. This really got Chris's name out there, helping to take his art to another level altogether. His pieces still sell today for huge sums of money. Back in 2011, for example, his God Save the Queen piece sold for £21,250. The original estimate of the piece – a heart featuring the Union Jack as a backdrop, with God Save the Queen in the foreground – had been considerably lower at £18,000. Chris became known under many guises, but the most popular of these were "The Neon Man" and "The Master of Glow".

It's never simple breaking into the art world for any artist. A lucky break came Chris's way in 2005 when renowned photographer David LaChappelle commissioned him to produce thirteen pieces for the window displays at London department store Selfridges. He worked with David for six months, helping to perfect his vision. The task was less than simple for a couple of reasons, one of which was LaChappelle's long absences due to other work commitments in Los Angeles or New York. However, things got there in the end. The window displays denoted the sleazier side of Las Vegas to London's shoppers. Given how God's Own Junkyard got its name, this was right up Chris and Linda's street. Thankfully, both David and the management team at Selfridges were delighted with the end product, and the company has continued to work with the department store on visual merchandising since then.

Chris's work has appeared in an incredible array of television shows and Hollywood blockbusters. Fans of the popular BBC crime drama *Luther*, for example, might remember one episode of the series that features a chase scene involving DCI John Luther (played by the incredible Idris Elba). The show's cameras whizzed past an eclectic mixture of old signs and garish neon creations, and any viewer would be forgiven for thinking that this was something that had been put together by set designers. Unfortunately, they'd be wrong, as this was God's Own Junkyard itself.

If you take a trip along to Shernhall Street – which you should, even if just for the killer Rolling Scones café at God's Own Junkyard – you'll find, in pride of place, a large neon rainbow sign. Sound familiar? Well, that's likely because it came from the last film that Stanley Kubrick worked on before he passed away, the mystery-thriller *Eyes Wide Shut*. Just one illustration of the repeated rainbow imagery in the film – purportedly nodding to the Illuminati – the sign sat above the entrance to a costume shop in a scene with Dr. William Harford (played by none other than Tom Cruise). Working on *Eyes Wide Shut* was such a privilege for Chris because Kubrick was one of his biggest idols. Chris was fascinated by the techniques used by the director, including the use of slow, protracted scenes, extreme camera angles, extreme wide-angle lenses, long tracking shots, extreme coldness and the use of natural light. Chris's work has appeared in loads of other big titles too, like *Tomorrow Never Dies, Mission Impossible, Batman, Blade Runner, Dark Night, Tomb Raider, Byzantium, Charlie and the Chocolate Factory* (the Tim Burton version, that is), and countless others.

So, this story begins with God's Own Junkyard because it was the dream of one of its protagonists, Chris Bracey. It was the point to which everything was leading, in some form or another. This story ends with God's Own Junkyard too, not because the place doesn't exist anymore, but because it's what Chris left behind when he departed from this world in 2014. It's his legacy! As famous as God's Own Junkyard may be, the history of the Bracey family business stretches further back than this much-loved icon. Chris's dream was built upon the successes of his father Richard, who established the family business back in 1952. And Chris only managed to realise his dream with a lot of help along the way, not just from Richard and Linda, but also from his son Matthew, among countless others. You'll hear more about Matthew in due course, but let's just say that this half-unlucky, half-jammy sod made the growth of the business pretty interesting. His entrepreneurial spirit would eventually take him and his dad across the world to China, chasing a million quid and giving Chris one final, crazy sunset ride before he left the world. This story is a shit sandwich, in essence. The two bits of bread are Chris's dream and that dream comes to fruition. The filling is the unimaginable shit that went down in China. Before getting to that, you need to understand the first bit of bread.

Chapter 2 – Richard Bracey (The Grandfather)

Born in Wales, one of five tough nut uncles and a sister, Richard cast his own dreams and desires aside as he found himself doing what his father and uncles had done before him: working down the mines. Falling into the same line of work as your father – and even your grandfather – was common back midway through the twentieth century. And so was working down the mines if you happened to come from Wales. Richard's cousins all followed suit too.

Richard spent his days hidden away, toiling in the dank, cold mines of the Black Mountains. Strewn across sections of Powys and Monmouthshire in the southeast part of Wales and stretching across the border with England into Herefordshire, this cluster of hills has been thought of as majestic to external observers for years. Highly popular with walkers and ramblers thanks to the stunning views from the numerous ridge trails, what lay beneath was anything but stunning. Day after day Richard turned up to work, extracting tonne after tonne of coal. For years he suffered through this life, one that he despised immensely, one that entailed days so long they felt like they would never end, one that meant the inhalation of several different toxic fumes, one that sent him home each night laced from head to toe in filth, one that meant a risk of death that soon followed after breakfast each morning. For most people today, for whom going deep into London's underground system is bad enough, such a life is unimaginable. The existence of most youngsters these days is highly privileged compared with what Richard endured as a young man. With all the whining you hear from millennials today about how crap their lives are, it really makes you wonder how they'd fare down those mines. Anyhow, complaining about millennials and how they expect everything to be handed to them on a silver platter could fill a whole book on its own.

Luckily for Richard, fate had something else in store for him, helped along by his own strength and determination. Such a length of time working in the dark, black filth of the coal face had chipped away at his spirit little by little until he couldn't tolerate it for a second longer. Deciding that enough was enough, and unable to bear the darkness, Richard desperately sought a state of being and a career that would bring light into his life.

He wasn't a materialistic man, not that he'd have had the money to be one even if he wanted to be, so he had very few belongings. He packed them up in a pair of tatty, brown leather suitcases that he'd swiped from his parents' attic, one buckle broken on each, and organised transportation out of his little Welsh village. Bound for the Big Smoke, off he went by horse and cart to begin the next chapter of his life. Of course, he was sad to wave goodbye to his family, but other than that all that he left behind were bad memories and a couple of items that fell out of his half-shut suitcases into the muddy road. The driver had been a grumpy old git, so he hadn't dared ask him to stop to rescue them.

On arrival in London in the late 40s, seeking employment in the world of light, he couldn't have chosen brighter lights to work with if he tried. Talk about going from one extreme to the other. With all the chat about neon lighting until this point, it's obvious that he started working with…you guessed it…NEON. Essentially, he decided that he was going to come out. Oh, hang on, it's not what you're thinking. No, no, he didn't come out of the closet. He'd been in the bloody mines, not Narnia. He came out into the light you plonkers; more specifically, out of the dark and into the light.

Incidentally, "Out of the Dark Into the Light" is the title of a neon piece that Chris crafted a while back in honour of his dad. The creation – which features "Out of the Dark" in unlit black script and "Into the Light" in white neon lighting (the reasons for which go without saying) with touches of blue, red and purple – was one of many presented in his first ever UK solo show at Scream Gallery in London's stylish Mayfair area.

Training as an electrician, Richard found a job at Power Neon, an established and experienced neon sign making company. His work there permitted him to learn the trade and master it himself. By all accounts it wasn't an easy trade to pick up, but the effort and time investment required to get to the level of skill he eventually acquired was made worth it by the vibrancy of the environment he was immersed in daily.

It may come as a surprise to many people that neon signs were around as far back as the 40s. Neon is actually a chemical element with the symbol Ne and the atomic number 10, for any science nerds out there who like the specifics. Discovered in 1889 by Scottish chemist William Ramsay, neon – named after the Greek word "neo" or "new" – wasn't used for the purposes of lighting until 1904. At that time, French engineer and inventor Georges Claude began to make illuminated tubes, combining the work of Ramsay and two others. The first was glassblower and physicist Heinrich Geissler, who had invented the "Geissler tube", a gas discharge tube used to demonstrate the principles of electrical glow discharge. The second was electrical engineer and inventor Daniel McFarlan Moore, who had come up with the "Moore lamp", an extension of the Geissler tube, the first commercially viable light source based on gas discharges rather than incandescence, and the predecessor to both neon and fluorescent lighting as they are known today. The first demonstration of a large neon light was much later at the 1920 Paris Motor Show. This signalled the dawn of the neon age, with neon lighting used widely in commercial advertising thereafter. So, there you have it, neon as a source of light has been kicking about for much longer than you might have expected. You learn something new every day.

While being stuck in the dirty mines of the Welsh Black Mountains had been massively restrictive, Richard's employment at Power Neon was anything but. His work took him all over the breadth of London. Even though the city was still reeling over the shock of destruction caused by the horrific bombings of The Blitz, the general vibe was one of positivity and hope. World War II propaganda posters remained plastered everywhere, and one particular design declared that "Freedom is in peril – defend it with all your might". This, taken alongside the especially bad devastation of industrial East London where he rented a room from a kindly old couple, had been a stark reminder to Richard of what had come before his arrival, and of his newfound freedom from the shackles of his past.

He loved darting around the bustling city, collaborating with various clients on a range of projects. He particularly enjoyed helping to maintain the thousands of neon lights at Piccadilly Circus, which included enormous, towering advertisements for many brands and products that are still around today – Wrigley's chewing gum, Bovril meat extract paste, Schweppes tonic water, Guinness dry stout (which they claimed to be "good for you") and Gordon's gin are but a few examples. Another of Richard's favourite projects was the neon sign at Walthamstow Stadium, a 30s art-deco building that made an appearance in too many films, album covers and music videos to name. Once called the "Victoria Line's Las Vegas", the stadium is steeped in history, and the sign speaks to the hard work and craftsmanship that went into its creation. It fell into disrepair in 2008 but is now back to its former glory following a 2009 restoration that cost £100,000, once again bathing the dog track in the same vivid neon glow as it used to back in the day.

Although he hadn't grown up in a formal family, Richard had mostly been known by his full name back in Wales. Not here in London, though, where everybody knew him more colloquially as Dick. Of course, Dick is short for Richard. As a sidebar, a lot of people believe that this came to be the shortened version of the name for certain reasons – that is, because the etymology of Richard, a man's name, can be traced back to Proto-Germanic "Rikharthu", more or less meaning "hard ruler", and because dick refers to…well…the thing that all men have that gets hard. Nonetheless, they'd be sorely mistaken. How Dick actually came to be short for Richard is one of those "knee bone connected to the thigh bone" sort of developments. Regrettably, it's pretty boring compared to the penis angle that most people go for. Basically, it's simply because, centuries ago, people loved to shorten names and use alternatives that rhymed. Thus, Richard became Rich, which gave rise to nicknames like Rick, which eventually became Dick.

Even though all his pals called him Dick, he'll remain Richard for the remainder of the story – high five for consistency! He was blessed with a character trait that has the power to carry a person far in their life: ambition. And his desire to do well for himself and achieve great things served him well. Not only did it take him to London, a land of greater opportunity in the first place, it also made him work his arse off at Power Neon until he got to the stage where he thought, "Hey, I can make it on my own." And, feeling grateful for everything that his employers at Power Neon had taught him, go it alone he did. He'd gained a high level of proficiency in the neon sign trade much faster than he could ever have hoped for. For that reason he truly believed in his abilities, lacking none of the confidence and gutsiness that make branching off a success.

With no doubt in his mind that he could make it work and make a decent living independently (a boss-free outcome that encourages a lot of people to put in a shift), Richard set up Electro Signs in 1952. He may have had a considerable arsenal of skills and knowledge in the trade to hand, but there was a problem. With limited financial resources he was unable to afford dedicated premises to house his own neon sign making business. By this time though, Richard had moved into his own home, a small but adequate bungalow in the fairly residential Highams Park area of London, just northeast of Walthamstow. The space around the property was the perfect solution to start with, and he developed improvised premises in a sturdy, wooden garage-cum-shed that sat down the side of the bungalow.

As it transpired, Richard's confidence in the venture wasn't unfounded, and things ran smoothly. The experience gained during his time at Power Neon proved to be invaluable, and when married with his strong work ethic it led to the production of at least one sign per week for several different carnivals and fairgrounds that operated in the cheerful seaside towns along the east coast. Richard had managed to get the gig through a contact that he made, and aside from being grateful for the work it gave him an excuse to get out of the city for a little bit at a time. Making loads of contacts and getting work through word of mouth was how Richard conducted business in general. Much of that was down to the fact that he was an affable guy who didn't make enemies easily and who became an integral part of the community he lived in. He was just a good man who people wanted to do business with – simple as that. Eventually, work began pouring in from all directions not only from other fairgrounds and carnivals but also from amusement arcades and pretty much anywhere that used neon for advertising or otherwise. Neon was increasing in popularity at a phenomenal rate, which meant that potential clientele was around almost every corner.

At the top of his game, Richard had formed a company that was quickly becoming one of the industry leaders in the southeast of England. Chris might have become the Master of Glow, but the truth is that he inherited his crown from his father. The reason that it all began, Richard essentially paved the way for the success of the Braceys for years to come.

Under the Electro Signs name, which became a bit of an institution itself, Richard made an abundance of signs. One that stood out to him as an accomplishment he was especially proud of was the huge, soaring sign that belonged to Raymond Revue Bar on Brewer Street in London's Soho district. The brainchild of property magnate, magazine publisher and true playboy Paul Raymond, this theatre and strip club was renowned for being the only one of its kind in London to (legally) offer patrons the sort of full-frontal nudity on the stage found in venues elsewhere in the world, including in the United States, Canada and a few European countries. Its giant, brightly lit neon sign – a true achievement for Richard – declared the club to be "The world centre of erotic entertainment". It made the club a local landmark and helped to put Electro Signs firmly on the map. By 2004 Raymond Revue bar was seen as unfashionable, and it couldn't compete with somewhat classier offerings like Stringfellows of Peter Stringfellow fame – one playboy overshadowing another. Yet, as the venue has exchanged hands (and names) over and again, the sign has remained in place. It fell into a sad state of disrepair but along came the Braceys to save the day. Some years ago, they restored the sign to its former glory and still maintains Richard's baby to this day.

Another sign that Richard talked a lot about over the years was the one above Bar Italia in Soho's Beak Street. This unique red and green neon sign – which features a large clock in the centre – was designed to be attached to the wall on its side, projecting out over the pavement and visible whichever direction people come along the street. While likely under new management now, Bar Italia has done well to stand the test of time, and the same can be said of the sign. Still in good nick, it stands there as a shining example of what anyone can achieve if they put their mind to it.

Chapter 3 – Chris Bracey Joins The Business

Life ticked along nicely for Richard after setting up shop. He'd found himself a lovely girlfriend, Doreen, who became his wife. Like all the women before her in the Bracey family and all the women to come, she was the matriarch of the family. Soon after, the stork delivered their first son, Kirk. He was to become an absolute firecracker, but more about him later.

On the 25th of December 1954, Chris was born. What are the chances of that? Someone being born on Christmas Day. Actually, the chances are relatively high. In 2017 alone, for example, midwives welcomed almost 1,400 babies into the world on Christmas Day across England and Wales. Overall, there were just under 680,000 births in England and Wales in 2017. That means that the babies born on Christmas Day that year accounted for 0.2% of the 680,000. It might not be a staggering figure to many, but if you imagine 1,400 babies all in one place, all screaming their heads off and pissing and shitting everywhere, that is definitely a whole load of babies. Interestingly, the NHS catering teams prepared 400,000 Christmas meals on the 25th the following year. The thought of those 400,000 more than likely rotten meals just about beats the idea of dealing with 1,400 babies at once. However, many people were born on Christmas Day 1954, Chris was one of them, along with Annie Lennox as a matter of fact. There must be something about coming into the world on that day and success because she's managed to flog over 80 million records worldwide, and she was even given an OBE in 2011 for her charity work. Well done Annie Lennox. Well done December the 25th 1954 for bringing that musical genius into existence at the same time as Chris Bracey. It was a sign that he would do amazing things. There are no two ways about it. And lest we forget, this is why he's called Chris in the first place. For Richard and Doreen, it was either Chris or Santa. No explanation is needed on that one, is it? No? Excellent, let's move on. Surprisingly, a fair amount of people in the world are called Santa. Ironically, in historical terms, one of the most popular occupations for people called Santa was coal mining. That's a bit too close to home to be a coincidence considering Richard's past.

Across the years Richard found himself juggling family life with growing the business. Both went well, give or take the occasional drop of a ball. He'd always been pretty tough, just like his father and every one of his uncles, and his parenting style mirrored that. To say that he was strict would be a massive understatement, but it wasn't like Chris and Kirk were living under some despotic rule; some super authoritarian regime where nobody got a say. It wasn't like that at all. Richard might have been stern by nature, rarely allowing himself to relax enough to just have a laugh or to have a bit of banter with his kids, but it would be unfair to say that he wasn't honest and fair. What is it they say? Firm but fair. That was Richard all the way.

Electro Signs was doing such a roaring trade that Richard was unable to keep things going by himself. He gave thought to taking someone on, like he'd been taken on by Power Neon many years before, but he was overcome by the idea of keeping it in the family. Chris was all grown up by then and the ideal situation was for him to get on board. Reflecting back on his younger years and how he'd merely been expected by everyone in his family to follow in his father's footsteps into the mines, this put Richard in a bit of a quandary. He flatly refused to be the sort of parent who forced his child into a career merely because that was his destiny in life. From his own experiences, he knew better than anyone how "square peg, round hole" such a move could be. Leaving the choice entirely up to Chris, he put his idea forward.

Thankfully, the gods were on Richard's side. After some careful consideration of the offer Chris agreed – albeit with some minor reservations. Working with Richard making neon signs wasn't even close to what Chris would have described as his ultimate life objective, but he didn't hate the prospect entirely. Since childhood, he'd been gifted with a real passion for anything related to art, and he wielded some spectacularly raw artistic talent. At the time his dad asked him to join Electro Signs, Chris was working at Parlour Wood Studios in Soho as a touch-up artist. This was before the days of Photoshop, and Chris was responsible for touching up artwork for the likes of Avon Advertising. Again, he didn't find this to be the most exciting work. He suspected that sign-making wouldn't fully address his artistic needs either, but he couldn't help but see the glaring artistic potential in sign making – especially if he made the most of it. He had never considered that it would be the medium that he poured his creative energies into, but the more he pondered on it, the more he realised that this could be the right move for him.

To date, Richard had crafted signs for companies of all sorts. Yes, they looked great – that much is for sure. The thing is that they were underpinned by commercial ideas and goals. In other words, they were made to give businesses a literal shining competitive advantage over their rivals – fundamentally, to make them more money. Now, let's get one thing straight: Chris liked having cash as much as the next person. After all, money makes a lot of life's pleasures possible. What he had trouble accepting was the primarily profit-driven nature of the clients that he'd be working for under Electro Signs. He might have seen the benefit of money, but he leaned much more towards the idea that sign making could become an art form rather than a mere way to increase the profits of businesses. He pushed his reservations to one side and embraced the opportunity to learn the trade as his father had done, and use the skills and knowledge garnered over time to further his own artistic interests.

It was lucky that Chris wasn't as motivated by money as most people around him, as Richard was paying him a paltry tenner a week. Obviously, this made things a little tighter than he'd imagined they'd be. Chris didn't lead an expensive life, though, so he just about managed to get by on his small income. Besides, he was still living at home, which meant he wasn't burdened by paying rent or having to stock a fridge and cupboards with food. On top of that, even though he'd been working for a while by then, his parents hadn't asked him to pay any keep either. Ah, the joys of living at home. All of that, along with the neat pile of ironed clothing that would magically appear on Chris's bed every couple of days, led to the conclusion that he had it pretty sweet. Life can also be very cheap when you're single, which Chris was.

His singledom wasn't destined to last for much longer. In his teens, Chris would soon meet the spirited Linda, and any guy who has ever had a girlfriend can attest to the fact that girlfriends are one expensive business. Chris was about to need a substantial increase in cash flow! But Linda, a total knockout and a natural beauty, was worth every penny he spent on taking her out. They'd kick about town together, going on all sorts of dates and getting up to all kinds of mischief. She was the best partner in crime that Chris could have asked for, and he fell for her hook, line and sinker. It was definitely love at first sight. That's for sure. Richard agreed to give Chris a small raise, which helped finance his new romance no end

Linda was shorter than Chris at five foot six, which wasn't difficult. He was a big guy at six foot, with a slim and slender but muscular build. Linda was slim and had long, dark hair. She would keep her hair like that right up until her thirties, when she fancied a change, dying her hair blonde, and deciding that was the look she'd maintain from then on. Although Chris loved what Linda looked like as a blonde, he often thought back to those early days, picturing that gorgeous brunette that exploded into his life at a young age. In the end, though, he didn't care what her hair looked like. That's the true beauty about being in love with another person: you don't give a fuck what they look like – you'd love them no matter what. Funnily enough, it's the major difference between being in love with someone else and being in love with yourself. When you fancy yourself as a bit of a looker you care about your appearance more than anything else. Besides, Chris was partial to a bit of bottle blonde himself. His hair was naturally brown with little hints of blonde here and there, but from his teen years onwards, he preferred to bleach it. Doing that was trendy in the 70s, but that's not why he did it. He just liked it that way – it made him feel like himself. On top of that, Chris kept his hair long, pulled back into a ponytail most of the time, and it was a real part of his identity, both from his own perspective and that of others who knew him.

Linda's hair had always been a bit of a curly, frizzy mess, so she was obsessed with making sure it was straight. Of course, back then, there was no such thing as hair straighteners. In fact, most women throughout history had been concerned with the exact opposite: curling their locks. Not Linda! She was a goth and goths liked straight hair, so she did what all the goth chicks were doing at the time in the absence of hair straighteners. She ironed it! What else? It was a common scene for her parents to walk into the living room to find the ironing board set up, Linda bent over it, steam billowing from her hair and the sizzling sound of it being frazzled.

Linda, who was fair-skinned and liked it that way, was a goth through and through. Chris was the total opposite, loved his skin tanned, and for that reason sunbathed at every opportunity. Linda would never be out and about without wearing a lot of eyeliner. What would any self-respecting goth be doing without their eyeliner? That'd be criminal. Other than that, though, Linda wasn't heavily into make-up, on the whole. Sure, on occasion, you might see her sporting a bit of lippy or a spot of light foundation (on special occasions). Aside from her staple eyeliner, though, she wasn't afraid to show the world her bare face. Linda smoked from a young age, and until this day she's always got a fag in her hand and puffing away. It's not been unknown for her to have her next one lit before the last one's been extinguished. That's just how it was and how it always will be.

When Chris met Linda she was working at a public relations firm called Brian Mitchell Ltd, based in Fetter Lane and just a five-minute walk from Chancery Lane Station. The company has long been dissolved now, but Linda enjoyed her job there and working in PR almost as much as heading into the hustle and bustle of Central London each day. Always the protector, Chris would see her safe on the bus every morning and meet her off the bus when she came home. Even though Linda could look after herself, she secretly loved that he did this for her.

The couple knew that they were right for each other right out of the gate, sure that it wasn't all just a fleeting dalliance – one in a long line of many. Na, they were both certain that the other was the one for them, the person that would be their life partner, the one that would be a rock for them through thick and thin until the very end. It was all so different back then, the world of dating. There were no apps like Tinder, or Bumble, or whatever, giving people endless choice like they're in some weird human supermarket with the biggest product variety imaginable. There wasn't the same feeling of, "Oh, what if I can do better?" that seems to be around in modern times. There was none of that crap. People met, they fell in love, they got married, they got their own place, and they had kids. For a lot of people, yeah, there were affairs along the road, and that road wasn't always smooth. The road wasn't always smooth for Chris and Linda, like any other couple, but there was no playing away. They remained just as in love with each other throughout their lives as they were when they met.

And the pair followed the usual path, if a little quicker than many others. Wasting zero time, they set about trying for their first child. It turned out that trying wasn't really something they had to bother with as they conceived on their first go, which was just one of many amazing things that went right for them. Linda used to joke about how Chris must have decent swimmers in him for her to get knocked up so fast. When they'd realised that Linda had a bun in the oven after a trip to her family doctor, they had one thing on their mind: SAVE, SAVE, SAVE. Not that he was looking forward to doing it, but Chris had been planning to go to his dad to ask for a further raise on his wages. When Richard heard the news that he was going to be a grandad for the first time ever, it was the best thing he'd heard since finding out he was to be a father all those years before. Richard's state of elation meant that there was no need for Chris to ask him for more money. Richard was more than aware of the costs involved in having a child and offered to pay Chris more money himself. This was the best possible news. With that salary bump and with Linda's wages from Brian Mitchell Ltd, they could put enough money aside to move into their own home and keep enough by to cover the cost of all the stuff they'd need to buy before Linda popped.

They scraped enough together to get their own flat. It wasn't much – a decent-sized high-rise flat in Leytonstone – but it was theirs and that was phenomenal. They put their own stamp on the flat, and it didn't take long until it felt like home. The location of the flat wasn't ideal for Chris getting to work back in Highams Park, but it was a good price and the residential, community feel of the area were all that mattered at that point. Every day he'd make the eight-mile return journey between the flat and his parents' house (where the business was still operated from the shed/garage down the side of the house).

Chapter 4 – Chris Bracey Takes Over And Reforms The Business

Just before Chris and Linda took the next step in 1973, getting married, Richard got to the point where he was ready to hang up his hat. He'd had a bellyful of the slog and took a back seat, leaving Electro Signs in the more than capable hands of Chris. He now knew the business and the industry like the back of his hand, and he was happy to take the reins. As he learned to relax, Richard's hard exterior softened a little.

Business was starting to pick up nicely and there was a regular flow of orders coming Chris's way. He didn't take full payment from his customers upfront, and it had always been that way even on Richard's watch. It just wasn't how things worked. The problem was that operating a payment system like this meant that it was often challenging getting the money from customers after their orders had been delivered. For some reason, the carnival and amusement arcade owners were the worst for this, and sometimes it could take anywhere up to three months to get full payment from them. It was so frustrating at points, like pulling teeth. Occasionally, Chris got close to blowing the house down with the selfish fuckers to let them know that they were messing with his ability to save up for the family that he was about to have to fund. Obviously, Linda would be off work for a while, staying at home with the baby. And yeah, they'd have help, both in terms of money and support, from their families, but money was money and Electro Signs was due it. Chris never came to blows with any of the clients because he had the power to keep his temper at bay (most of the time). Nevertheless, to say that no strong words were ever exchanged would be a big, fat lie.

When all is said and done, Chris was sick to the stomach with chasing money from their most evasive clients. He'd lay awake at night mulling the situation over. There has to be another solution,

Chris would think, there just has to be. But what was that solution? Above anything, the fundamental nature of the business wouldn't change. It would always sell neon signs. OK, so where could he go with that? Electro Signs would have to start selling something that people wanted to buy, something that there was a big market for. So, what was that? He already had a product, but how could he alter it easily to make more people want to buy it?

It took Chris a fair whack of time to come up with the answer. After many a sleepless night, going over everything in his head again and again, he concluded that his thought process was too restricted. He'd have to think outside the box. A bit of brainstorming later and it finally hit him like a pleasurable punch in the coupon. It came to him that he'd have to sell something that wasn't a product, as such, but more of a concept if you will. He'd sell sex! It was ingenious if he did say so himself.

Praise the lord that Richard was no longer running the show because he would never have gone for this pretty eccentric idea to take the business in a risqué new direction. Chris was baffled that the idea had never sprung to mind before. After all, he had a pretty major connection to the sex industry: his older brother Kirk.

Kirk had forged a successful career working in Soho within the industry and went on about it until he was blue in the face. He was a real old-school hustler who took nothing seriously. He had the gift of the gab and could sell sand to Arabs. Hell, he could sell a bag of dildos to a nun – no joke. Remember that scene in *Lock, Stock and Two Smoking Barrels* when a gangster does some poor sod in with a dildo? That's Kirk in a nutshell. He once beat up five gangsters single-handedly with nothing but a rolling pin and a cucumber after they'd confronted him for banging a bird that one of them was engaged to. They were wielding machetes, and he lost a few fingers during the struggle, but he was a fearless fucker. That night he was like a psychotic Delia Smith after taking a bad pill. Two guesses as to why he had a couple of phallic objects at hand. Let's just say they weren't for food prep or eating. Enough said. Kirk was a ladies' man and managed to land dates with the hottest women around. He was once going about town with some sexy female mud wrestler, and he had some celebrities in his little black book. The hustle eventually got him into serious bother down the line when he screwed over the wrong crime family in Soho over a shipment of sex toys, and he was forced to do a runner from the UK.

Back when Chris worked in Soho he'd walk the streets after work, taking in all the sex shops and strip clubs (from the outside, of course). They were ten a penny in the 70s, in general, and the streets of Soho were especially crammed full of them. He could never pinpoint exactly why he felt some affinity for Soho and the sex industry, but he always knew that he'd be tied in with it one day somehow.

It's funny, an area that eventually became famed for its connection to sex and debauchery had been fashionable years before with the aristocracy. Those are two extreme ends of the spectrum.

One of London's key entertainment districts since the nineteenth century, Soho developed a reputation for being the epicentre of London's sex industry with help from venues like the Raymond Revue bar and others. Sadly, like many areas that used to be much grittier, Soho is now unrecognisable. It's mainly frequented by the upwardly mobile, who flock there for its restaurant and coffee shop culture. Soho is still vibrant at night, especially along Old Compton Street, host to the majority of London's gay scene. But it's not what it used to be, and only traces of the sex industry from old remain. Chris got in there at just the right time before any of this sad gentrification took hold of the area.

The day after his brainwave Chris made his way down to Soho, determined to find some way of making at least one meaningful connection that day. He was positive that he'd be able to sell neon signs to businesses firmly embedded in the sex industry. His expectations took a battering across the day. As morning became afternoon, and as afternoon then fell into the evening, he got more and more despondent. Not a single proprietor was interested in doing business with him. It was so strange.

Half of the establishments he went into, he was made to feel the same way a stranger feels when they wander into the wrong pub in the wrong part of town. You know that feeling. It's almost like they were scenes pulled right out of that comedy show, *The League of Gentlemen*: "This is a local place for local people."

All the business owners were cagey as anything, uninterested in making a deal with someone they'd never met before, and worried that it could all go tits up for one reason or another. Chris had never imagined that the sex industry would be so insular; so cliquey. It was clearly just a trait of that world that he'd never stumbled upon before.

Even in the face of this frosty welcome, there was no chance that Chris would give up. Not only did he need these businesses, but they also needed him. Their signage was as dull as dishwater, more boring than a wet Wednesday in Milton Keynes. They were totally stuck in a bygone era, the facias of their shops, bars and clubs hanging onto the glory days of Perspex. The material might have been perfect in the 60s, but time had moved on, Electro Signs was moving on and the sex industry needed to move on too. Chris was resolute that he'd be the one to revolutionise their signage and drag them – if necessary, kicking and screaming – into more contemporary times.

A few weeks went by with Chris biding his time until he figured out his grand plan to win the hearts of Soho's sex industry. On a freezing cold day, when he was working on the sign for a shop on Brewer Street, things heated up unexpectedly. Chris was working up a ladder when he was approached out of the blue by a random guy on the street. The guy shouted up at him.

"Hey, mate. Come here," he beckoned with his index finger.

He started to wander away, and while Chris tried to shout after him he carried on walking. Chris descended the ladder, and once he was down at street level he followed the guy around the corner, desperately curious as to what was going on. When they were closer to each other, Chris realised that he recognised the fella. It was one of the shop owners that he'd canvassed a few weeks before. He got excited thinking that something good was going to come from it, and he wasn't half right. As they stood outside a strip bar, the guy pointed up at the sign above the door, a neon "Girls" sign mounted against a black backdrop. Even with the neon present it was lacking oomph, and Chris knew that he could breathe a bit of life into it.

"You're the guy who came knocking the other day, right? Looking to make signs for the shop?" He was stating, really, not asking. He knew exactly who Chris was and wanted to know what magic he could work to get the place looking better, to get the punters in. Chris didn't have to think for a second about his answer.

How he could revamp these joints was literally all he'd been thinking about for weeks.

"You've already got a sign up there saying you've got girls, right? Who wants girls when they could have 'GIRLS GIRLS GIRLS'?" Chris almost shouted the last part at the guy for the sake of emphasis. "Sorry for shouting, but you need to shout about the girls. And why stop at that? Everyone can see the door, yeah, but why not have a big, fuck off arrow border around it all with flashing lights pointing down at the door? Tell the punters exactly where they go to get what they want. Show them where it's at. You see what I'm saying?"

Chris's enthusiasm, creativity and ingenuity shone through immediately and the guy was bowled over. He was completely taken with the ideas Chris had thrown at him on the spot and signed off on it. And it was the ideal set up. He took a back seat throughout giving Chris free rein with regards to every aspect of the sign. All elements of the design were up to him: colour, style, shape, size. Everything!

This chance encounter gave Chris the opportunity to showcase his artistic flair. He knew that this was his chance to produce something so good that other sex industry businesses would be queuing up for his services. Well, the sign was a huge hit, and the proprietors of every sex shop, strip bar, cabaret bar and peepshow in Soho and beyond were shoving each other out of the way trying to get to Chris. How things can change in an instant. From then on, the most sought-after neon sign maker in London, Chris was inundated with orders. Almost every client allowed him the artistic licence to do whatever he thought would work best to make their establishments bright enough to throw the competition into the shadows – both literally and metaphorically.

Chris developed a signature style which incorporated the use of fluorescent green and pink together – something that had never been done before. Well-known sex establishments like "Doc" Johnson's Love Shop and Cinema (now Soho's Original XXX Bookshop) absolutely lapped it up. And there were so many more too, all of them without a single creative idea of their own, and so in need of Chris that it hurt. To name but just some: The Triple X, Sexual Cinema, Sex Supermarket, Rude Encounter, Models, Peep Show, Lunatics Strip, The Astral Cinema (now the gay sex shop Prowler),

Video Battle Centre (now a healthy yogurt shop and a prime example of damn gentrification), Madame Jojo's, and The Windmill Theatre (now Windmill International). Chris was even permitted to pick the names of some places. In doing so, he made sure to inject a snifter of his own humour into the names, with just a few being: Dreaming Lips, Sinsexual Cinematic Sex, Cinema Blue, Tunnels of Love, and The Pink Pussycat. Over the years Chris would eventually resign about 90% of the sex establishments in Soho. From being someone whose face business owners slammed their doors on, Chris went to being "The Neon Man". There's a couple of words that could describe how he felt about this. Pride and accomplishment are just two that scratch the surface of what happened.

Business was booming and Electro Signs was now knocking out three signs a week. Even though production had upped the quality of the signs stayed the same, Chris making sure that they were of the highest standard. And family life was even better. By then Chris and Linda's first son had been born, and they'd got through that terrifying period as first-time parents. Linda had gone through pregnancy and labour like a trooper, and by the time she came home with the baby she took to motherhood with relative ease. She and Chris managed to cope with all the shitty nappies, all the crying and all the sleepless nights, coming out the other end alright. They'd learned a good few lessons before their second son Matthew was born, and the second time around was a bit more ironed out.

Richard could see how well Chris was doing at the head of the company and the head of his family. He wanted to help in some way, whatever way he could. After thinking about it for some time and going over the figures, Richard assessed that he could probably swing buying a property to help the business. This wouldn't only boost the business, it would also give Chris a nice leg up, giving him a more suitable place to work from. With production levels at Electro Signs so high, largely thanks to Chris's efforts to reform the business, it was no longer a viable option to operate out of the shed/garage down the side of Richard and Doreen's bungalow in Highams Park. Together, he and Chris shopped around, scoping out what was on offer. The pickings were pretty slim, unfortunately. While a fair number of properties were available, few suited their needs. They required somewhere that could be used as business premises but somewhere that would equally be suitable as somewhere for Chris and his lot to live. They held on until the right property came along, and sure enough it did. It was an old cottage in Marlow Road, near Walthamstow's Wood Street, and just a stone's throw from both Vallentin Road and Shernhall Street. You can tell that, other than its connection with Highhams Park, the business has stayed pretty true to Walthamstow.

The cottage was a tiny little place clad in bright white wood on the outside, featuring just two windows – with small panes of glass – and a low doorway at the front. Getting through the entrance was always fun and games for Chris and Richard, both tall guys. It was right opposite the famous Duke's Head pub, which hasn't changed much between the 70s and now other than a dramatic switch in colour from a bright white to dark blue and now black. Sat beside a newer and bigger building made of bricks, which was a travel agency back in the 70s and 80s, the little cottage has stood the test of time. Like the pub, it hasn't changed all that much itself. Mentions of it can be found in a couple of different history books, but the nicest description is in a book called *Right Up Your Street: A Short History of Wood Street*. The Walthamstow Historical Society describes the wooden-boarded cottage as being overshadowed by the buildings that surround it on account of its minuscule nature and salutes its ability to escape demolition across the years. The book refers to the small windows, imagining that they have taken in so much change as the decades have rolled past, as more gentle, older times have been replaced by the harsher, modern world, all the while the cottage insisting on remaining the same. Very little is known about the history of this property before the Braceys took ownership, even though its walls are bound to conceal some tales, but Chris and his family managed to fill the place with plenty of history.

The cottage became Electro Signs' base of operations, with enough space left over for accommodation. There were two bedrooms upstairs (one for Chris and Linda and the other for the boys), a living room and a kitchen. The office was set up in the open-plan hallway. A lot was going on in there and it could look a bit of a jumble at the best of times. However, it's what would have been classed as an organised mess.

The move into new premises spelled the start of something new, representing a shift towards Electro Signs becoming more of a family affair. Chris's mum Doreen had been doing the accounts for the business for years. She had a great head on her for numbers and never made a single mistake in all her years doing the accounts. Linda was looking at getting more involved, and Doreen offered to teach her daughter-in-law the office side of running the business, leaving all the other stuff to Chris and Richard.

Living in the cottage gave Linda the opportunity to work for Electro Signs at the same time as looking after her young boys. Under Doreen's guidance, she learned the ins-and-outs of the business, and it was thanks to Doreen that Linda became a pretty tough businesswoman, eventually going on to study a degree in law. She was firm but fair, kind of in the same way that her father-in-law Richard was. Yet, there was a key difference between their firm but fair approaches; Linda was a much warmer sort of person than Richard, a lot more of a kind-hearted character.

At the back of the property, accessible through an arched brick and iron gate and down a narrow alleyway, there was a sizeable garden. In its current form, it was essentially a junkyard stuffed to the gunwales with scrap metal, a lot of which was old, rusting, scrapped cars. Chris and Richard had inherited all of this along with the cottage, which accounts for the slightly lower price they managed to negotiate with the vendors. It didn't pose a significant problem, though, as all that scrap metal could be flogged for a tidy little profit. Others would have despaired at the sight of it, but Chris could see past all the scrap, envisaging a space that would allow the business to grow even more.

To Matthew and his brother, the junkyard represented something else altogether. They were too young to care about what their parents were doing. They looked at the junkyard with wide, excited eyes, seeing the serious potential for play it offered. For the boys, the junkyard was one big, metallic, rust-covered playground, a land of adventure, somewhere to cause mischief.

Their mum would give them a bunch of keys, sending them out into the yard to drive the old cars. They were oblivious to the fact that the keys didn't belong to the cars, but colourful imagination reigned there; dull reality played second fiddle. The boys would climb into the cars using the keys to "start" the engines.

From the office Linda and Doreen would hear it all, all the "vroom vrooms", all the mimicking of car tyres screeching, the "pcchheeeeow" of fake collisions and they pretended to crash the cars. And on occasion one of them would have to go out to intervene in one of the many "no it's my turn" altercations that would erupt in the garden.

Their favourite playground was snatched away from them when Chris sold off all the scrap. They were gutted, but it's what was meant to be. With the scrap gone, Chris was able to construct a significantly larger garage and workshop that covered the entire space of the garden and scrapyard. With a bigger workspace it was possible to increase production from three signs a week to five a week, and business just kept on getting better.

Chapter 5 – The (Mostly) Unlucky Matthew Bracey

Behind the cottage there was a big play park. It wasn't incredible, just a large tarmac area surrounded by railings and in the middle sat dark green swings, a seesaw of the same colour, a tall slide and a dodgy roundabout that had been covered in blue, red and yellow graffiti. Matthew loved it up there regardless and used to cycle there all the time on a little three-wheeler bike his parents bought for Christmas the previous year.

Somehow, one day, he succeeded in catching his ankle between the frame and one of the wheels. Nobody could work out how he'd managed it. It looked absolutely impossible, but then again that was Matthew in and out. He was always getting into impossible situations from a young age which gives you a corker of a clue as to where this story is going. Basically, it's leading up to Matthew's all-time biggest clanger, a situation gone so fucking wrong that it totally belies any sense of belief: the steel deal from hell! His leg caught among metal as he screamed in pain was a sign as to what part of Matthew's future would hold. Of course, he had no idea about that at the time. Linda called the fire brigade who arrived – loud sirens blaring – on the scene quickly. The flashing blue lights of the fire trucks would have given Chris's neon creations a run for their money, and the involvement of both light and metal in this farce couldn't have been any more apt for what was to come in many years. The firemen had a commendable go at trying to release Matthews's ankle from the frame of the bike. Even though they tried their best, their efforts were in vain. The scene continued to get more and more extreme and ridiculous as the firemen drafted in another fire engine to assist them. Two fire trucks and eight firemen now on the scene, all because of one clumsy little boy, success was still far from hand. You might wonder what came next. Well, if you'd hasten a guess that another fire truck was called in to help then your guess would be spot on. The ankle was finally released. Woohoo! This was met with a huge round of applause and loud whistles and cheers from the massive crowd that had gathered around to watch the fate of this young lad. It just took a grand total of three fire engines and twelve firemen over two hours to accomplish. As they left the scene and as the crowd dissipated, Linda had contemplated on how much that would all have cost the fire service. A good few grand at least, she'd thought.

A few weeks went by and Matthew asked if he could go the play park again. Linda had been snowed under with paperwork that day and it was both cold and spitting outside, but she felt too bad to say no to his little face.

"OK, OK. Come on, get your bike," she said to his joy.

She abandoned her work for a while, threw on a warm coat and took him up to the park. It was the first time that they'd been there since the fire engines debacle the previous month. The bad luck was out of the way now. What could go wrong, eh? Ahem, well, quite a bit as it turns out. While Linda was sitting on a bench, her hood up and watching Matthew play, he leaned his head against the railings around the perimeter of the park – you know, the kind that has those spikes on top, which look like loads of little spears lined up. Of course, what else happened but Matthew's head slipping between two of the railings and getting stuck there. Linda could not believe it. Matthew screamed for her.

"For Christ sake. Not again," she muttered, rolling her eyes as she ran over to help him. "Oh, Matthew, what have you done?"

Linda tried her hardest to release Matthew's head by herself and even enlisted the help from another mother in the park. Between the two of them they failed in getting it out. When they got close to thinking it might slip out, Matthew yelped in pain as the pressure of the bars on his ears hurt him too much. He felt like his ears were going to be torn off. Not that he had a particularly big head, but it seemed to defy physics him getting his head wedged in there like that. Once again, Matthew's accident-prone nature had got him into a bit of a pickle.

Unable to release his head, Linda was finally forced to call the fire brigade once again. As luck would have it, it was the same crew as before, and what a laugh they had about it. They named Matthew "Clumsy Clara", which he didn't get. First, he had no idea what the word "clumsy" meant, secondly, he was confused that they were calling him a girl's name. Anyway, he has bigger fish to fry than being given the name of a girl, what with his head being trapped between bars and all that jazz.

In this sequel to *Play park-gate*, events unfolded similarly as before, with the first crew being unable to solve the problem alone. For that reason, they called in a second fire engine and then a third. Once more, there were three fire trucks and twelve firemen. Only this time, this wasn't enough! Would you believe it? Not to disparage the efforts of the hard-working fire service, who more than likely had better places to be than the play park – such as, you know, putting out fires – but come on. How many electricians does it take to change a light bulb? So, along came a fourth (and final) fire engine, along with an ambulance.

With the aid of an air jack, which is basically a mechanism designed to lift heavy objects (such as cars) off the ground by means of an inflatable support, they managed to free Matthew's head from the railings. All in, it took five emergency services vehicles, in addition to a huge team comprising of sixteen firemen and two paramedics, to force the bars of the fence apart. It seems that Matthew's future-self had once again hopped in a time machine, journeyed back to his childhood and offered him an unmistakable indication of what to expect from later life. This steel deal from hell really was locked into this unlucky kid's future.

Another few weeks later, back in the park…Ahh, I got you there, didn't I? Just pulling your leg. There were no further predicaments involving that little play park. Sure, plenty of mishaps through life for Matthew, but no more in the park.

Loads of kids are scared of things, reasonable or otherwise. For instance, there was a kid who lived near Matthew who had an intense phobia of masking tape. Everyone used to think that he was a complete weirdo because of that. Until they found out why that is. His mum says that it stemmed back to when his big sister locked him in a dark cupboard wrapped up in the stuff. What a twisted little madam, right? No wonder he was scarred for life by that.

With everything that had happened in the play park, you'd imagine that Matthew might have developed a crippling, life-altering fear of play parks, or bicycles, or metal fences. Oh no, his primary phobia was much darker and more terrifying than that. Was it killer clowns hiding under the bed? Nope – that wasn't it. Was it the boogieman in the closet? Nope – you're still wrong. Was it giant, flesh-eating spiders? Nope – and you're now out of turns.

Ladies and gentlemen, Matthew Bracey was terrified of buttons. This may sound totally unreasonable, but hang on. As any human on the planet who has ever been forced to wear scratchy, itchy, hand-knitted woollen jumpers can confirm, any association with these things haunts a person until their deathbed. Jumpers like that are the product of the devil, instruments of torture sent from the depths of Satan's lair. Matthew was no different.

His mum and nan had insisted on knitting the bulk of his clothing so that the family could save some money. After all, a few balls of wool and a couple of knitting needles were miles cheaper than the expensive, poor quality clothes in high street stores.

Besides, there were two kids to clothe, so any savings were important. Even though Electro Signs was doing well, Chris didn't take much money for himself and the family, instead preferring to pour as much as he could back into the business to buy better machines and materials and so on.

The jumpers were outfitted with these awful pearl buttons that were definitely designed to go on girl's clothes. To this day Matthew gags at the thought of wearing them. Unfortunately, because Chris ruled the roost as a pretty strict disciplinarian, there was absolutely no getting out of it. And so, Matthew's fear of buttons was born. And a fear of something he couldn't escape wearing simply represented one more thing to add to this kid's increasingly burgeoning inventory of bad luck.

It was actually a god-sent relief when his mum dressed him in clothes that had been purchased in various charity shops across London or in the flea markets and market stalls on Brick Lane Market. Even though he'd end up milling about dressed like a flower child looking like he'd just stumbled out of a hippy enclave in some far-flung corner of the world, this was better luck than being stuck with buttons – and considering how holey some of those were, that's saying something!

From the age of eight onwards Matthew would help Chris to design the signs. Chris loved having his son's input and incorporated a lot of the ideas that Matthew proposed into his work. Even as a youngster, Matthew had a fairly creative way of thinking. That was a characteristic that seemed to run throughout the Bracey clan – every new generation proved to be a chip off the old block, as they say. Whenever he could, Matthew would get into the workshop to watch his dad manufacturing the signs, and he often helped to make them after school and at the weekends. That all sounds pretty great, doesn't it? And it was, but it was this participation that would ultimately lead the ill-fated Matthew hurtling towards his steely, Asian destiny.

Despite the fact that moving into the cottage had worked out for the Braceys in so many different ways, it was around that time that Matthew's luck really started to dwindle. The Dukes Head – remember, the pub opposite the house – was insanely noisy at night, especially at the weekends. The family would huddle up in front of the TV in the evenings to watch their favourite programmes. Naturally, televisions looked different then. They were big, unwieldy things that were items of furniture in their own right.

Two TV shows that were a regular feature in the viewing schedule were *Monkey Magic* and *The Young Ones*. For anyone not old enough to remember these, what a sad life you must have led because they were awesome. *Monkey Magic* – known to some just as *Monkey* – was a Japanese drama series dubbed in English. If you got over the dubbing, which, although not ideal, was reasonably well synchronised as far as dubbing goes, then this cult classic was really enjoyable. An adaptation of a Chinese folktale and a sixteenth century Chinese novel called *Journey to the West* by Wu Cheng'en, the show was about a pilgrimage to the West undertaken by a monk and his divine guardians. The show's theme tune refers to the central character, Monkey, as "the funkiest monkey that ever popped", and they might very well have been correct. He was one cool dude. It was a hugely entertaining programme that gave youngsters like Matthew in England their first taste of Asian fantasy action.

The Young Ones couldn't have been any more different from *Monkey Magic* if it tried to be, but it had the same entertainment value all the same. About the hilariously mad and occasionally bizarre trials and tribulations of a group of wildly different student flatmates – an aggressive punk; a conceited, wannabe anarchist; an oppressed, paranoid hippy; and a charming would-be mobster – living during Margaret Thatcher's tenure as the country's dictator…ahem…Prime Minister. Few people liked Mags at the time, and for many adults it was a nice, light-hearted way of indulging in some offbeat anarchy and escapism from the realities of the early 80s. For kids like Matthew, it was just a funny-as-fuck load of slapstick humour.

Those nights gathered around the TV, watching these programmes and others, were scary stuff in all truth. The disruption caused by the noise of the pub over the road was just one aspect of it. The living room window in the cottage was right on the street, without any front garden, driveway or anything else acting as a buffer zone between the front of the house and the street. Without fail, the patrons of the Dukes Head could be relied upon to bring the whole street into a state of utter chaos every Friday and Saturday night.

Now, there's the good kind of reliable, like always being somewhere when you say you will or doing the dishes when you say you're going to. You know? Then there's the other sort of reliable, the really cunty sort that entails the drunkest twats you could conceive in your mind invariably getting boozed up, puffing their pigeon chests out and starting unnecessary brawls.

It was just Matthew's luck to end up in a home nestled right in that spot, a spot to which the brawls would consistently spill over. Usually, the fights would calm down, friends of the parties involved calming them down. Other times the friends would join in making matters all the worse. On those occasions, the unshakeable and fearless Chris would tell his frightened wife and kids to stay as far back and away from the window as possible as he went out to stand guard at the window.

He'd position himself in front of the cottage wielding his trusty shovel, Daisy. It was a pretty feminine moniker for what was essentially being used as a dangerous weapon. Fans of *The Walking*

Dead won't have forgotten the nefarious Negan of season 8 and his gruesome barbed wire covered baseball bat, Lucille. Well, Daisy was the original Lucille, but Chris wasn't motivated by evil self-gain, just the strong urge to protect his family and his home from angry, pissed arseholes. Without Daisy, a string of glasses, bottles and bins – pretty much anything that the brawlers could hurl at each other – would have come crashing through the living room window, no doubt as well as heads and fists.

Chris was a real protector, not just with his family but with his employees too. Chris had always been a firm believer in helping people change their lives for the better. Many of the workers that he took on over the years were criminals – current or former. He had all sorts on top of that: heroin addicts, alcoholics, sex addicts, transvestites, homeless people. You name it, he had it. Chris didn't judge them, wanting to open his doors to give people a second (or third or fourth) chance in life.

Many of the young guys who came to work for the Bracey family business had a dark story to tell, and they had done a lot of things that would make most people run a mile. But they were open with Chris from the beginning, knowing what kind of guy he was from the reputation that preceded him. Their stories didn't faze Chris in the slightest, as he knew how to handle that sort from the Soho days.

There was one problem, though. Remember the different kinds of reliability? Good and bad? Well, these guys were the bad kind. Much of the time the guys didn't show up to work when the business was right in the middle of a really important order. They would go AWOL a lot of the time, refusing to answer their phones to explain what the fuck was going on. Chris wouldn't take any shit from them. If he was to give them a chance they'd have to work with him on that. Hellbent, Chris would often track them down wherever they were, kicking the door down, dragging them out of bed, or pulling them out of a druggy situation and straightening them out.

This might sound harsh but it worked, and they grew to respect Chris for it. Chris, the born protector that he was with his own kids, was more like a father figure to his employees. He saw the best in them, identifying their skills and nurturing them. It was all in a day's work for him. The health and prison systems continue to fail people like this now, but Chris was a solution that none of the broken, useless systems could equal. They'd learn how to respect others, managing to ditch their drug habits, get an honest day's work done, and see how good it feels to be a valid, contributing member of society.

Alas, Chris occasionally had to do stuff he hated just to get the work done. Ricky, his scalpel guy and vinyl king at one point, was a serious alcoholic. Amid a huge job, Ricky had turned up to work after an all-night bender, his hands shaking and arguing that he was in desperate need of some cocaine or booze. It took some convincing but Chris allowed it to happen on his watch.

"Look, Ricky, this job is too fucking important to screw up, so just this once I'll let you have a drink and a line to steady your hand. One! Agreed?"

Chris was deadly serious and Ricky knew it. It didn't take him thirty seconds to have a swig of vodka and a hefty sniff before his hands were as steady as a bloke with his bollocks caught in a zip. As you can imagine, the job got done. Chris absolutely did not make a habit of letting that sort of shit go on, and Ricky got a stern warning after that.

Chris wasn't just a protector, but a teacher too. He got off on facilitating learning, teaching his kids things, helping them pick up information, knowledge and skills that they could put to use at the time or later in life. Chris was a pure swimming fanatic and had been since he was young. It was something that gave him intense satisfaction throughout his entire life.

Like Richard, he'd never been one to force a way of life onto his kids, but the rules went out of the window when it came to swimming. He was so aware of all the benefits that come from it that he wanted to make sure that Matthew would be taught to swim – and swim well.

He'd flick on the lights and shake Matthew awake at the ungodly hour of 5.30am every day for eight long years. This was hell at first but Matthew quickly got used to the early starts. Eventually, he'd wake up feeling alert and raring to go rather than feeling like he'd been shot by a tranquilliser dart full of enough serum to put down a prehistoric woolly mammoth for a few hours.

Chris would make him swim at least 100 lengths during every morning, and as if that wasn't enough, there was an evening session too. That was another 100 lengths minimum. If Chris wasn't able to take him for any given reason, which was usually to do with work, then Linda would drive him there.

As he got used to the gruelling schedule imposed by Chris, Matthew began to adore swimming, along with everything that it did to a person's body, in both physical and psychological terms. Not only was it fun, but he found himself getting really fit as the months rolled on. It made him feel healthier than he'd ever felt before, and he was able to eat pretty much anything he wanted without it having a physical impact on his body.

He noticed other kids at school getting chubby the more junk food they stuffed down their throttles, but not him. He felt more switched on all the time, he felt cheery every day, and he made so many pals through it. It made Matthew a real hard worker too. Seeing the benefits that could be attained through making the effort with swimming, or anything for that matter, it made him want to put his all into anything he did. In adulthood, that would work both to his advantage and to his detriment.

Matthew progressed with swimming over the years and became an extraordinarily talented swimmer by anyone's standards. His hard work was complemented by his slim physique and incredibly long feet. When his dad first told him that long feet would be his making, like long fingers are for a piano player, he was baffled.

What on earth is he banging on about? Matthew would think.

Chris wasn't half right, though, as those kickers helped Matthew reach the nationals and he won a stack of races, one after another, mostly coming in first place and sometimes second. There's a box of gold and silver medals and trophies hidden away in a dark corner of his loft to this day. Matthew was even inches away from being chosen to compete for his country in the Olympics.

His accomplishments were also attributable to his dad's insistence from early on that he must wear swimming trunks instead of swim shorts. Chris argued that, on one hand, shorts – which were undoubtedly heavier – would weigh Matthew down and hold him back. On the other hand, trunks would make him lighter and more streamlined, allowing him to get through the water faster. That wasn't all there was to that, though. From somewhere, Chris had picked up a little nugget of information that wearing trunks a size smaller would be even more helpful in this respect.

"The tighter the better, son," Chris would say, serious as a heart attack. "If you want to move like a fish, it's what you need to do."

Matthew, sceptical at first, was surprised to find out that his dad was right all along. It might not seem like much but wearing tighter trunks must have knocked off a second in total on final race times. That was a big deal as that second could mean the difference between gold and silver, between gold and bronze, or even between gold and fuck all. If it hadn't been for that piece of wisdom, wherever Chris had picked it up from, Matthew would have lost a lot of the races he competed in.

The only issue with the tight trunks was that they were a nightmare to get on, which was problematic right before races. It was bad enough struggling to get them on, having to grease up just to get them over the calves and thighs – which were pretty chunky by then – and up to the hips. These "budgie smugglers" as Chris called them, were also really restrictive once they were on. Matthew was in agony wearing them, his penis and balls squashed down like a woman's waist in a corset.

By the age of fifteen, with a touch of self-destruction, Matthew made the poor decision not to take the sport any further. He told Chris that he had simply lost interest in it all. Although Chris was absolutely gutted knowing how far Matthew could take his talent, he told him that the decision was his to make.

Matthew's decision led to some embarrassment for Chris who had coordinated a lot over the years with Matthew's swimming coach. Alan Peters had invested so much time and effort into Matthew's success, and Chris was mortified that it had all been in vain.

Chris was willing to accept Matthew's decision, but he had one and only one stipulation, that Matthew wrote a meaningful and heartfelt letter of apology to Alan, documenting and justifying his reasons for ditching his passion. He cited the same reason that he'd given his dad, but it was bullshit in reality. The truth was that Matthew was making a crap decision, one based on the fact that, as a fifteen year old lad, he'd just discovered the world of pubs, alcohol, clubbing, and most importantly: GIRLS.

These pursuits brought a whole new level of satisfaction into his life that swimming just couldn't come near to matching. Incidentally, as well as all the health benefits that were attached to swimming, all that stuff is what Chris had been trying so hard to keep Matthew away from.

Before then, yeah, he thought girls were pretty, but he didn't get distracted by them. Chris would egg him on as he'd squeeze himself into the tight, brightly coloured trunks.

"Come on, get those budgie smugglers on," he'd shout as Matthew tried his hardest, then repeating some of the best-known lines of Mickey Goldmill, Rocky Balboa's coach in the unforgettable *Rocky* franchise.

"You're a greasy, fast, Italian tank," he'd yell.

"You're gonna eat lightning, you're gonna crap thunder," he'd add, pumping Matthew up.

With a hard slap on the back, he'd round off with a reference to Rocky catching the chicken in *Rocky II*: "If you can catch this thing, you can catch greased lightning."

There was no chicken, obviously, but the sentiment was there. And it worked to get the adrenaline pumping. Matthew was the one to beat, the key target. His competitors would play dirty, trying to distract him using all the tricks in the book. One team, The Killer Whales, had a lot of the best swimmers and won loads of galas, would send over hot girls to put him off. He was young and full of cum, but he'd hold his hand up to them letting them know he had bigger priorities than their pretty faces…and everything else they had going for them. They weren't used to being knocked back and were often shocked, but Matthew's mind was one track.

Besides, as puberty had hit and as he'd become sexually aware, Matthew started to knock one out before events. He thought that this would allow him to keep his eyes on the prize, guaranteeing that he'd win and beat his personal best. He learned the hard way that he was sorely mistaken. His times got a bit stagnant and he became sluggish, but he couldn't for the life of him figure out why. Always perceptive, Chris had an inkling as to what was going on.

"Son, are you shaking the one-eyed trouser snake?"

Matthew was puzzled, to say the least. "Eh, Dad?"

"Are you beating the meat? Flogging the bishop? Spanking the monkey? You know. Are you having a five-knuckle shuffle?"

The penny finally dropped. Matthew hadn't come across – excuse the pun – most of these terms, but "five-knuckle shuffle" was one he was familiar with for sure. A deep crimson crept across his face as embarrassment set in. He couldn't believe he was having this conversation with his dad. Matthew came clean, admitting that, yeah, he did often have a wank before races. And what of it?

"You NEVER do that within forty-eight hours of a competition as a bare minimum. You'll be sure to lose," he stated, explaining that it drains the stamina, weakens the arms, and makes swimming feel about five times more difficult.

It all made sense, why Matthew had hit a wall, why his arms felt like fat logs after only a single length, and why he felt like someone was pulling him back as he tried to move forwards. Never again did he knock one out within a few days before a race, and it went back to business as usual. The problem with that: girls did become a real distraction! And not just in swimming, but in his social life too. In the end, being a horny teen, one looking for a boozy time with his mates, was the undoing of his swimming career.

Although girls were a major contributor to Matthew's decision to pack in the swimming, the persistence and tenacity that the sport taught him remained into adulthood. Quitting might have been a bad decision, but those qualities would serve him well – sometimes!

Chapter 6 – The Braceys Get Tighter With Soho

As part and parcel of his nature as a teacher, not only did Chris seek design help from Matthew for the signs and encourage him to both watch and help out in the workshop, he also took him out in his typically East London "man-with-a-van" Ford Transit.

During the same period as all the swimming stuff, they'd go about together, working with the older customers at the amusements, carnivals and fairgrounds or "the shows" as Chris called them sometimes – all along the east coast. Chris didn't shy away from taking Matthew along on the Soho jobs too, helping to design and create neon signs for the newer, sex industry clients.

Matthew's eyes were opened from a young age. To say that he got an education early on doesn't even come close to covering it. Oddly, if Chris has been trying to keep Matthew away from that sort of stuff by encouraging him to put his all into swimming, he might have undone some of his good work by immersing Matthew in this grittier side of London.

Chris was a right cockney geezer right down to his bones. He couldn't have hidden it if he tried to. His vocabulary mainly comprised of cockney slang, and anyone unfamiliar with it would be totally lost talking to him. He always had a laugh about that, though. Unlike a lot of other guys who are cockney born and bred – traditionally, anyone from London's east end, and more recently any Londoners with working-class roots – Chris didn't just speak cockney slang. He added to it, making up his own words for the banter. He had such a quick thinking mind and he thought up some really funny shit on the spot. It was these lightning reactions that helped him make a name selling signs in Soho's sex industry in the first place, and it served him well throughout the rest of his life and career.

Back when he'd been working with his dad, where possible, Chris tried to avoid getting into arguments with business owners over delayed payments. However, now that he'd become more of a hardened businessman, joined by the gutsy Linda as his new "wingman" in the business, he didn't suffer fools as gladly as he used to be willing to.

This led to a lot of arguments and fights with the owners of Soho's sex shops, bars, and so on, and he got into some sticky situations with gangsters too. Many a time Matthew watched his dad argue over money. Mostly, the proprietors respected Chris's honesty, courage and front, admiring his refusal to back down to threats, but things often got heavy.

Once, a few gang members roughed Chris up a bit, pinning him against a wall and giving him a few slaps. Chris avoided getting hot-headed, though, knowing that the clever thing wasn't to respond immediately. Instead, he walked out of the place, appearing calm and collected and as if he'd got the message. He returned from his van, which had been parked outside, with his preferred weapon of choice – you got it, Daisy the garden spade. He gave the heavies a chance to pay up, but their refusal led to Daisy being put to work, Chris eventually walking out the victor with what he was owed.

Chris always made sure never to cross Paul Raymond, though, whatever the circumstances. Thankfully, they had a good working relationship that had carried on since Richard had worked on Raymond Revue bar's famous sign years before. Moreover, he usually paid on time, so there was never a need to confront him for any reason. Raymond was considered by everyone to be the godfather of Soho, a right Don Vito Corleone sort of character and one that you just didn't fuck with. He had power and he had money. The latter was evident both from his lavish venue and the hand-made, velvet jackets he sported. If you messed with him, he'd ruin your life. By the same token, Chris avoided any conflicts with other renowned thugs – the top dogs.

Once Raymond had faded off the Soho scene, the area was unofficially run by a number of ruthless English and Maltese gangs. They were in fierce competition with each other and it was so obvious to anyone who fell into their path that a struggle for power was going on there. They were both vying for the best sex establishments, hoping that their punters would make them a fortune. Chris worked hard to avoid getting sucked into this power vacuum, at the same time holding his own so he didn't get squeezed. This was no mean feat as the middle ground between the two was a narrow plank that Chris had to tread very carefully. The alternative: very hot water. Somehow, he navigated and survived in this treacherous world by following what he felt was the "right way".

Chris taught Matthew about the "right way" to make money, giving him possibly the sagest advice he'd ever give him across his lifetime.

"Always be honest and, if possible, always tell the truth," Chris would state with a look on his face so earnest that the importance of his guidance was as clear as day.

And he lived by this rule without exception, never allowing himself to get involved with any shady deals no matter how tempting they were, and irrespective of the shiny outcomes those deals may offer.

While Chris never got into shady deals, he got tied up with some shady characters. They were really difficult people to work with, and Chris had to accept that it was they who set the terms of their deals, not him. He might have been willing to battle with a lot of people in Soho, demanding payment, but things just didn't work like that with his most sinister clients. Chris wanted their business and he just had to get on with it. They weren't totally unreasonable and always paid after some time.

Payment wasn't always made with money. That was how the whole of Soho rolled. If you wanted to do well there, getting repeat business, you had to know when to accept 100 dildos instead of £200. Chris would always get his money that way, and sometimes even more from selling the dildos (or whatever had been given to him as payment). It would just take longer.

The owners of sex establishments were bad people who did bad things. Many a punter would get tricked into the sex shops, peepshows and striptease bars, thinking their hunt for girls was over, only to find a fist in their face. Chris used to have a laugh at their expense.

"The punters aren't the hunters, Matthew. They're the hunted," he'd say mocking them, knowing full well it wasn't really funny what was happening to them.

These guys were heavy-handed and merciless, stopping at nothing to extort money from innocent people, threatening them with the most brutal forms of violence conceivable. In some of the bars men would dress up convincingly as women and flirt or bat their eyelashes into having a drink bought for them by a punter. When the punter obliged, the drink was made by the bar staff and put down in front of the "lady" and the punter would be stiffed with an exorbitant price.

Obviously gullible, unseasoned individuals who had no idea about the way Soho ticked over, they realised what sort of a situation they were in. They either paid up or they paid the price in another way. And it wasn't 100 dildos instead of £200 kind of a deal. If they didn't pay, the gangsters would have no qualms about breaking a digit or two. Fingers or toes – it was all the same to them.

That wasn't all that used to go on. Plenty of other scams were being run on top of that. The proprietors and their henchmen knew that they could pretty much get away with doing whatever they wanted. The punters wouldn't go crawling to the fuzz because they were more than aware that, if they did, they'd end up with more than a broken finger or two. How many fingers might break when you dump the bound and gagged body of a snitch into a grave while he's still breathing? The thought speaks for itself, doesn't it? Even if the punter did run squealing to the police about what happened to them, there was no way of proving it. That being the case, these gangs went about their business, uninterrupted by the authorities and doing over anyone who stood up against them.

The gangs hadn't learned their lesson from the fate of the infamous Kray twins, Ronnie and Reggie, who'd been sentenced to life imprisonment for murder in 1969. Speaking of the Krays, they were released from their respective prisons to attend a funeral held for their mother, Violet. It was the first time that the twins had been seen in public since they were imprisoned, and security for the funeral was very tight. This wasn't only to ensure Ronnie and Reggie kept in line, but also because of the large number of underworld figures that were in attendance. Chris wasn't at the funeral but it was all over the news. In every newspaper and on every channel's news programmes, there they were, each and every one of his clients. About 80% of his client base had been there that day, which goes to show the spheres Chris was operating in.

The way Chris expertly treaded a fine line between standing up for himself and maintaining the precise degree of respect for his hot-tempered customers was nothing short of an almost implausible display of bravura. It earned him a strong reputation in Soho. Everybody trusted Chris, they knew that it wasn't in his nature to be a grass as long as fairness was present in the equation. If he got what he was owed, everything would be gravy. If he didn't, they'd get what was coming to them. His approach got him known as a force to be reckoned with.

On top of working in the office at Electro Signs, Linda took on a second job at Harmony Time – a sex shop in Soho – for a bit of extra cash. The shop sold sex aids, amongst other kinky paraphernalia. Rather than working in the shop itself, Linda ran Ann Summers' style sex parties, keeping all the stock in the cottage and coordinating all the girls involved. This only lasted for a year or so, but while she was doing it she put a lot of the business acumen she'd acquired from Doreen to good use. She was a formidable woman and had to take a tough approach with the girls. She had no other choice but to be like that, or the girls wouldn't have thought twice about short changing her whenever possible. Like Chris, she wasn't someone you'd want to mess with. A true cockney bird who hadn't had the best childhood, she could handle herself.

Handling yourself was a common theme among the Braceys. They could all look after themselves without any problem when it came to difficult situations. From a young age Chris taught Matthew how to defend himself, irrespective of how big the boys picking on him were. His motivational speeches about how to deal with bullies were pretty similar to those he'd give Matthew to get him worked up for his swimming races, and they were accompanied by some extreme action.

Matthew's first lesson in this sense came when he was about 9. While it was nowhere near as bad as Vallentin Street would come to be known, Wood street and the surrounding area had a disproportionately high population of youths in gangs. Close to the family's little cottage, he'd been picked on by a group of older kids.

He'd never understood why kids could be so cruel. Not that it was right, but it even made more sense if they were after money or something like that. The thugs in Soho weren't the best examples of humans, but at least they reserved the majority of their violence to extort money from people rather than just to get their kicks. But these kids in the street were just twats, out looking to beat on someone smaller than them for some cheap thrills. Kids like that go for the ones they think are defenceless – it increases their chances of getting away without any marks on themselves.

Out and about playing, Matthew was just minding his own business, when, from nowhere, he got whacked in the mug with a big C-sized battery. It gave him a cut in his face that measured over an inch, and it was bloody sore. The kids who'd hurled the battery at him stood there pissing themselves with laughter, threatening him with some more if he didn't bugger off "their patch." Matthew thought it would be in his best interests to do as they said and scarpered as quick as he could, his tail between his legs and tears streaming down his cut-up, bloody face.

When Matthew had made it back to the cottage, he walked in the door to be met by Chris.

"What the hell's happened here?" he said, with rage in his voice – not at Matthew, but at the unknown perpetrators.

Matthew had thought about lying, embarrassed at what had gone down outside, but he reluctantly came clean. Without a thought, Chris put a hand on Matthew's back and together they marched back down the street.

"Dad, why are we going back?" Matthew asked, terrified of what was coming.

"You're gonna go back and face up to the little fucktards. That's why we're going back. You DO NOT give in to bullies, no matter what, no matter how big they are. Understand me?"

With Chris towering above them, the boys hadn't looked so tough any more, and Matthew could see that they had suddenly become the vulnerable ones. Like the punters in Soho, who had started out as the hunters, the predators, these bullies had been made the hunted, the prey.

"Go on, punch him," Chris urged, nodding his head towards the biggest one.

The boy braced himself. As Matthew's clenched fist landed on his face with a thud, he looked like a scared little rabbit. The boy started to fight back. Something had been unlocked inside Matthew, and he went for the boy with the same vigour as he put into his swimming. He carried on punching the boy until he begged him to stop.

Matthew might have taken a few punches, but he'd won fair and square. After this, word must have got around that he wasn't one to fuck with, because he was left alone by all the other youths as well as these kids. Matthew has always appreciated being taught that old-fashioned but vital lesson: stick up for yourself or you'll be a victim.

Chapter 7 – The Braceys Get Into The Movies

While doing his rounds in Soho, Chris was approached by another guy called Chris Townsend (we'll call him Townsend for the sake of avoiding confusion here) working with a film unit. He and his team wanted to know if Chris could help them get inside the strip joint whose sign he was working on to do some filming inside.

Townsend had already asked the proprietor, Mike, who'd knocked him back. Mike didn't trust that they were really a film team, instead suspicious that they were really from the Inland Revenue or such like. Chris believed that it wasn't anything like that, though. There's no way that the Inland Revenue, or any other government organisation, the police or whatever, would go to the lengths of hiring so much expensive camera equipment and so on, as well as organising the gigantic, professional film location van they had with them.

No way, these guys were the real deal. Just as luck had come his way when he'd been up that ladder and approached by his first Soho client, an opportunity had landed in front of him there. Chris promised the crew that he could get them inside on the proviso that he could do all the neon signage for whatever film it was they were working on. The deal was struck, the film crew got their location, and Chris got to do the signs for the movie.

It only turned out to be the 1986 film *Mona Lisa* by Neil Jordan starring Bob Hoskins. If you haven't seen the film, go watch it. About a call girl and the ex-convict driver she's hired to take her from one dangerous job to another, this British neo-noir crime drama has been called "classy kitsch" and "an unsavoury yarn" among other insults, but the performances of Hoskins, Cathy Tyson, Robbie Coltrane and Michael Caine are amazing.

In the movie game fat wallets were everywhere and nothing was too expensive. It might not be the same today, but that's certainly what it was like back in the 80s. Handmade Films, the production company who made *Mona Lisa,* really appreciated the help that Chris had given them and loved his neon work. It was a landmark moment, not just for Chris, but for the Soho sex scene too. This was the first time they had opened their doors to a film crew, and nothing had gone wrong.

With the money Chris made working on *Mona Lisa*, he was able to purchase larger premises further up Wood Street on Vallentin Road. He knew things were about to move to the next level and he'd need the additional space. The building was an old war bunker that had been converted into a factory. Before they took it over, the factory had been used for printing fake money. Sadly, for the owners of the racket, they'd been busted by the police a little while before. To Chris's benefit that meant the building was going for a complete song, and he snapped it right up.

When the business moved into the factory there was fake money everywhere, stashed into the walls and the ceiling. Chris couldn't believe that the police had missed it and left it there. Naturally, he disposed of the counterfeit currency. Even if he'd had no qualms about using it, he couldn't have done if he wanted to as it was of such shoddy quality. No wonder they'd been rumbled.

In the far corner the old war bunker was still there, as the building had just been constructed around it. Chris supposed that it must have been easier to do that than going to the effort of knocking it down and filling it in. And he was right because when he made the decision to knock the thing down himself, to free up some more space, it was the end of him. It took Chris six solid weeks of intensive labour to raze it. Even though it nearly killed him, he was glad that he'd done it.

This was the beginning of a whole new chapter for the business, with the business working on loads of different films, television shows, commercials, music videos, and much more. The company signed a lot of deals with Elstree Studios, Pinewood Studios, and a number of others too, working on a host of familiar titles including *Roger Rabbit, Superman IV: The Quest For Peace, Teenage Mutant Ninja Turtles,* and *Judge Dredd.* Working on the films really changed the lives of the Braceys in so many different ways, and it allowed them to make the most unexpected connections with famous people from all over the world.

Matthew's younger brother Max actually played baby Superman in *Superman IV* in the scene where baby Superman is sent to Earth from the planet Krypton in a crystal by his parents. This had come about by chance after Chris overheard a conversation on set about a baby being needed. Peter Young, the film's set designer and two time Oscar winner, piped up that Chris and his wife had just had a baby who was the perfect age for the role. And that was that. Even though the scene was cut, it can still be seen in the director's cut. Pretty cool claim to fame for Max nonetheless, huh? It's certainly one he tells on dates, and it serves him well. Until today, he gets invited to conventions to sign autographs and he is technically the only actor alive who plays Superman in any of the franchise's iterations from the original movies.

Matthew was ten at the time and allowed on the set. With wide eyes that chuffed little boy got to watch the frenzied battle scenes between Superman and Nuclear Man (although there were actually two nuclear men in the original cut). It would become one of Matthew's favourite films of all time.

Chris and Peter Young came to be good pals. You could say that Peter was a "superfan". Get it? Oh, OK, terrible pun. Regardless, he loved Chris's work so much that he put "Bracey's" on a shop sign in one scene of *Superman IV*. The shop gets absolutely destroyed by Nuclear Man (horrible sod). Goes to show: nukes are no good for anyone! A sign that Chris once made for the Hard Rock Café, London, which says "No drugs or nuclear weapons allowed in here", confirms that.

Later that year, Max also played an infant Barbara Hutton in *Poor Little Rich Girl: The Barbara Hutton Story*, the adult version of whom was played by none other than Farrah Fawcett. No, you didn't misread. Max played a little girl even though he's a boy, but at that age it's pretty difficult to assess a baby's sex. That explains why so many parents go down the route of blue clothes for boys and pink for girls.

Although Matthew had been helping out for years with design ideas and other bits and pieces, he was eventually old enough to contribute in a much bigger way. No longer as slim as he'd been back in his swimming days, he'd bulked out and grown a ponytail like his dad's and got to a whopping six foot two. Chris stepped aside and let Matthew take over in terms of going out on the tools and dealing with customers "out in the field" so to speak. At this point Chris also moved into the office, significantly reducing his role in the workshop. He wanted to concentrate on growing the business and took on some workmen to take over the more physical stuff in the workshop. With Chris putting in more time in the office, and with Matthew out and about dealing with the Soho customers, other movie work started to pour in.

While on the set of *Interview With A Vampire*, there on standby just in case any of the neon lights blew up or ran a fault, Matthew would stand at the back of the set smoking with Brad Pitt between takes. Christian Slater would join them for the odd puff here and there. It was all par for the course, you know, casual cigarette breaks with Brad Pitt and Christian Slater. As he stood there in a cloud of smoke one day, Matthew wondered what that unlucky kid in the playground would think of his older self hobnobbing with celebrities.

After many years Chris asked Matthew to move into the office. Things had changed a lot for the business and Soho was almost unrecognisable now. The old-school, East London gangster style of doing things had come to an end. This was unsurprising as everyone knew it couldn't go on like that forever. The police, who had overlooked a lot of stuff in Soho's heyday, had increased their presence in the area, taking a heavier hand with licensing. The gangs from London and Malta had more (and stronger competition) from gangs of other nationalities who had started to arrive on the scene, with more elaborate scams, better connections, more resources, and an even more vicious, take-no-prisoners approach to conducting business than Soho had seen before.

With all that change in Soho and everything that had happened for the family business, a fresh take was called for. Chris needed someone he could trust in the office and Matthew was the man for the job.

Chapter 8 –
The Years Leading To The Steel Deal

Matthew had agreed to take the office role within the company which he was happy about. However, he was less than pleased with the space. Basically, his dad had asked him to come to work in the dark and dusty corner of the workshop, a disorganised mess of papers and filing cabinets. Matthew, a decent negotiator by then, persuaded Chris to build him an office so that he could have a decent place to work from.

The office would be built by extending the first floor. Matthew was elated that his dad had agreed to this, but that elation soon faded away once he realised the outcome of it. The result was a sad shed plonked into the roof. They nicknamed this "the hole in the wall". If you think of Harry Potter's cupboard under the stairs, you wouldn't be far off.

Looking at the rest of the building, which was in a state just as poor as Charlie's house in the *Charlie and the Chocolate Factory* remake, Matthew could actually consider himself as lucky even though it didn't offer him much more space than the dusty corner downstairs. The building was pretty tatty overall. Located on a corner, right in front of a big block of flats, it was covered in pebble dash all round. There were a couple of windows at the front on the first floor and both a shop front door and a couple of garage doors (covered in graffiti) at the front downstairs.

Matthew complained to his dad about the space he'd been given, but Chris, being both a tough boss and father, wouldn't hear any of it.

He went on a rant.

"I gave you a fucking window. What more do you want? OK, so it looks at Northwood Tower which holds the most ruthless bunch of pirates and villains in East London, but it's a fucking window, isn't it? That's something no other cunt in this place has got."

Unreasonable or not, he was right. It did have a window. Then he started going on about how the block of flats had housed a celebrity at some point since it was put up.

"If Brian Harvey from East 17 has lived there, it can't be that fucking bad."

It was a weak argument from Chris's end, but he wasn't going to change his mind. Matthew knew that this was his lot. He wasn't going to get anything better out of his dad. Matthew would just have to make the most of his hole in the wall. He set about making it as nice as he could, which wasn't that nice. It would come to be stuffed full of paperwork, old filing cabinets, a couple of battered desks, and a threadbare carpet. Every inch of the walls was covered in pictures of movies that the company had worked on and celebrities the family had mingled with over the years through work connections. There were cobwebs in every corner and neon signs everywhere. To this day, the office hasn't changed a bit.

The building remains there too, cracking and derelict, the floor higher in places than others, squeaky floorboards and all. The exterior got tarted up over the years painted a deep blue colour with a red awning being added to the left window of the office, and a massive print of Chris added on the side flanked by angel's wings. Even so, the place is like nothing else that you'd find in this day and age. Battered and broken, it lives on.

While Matthew was set up in his less than modern office, the world was modernising at a rapid pace. Part of this was the rise of the internet. Chris was an old-fashioned sort of bloke and despised all the technological advancements that were coming in then. Not only did he resist new technology, but he got mad whenever anyone around him would talk about technology.

"If I had my own way the world would stay exactly like it is. All these developments, so-called progress, they're just taking a shit all over the world. And it's fine like it is," he'd say, over and over, or words to the effect at least.

His attitude towards technology meant that he preferred to keep things traditional with the business, employing sign-makers whose methods were a bit more dated than some more contemporary sign-makers.

Matthew, however, embraced technology, seeing it as something that could take the family business into the future. His hole in the wall might not have been his ideal workspace, but he could open the door to technology making his job a lot easier and working to the advantage of the company. Matthew wouldn't let his dad's resistance to technology stand in the way of essential progress. Chris would thank him in the end once he saw what "all those new-fangled devices" could achieve. Until then everything had been written up by hand or on a typewriter and sent by good old snail mail – or sent by fax machine at best. Matthew bought a few PCs, keeping one for himself and giving the others to the office staff that now worked there. When he first broke into Soho, Chris had been intent on modernising the signage of the sex establishments, taking them away from outmoded acrylic and introducing them to fashionable neon. Similarly, Matthew was now set on bringing Electro Signs in line with the practices of modern businesses even if Chris was displeased with the changes.

Matthew didn't just want to stop at implementing technological changes in the business. He wanted to get far more radical than that. He pitched the idea of Signbuyer to Chris which he'd been thinking about for some time. This would be an internet shop, e-commerce, something far removed from Chris's comfort zone. Knowing about his dad's relationship with technology, it was clear that the proposition wasn't going to be one he'd welcome with open arms. If the pitch had been on *Dragon's Den*, Deborah Meaden, Peter Jones, Duncan Bannatyne, and any of the newer dragons might have gone for it straight away, but if Chris was a dragon he'd definitely shout, "I'm out!" As anticipated, it took some persuasion. Chris had no clue what Matthew was on about.

"The web? What the fuck are you on about? Have you lost your fucking marbles, boy?"

Matthew endeavoured to explain the world wide web to his dad.

"Right. How do I put it? It's basically an information system that anyone can access from anywhere on the internet, which is an invisible network that stores all the information. You can go online on your computer, read things, do things, send electronic mail, buy things. You see?"

Chris did not see. He couldn't get it at all

"So, it's in the air floating around, is it? Information just bobbing about in the air? Makes no sense, Matthew."

It took the best part of a weekend getting the concepts of the internet and the web across to Chris, and Matthew told a couple of porkies. One was that, yes, the internet is in the air. Well, it is, sort of. One of his dad's key concerns was the information being intercepted by dodgy bastards.

"Dad, don't worry. Your private information is encrypted. That means the Russians can't get to it. That's all you need to know."

Two gruelling days later and Chris was vaguely on board with the idea. He trusted Matthew and knew that he wouldn't do anything he thought could harm the business. It was time to see what Matthew could really bring to the table if he was given free rein.

By this time Matthew was married to Sarah. They'd met when she was eleven and he was thirteen. Some cynics argue that love at first sight isn't possible, but it had happened to Matthew's parents and it had happened again with Sarah. There's a neon sign in their kitchen that depicts how they felt about each other on first sight: "When I saw you I fell in love and you smiled because you knew." Even though they had feelings for each other they'd remained friends for years before getting together, attending the school youth club, drinking milkshakes from the tuck shop, watching *Eastenders*, and taking walks around Highams Park forest and lake.

Four years later, at new year, they bumped into each other in a club. Matthew had obviously been keen but Sarah was playing it cool. That went down the drain when the table she was sitting on collapsed, leaving her on her back and arse rolling around on the floor. They erupted in hysterics, her face bright red. Matthew was always making a twat of himself, so it was nice not to be him for a change. They had their first kiss that night and they've been together ever since. They moved in together at sixteen, had their first son three years later, and their second four years after that.

In a fitting tribute to Sarah's scarlet face after she fell off the table that night in the club, on their wedding day a wasp had found its way into her veil and stung her, leaving her face all red and swollen.

Unfortunately, that wasn't the only stroke of bad luck the couple had the day they got married. A bit of the Matthew Bracey curse made an appearance that day. It was roasting hot at thirty-five degrees, so much so that everyone was dripping with sweat. The air conditioning in the reception hall was bust too. Just after the first dance, Sarah's aunt even collapsed with heat exhaustion and had to be whisked off to the hospital. Poor bird. Vinyl king Ricky, long since gone from Electro Signs, miraculously and unluckily turned up as their chauffeur, still boozy and shaky as hell. They just about made it to the reception, albeit forty-five minutes late, after taking the wrong route twice.

Anyway, Chris had given the go ahead for Signbuyer which would later become signbuyer.co.uk displayed in a huge sign on the premises – yup, a neon one. A year in the making, Matthew's vision became a reality. It was an instant success, its first order coming in only three hours of the website going live. It had paid off. Phew! Chris was brimming with pride at his son's handiwork, and unexpectedly at Matthew's technological prowess. When asked about his computer abilities by anyone Chris would just shrug.

"I don't need to learn about computers and the internet. My sperm does it for me."

Chris's pride was indisputable. He saw his son as an extension of himself. That made Matthew feel really good about himself.

With Matthew's help the company grew. Increasingly, Chris had more time to focus on his neon art. With neon in his blood and argon in his eyes, he brought his incredible ideas to life. As he poured himself into his art, and work to some extent too, Chris became somebody else. Jobs were getting tougher, clients more challenging to deal with and expectations of quality were at an all-time high.

He was in huge demand and rarely had time for anyone. Everyone wanted a piece of him and it was stressing him out to the max. Nearly at breaking point, he'd allocate fifteen seconds to anyone wanting his attention.

"NEXT!" he'd holler as their time ran out and it was somebody else's turn.

That said, he always found time for Matthew, prioritising him over anyone else and never failing to welcome him with a warm smile and a cheerful greeting. They were rarely at odds with one another, and it was as if Matthew couldn't put a foot wrong. Chris constantly bragged about how the enterprising Matthew could buy 1000 cheap signs from China and sell them in thin air. Of course, he meant the web. Be that as it may, the steel deal was about to turn Matthew's good business record on its head.

Chapter 9 – The Steel Deal

Matthew had been working in the office for many years. Business was ticking along nicely, but Matthew became twitchy. Although Signbuyer represented a major departure from anything the business had done in the past, Matthew had never taken any real risks. He knew that the venture would work out, even if Chris had some initial reservations. On the whole, he'd always played safe and done things the way his dad wanted them done. It was now time for a new challenge.

In early 2007, Matthew was deep in the depths of the internet when he stumbled upon something that aroused his curiosity. It was a website with advertisements seeking parties to fulfil unbelievably huge orders for metals and minerals. Matthew was accustomed to orders with a value of between £50 and £10,000, but the orders on this site ran into the millions. He became excited, thinking to himself, "One order. Getting the product from A to B. How hard can it be?"

He couldn't help but wonder if there was something he wasn't understanding about it all. There were hundreds, if not thousands of orders for raw materials just sitting there, ready for the taking and nobody fulfilling them. He trawled through the list eventually finding one that sounded relatively simple:

£2,000,000 STEEL DEAL NEEDED FOR IRAN URGENTLY!

Matthew was oblivious to the fact that Iran was sanctioned by many countries at the time, with rising fears as to their nuclear intentions with regards to its nuclear energy programme. Once again, thinking back to Nuclear Man destroying the fictional Bracey's store in *Superman IV,* nukes are no good for anyone!

In his ignorance Matthew began calling most of the major steel firms in the UK, trying to source a company that could supply the steel and find out at what price. This is when Matthew learned that

Iran was sanctioned and that it wouldn't be possible to ship steel there – legally, that is. Matthew had never been one to give up easily, usually operating on the basis that there's a way around any obstacle. A couple of days went by and then Matthew received an ominous phone call from an unknown man. His voice was deep and his tone threatening.

"Stop looking into sending steel to Iran or you will regret it!" he warned.

Matthew gulped and said, "OK," before the phone went dead. He never found out the identity of the mystery caller, but he wasn't planning on letting some invisible man put him off his grand scheme. Matthew was a little wary but certainly not scared enough to go off the idea. There were seven-figure sums of money to be made and like fuck was he going to back away from that. Pumped full of the same adrenaline and butterflies that he used to feel right before a big swimming race, Matthew pressed on.

He'd had zilch success with the UK steel firms. None of them was up for it due to the sanctions, and the prices they had mentioned were extortionate anyhow. He figured that he'd have to take his search outside the country's borders and look elsewhere.

In retrospect, on some level, the phone call had left him afraid of pursuing the matter in the UK. Matthew racked his mind as to where he could source large quantities of steel at low prices, and then, like a meteor ploughing into the planet at full pelt, it hit him: China!

If he could buy cheap signs from China and sell them at signbuyer.co.uk for a big profit, then why couldn't he buy cheap steel there? It was perfect. He started to send countless emails to steel firms across the country, with his first bite coming a few days later.

The response was from a man called Henri who claimed that his firm has all the steel that Matthew needed and could fulfil every part of the order. Matthew was thrilled as it all seemed to be heading in the right direction. The whole deal seemed legit, the potential profit was amazing, and the supplier seemed professional enough.

There was just one tiny hitch: he didn't have the cash himself. There was only one place he could go for the large investment he needed, so he invited Chris out to dinner. It was time to get his backer on board this money train.

Matthew booked a table for two at his favourite Italian restaurant, Pizzeria Bel-Sit in Woodford. They ordered some beers and a couple of pizzas and gabbed for a bit. Matthew was planning on getting at least halfway through the meal before putting the idea on the table, but the restaurant was busy, noisy and he could barely hear himself think. It was getting him stressed out, and soon after their starters arrived he decided to get it over and done with.

"Dad, I've been thinking."

"That's a dangerous game to play, son," Chris said smirking.

Matthew didn't even break a smile, desperate to come out with it all. "How about we sell some big orders to another country? We can buy from China and sell to Kuwait, etcetera."

Chris, only half listening as he wolfed down a garlic-smothered langoustine, said, "Yeah, sounds good to me. What are we selling?"

"Steel, Dad!"

"Right, I see. And how much wedge do you need?"

There was a brief pause before Matthew answered. "A million."

Chris almost spat out the mouthful of beer he'd just swigged. "You've got to be fucking kidding me. Where the fuck do you think I'm going to find that kind of money? I don't run a fucking brothel!"

"Dad, we can make £500,000 each if this works out. Can you find the money from somewhere?" Matthew pleaded.

Chris trusted Matthew, he had no reason not to as he had never disappointed him before. Well, other than ditching his swimming career. He believed that Matthew had it all in hand, and with a bit of a head bob indicated that he might just about be able to swing it. They chatted about the details over the remainder of their grub before Chris appeared to be in.

"We've got to get it past the governor first."

Of course, Chris was talking about Linda. Her business head had only got stronger as the years had gone on and she was the sharpest thinker of the Bracey bunch. Matthew knew that his mum could easily put the kibosh on the whole thing, given that she was the one who was essentially in charge of the money. Like Doreen had once been, she was the accountant, and also like her mother-in-law had been she was the matriarch of her family unit. The true backbone of the family and the business, not a single thing went ahead without

Linda's approval, and Chris and Matthew would have to tread very carefully with this one.

Matthew waited for just the right time to fly the idea past his mum, and a sunny September's day when everyone was in a good mood seemed as good a time as any. It was the weekend and Matthew had popped in to his parents' home. He approached Linda, her head deep in the company books, while Chris was painting in the background.

Matthew put the kettle on and deftly popped a cup of tea, just how she likes it, in front of Linda. He pushed her fags and lighter towards her knowing the best way to calm her down before the big ask.

"Mum, I have a business venture that needs your approval."

"OK, dear, what is it?" she asked, intrigued.

"I have this huge deal that I need Dad to invest in. Basically, it's making steel parts for a Chinese client."

This was a huge lie, but the worst was yet to come. Linda wasn't keen.

"Listen, son, we don't have money for silly fucking ideas. We worked hard in this family to get where we are today. Throwing money away in these difficult times is stupid!"

Matthew wasn't deterred. His mum would always disparage any idea at first, it was just her way. She would blow even the best of ideas out of the sky, tearing it to shreds, all the while swearing the house down, blowing smoky clouds in the air, and sipping a cuppa. This time was no different. Chris continued to paint, not saying a word throughout the whole conversation between his son and wife.

An hour went by, Matthew holding his cool and not betraying his nerves, in the knowledge that his mum might cotton on to his lies or to the fact that the venture could be dangerous. He'd come bearing some forged documents that simplified the deal, hiding its link with Iran and that it would cost a million squid. He just wanted her to agree to it and to get his dad on a plane to China to get the ball rolling. Any difficulties that arose, they could iron out once they were there. That was the plan anyway. Linda seemed to buy into the plan a little more once she realised that nothing would be agreed upon before Matthew and Chris flew out to China to scope it all out. However, some scepticism remained.

"So, let me see if I've got this right. You want to fly to China with your father on some dream that you're going to make a million between you?"

"Erm, yeah. I suppose that's the long and short of it."

Linda paused, her face blank. Matthew wondered if they had her.

"Well, if you think that I'm that fucking stupid, you've got another thing coming." They didn't have her. By this time, she was standing up, waving her fag around and ashes flying all over the show. Chris finally decided to chip in to help a rapidly sinking Matthew.

"Lin, I love you and you know I always think that you're right, but give the boy some space. He's not proven us wrong yet, has he? Do you want him going to the other side of the world without me on this deal? He's a persistent little bastard and he'll go whether you say yes or not. Right?"

That was all it took. Linda stood for a moment, paused and launched at Matthew with a hug.

"OK, son. If your dad's behind you on this and you really want to do it, then go for it. But I have to be involved with every aspect of the arrangements. Clear?"

It was clear as fucking crystal. Matthew couldn't believe it. She'd agreed to the deal, it was basically signed and done. The sound of money pinged through Matthew's mind.

We'll be laughing all the way to the bank, he thought. Would they, though? Would they really?

Matthew got in touch with the Iranian organisation that had posted the ad for the steel order and they agreed that he'd fulfil it within the space of three months. When they sent him the details, he noticed that it entailed multiple different parts of steel of different shapes and sizes. It appeared to be parts for machinery of some kind.

He sent the specifics to Henri who then dropped the bombshell that Matthew would have to bring the tooling for the parts to check quality expectations and grade of steel. This threw Matthew into turmoil. After that mysterious, threatening call he'd had, how would he swing organising tooling with a UK steel firm? He was terrified that he was being watched. It was a possibility for sure. He wondered if it could be a competitor.

He set about trying to find a components manufacturer to sort out the tooling, and amazingly he got one just at the bottom of Wood

Street called Goss Components. He rocked up there on foot minutes later, laying out his plans only to be told that the components would take six weeks minimum and that they would cost 30 grand alone.

This was a major setback. For a start, Matthew needed them within three weeks, and there was no way he could shell out £30,000 for something that might not even happen. Some speedy problem solving was required. Quick thinking Matthew offered the manufacturer a 5% cut assuming it came off. They bought it and the contract was soon drawn up and signed. Things were back on track.

The tooling was completed in two short weeks and Matthew arranged a meeting with China. Matthew was no fool, aware that everything would have to be planned down to the final detail. Not only would they need flights, transport on the ground and accommodation, but they'd also need a translator. The communication he'd had with Henri so far had been in broken English, so he wasn't confident that a deal of this value could be negotiated safely without a translator.

Matthew was in the office with his parents when he thought he'd get Chris's thoughts on a translator. Linda chimed in, though.

"No fucking translator, that costs money. You'll just have to talk in Chinese," she said sternly.

"Mum, come on. Really? I'll just conduct a 2 million quid deal using this, will I?" Matthew retorted while waving a Chinese dictionary in her face. Her face was expressionless and Matthew realised she wasn't joking. Chris to the rescue once more.

"Don't worry. I have a friend in China. You remember, Lin? That bloke Arthur Chang? The Buddhist monk from Hong Kong?" Matthew burst out laughing, about to comment when Linda answered her husband.

"Oh yes, I remember. You don't get much better than him. He loves a deal, that guy. If you cut him in on the deal then he'll travel with you for free anywhere. I bet he'd even sort out your transport and tell you what hotels to stay in." Linda had been placated. Praise be.

"Dad, is there anyone you don't fucking know? A fucking Buddhist monk from China. Are you kidding me? What's next? A camel specialist in Kuwait?" Matthew wouldn't have been surprised if the answer to that had been yes!

Matthew emailed Arthur Chang, offering 5% for his help. When he replied, he came back with a counter-offer of 15% and the cost of his flight from Hong Kong and accommodation. Matthew caved as they needed him. When he told Chris about this Chris wasn't surprised saying that Arthur was a shrewd player, someone you couldn't squeeze a penny out of. Apparently, Arthur told Chris a story once that made him understand how things work in Hong Kong.

He'd said, "Chris, you want me to live in a shack like some skinny dog? You want me to starve my family because you want more money? If I want to get anywhere in this country, I have to move up! And I mean up! The richest live at the top of the buildings and the poorest at the bottom. I'm on the seventh floor and I want to be on the thirty-third. Now pay me what's right and we got a deal!" And that's Arthur Chang.

A date was set, the meeting was locked down, and hundreds of emails were sent back and forth making the necessary arrangements and coordinating everyone involved. Henri requested that the meeting be held in Tianjin where he was based. Matthew could only get flights to Beijing, though, so that's just how it would have to be. Arthur was decent enough to arrange some transportation between Beijing and Tianjin as well as the hotels, not giving any specifics but stating that it would all be satisfactory. With a few bumps along the road everything had fallen into place neatly. That was it, nothing could go tits up from that point onwards. Or so Matthew believed.

Two days later the lads set off to Heathrow Airport where they bought some unnecessary crap in the shops through security, knocked back a few swift halves, and boarded their eleven-hour flight to Beijing. All that was left to do was enjoy some free booze, force down a shitty meal served on a plastic tray, take in a couple of movies, check out a couple of air stewardesses, and nod off to dreams of a million fucking quid. Little did they know that Matthew's bad luck monster was about to rear its ugly head again, returning with a greater vengeance than ever before ready to unleash all hell on them. As the tin capsule hurtled over Iran, Matthew and Chris zizzed away blissfully unaware of the absolute circus that awaited them.

Chapter 10 – And So It Begins

Matthew prised his eyes open just about an hour before landing. A stewardess called Tina was standing in front of him. She had a massive shock of ginger hair and a face littered with freckles. Apparently, she had been nudging him for about two minutes to wake him up for breakfast. Ordinarily, Tina wouldn't waste so much time trying to awaken a passenger who clearly wanted to carry on sleeping, but Matthew had given her direct instructions not to let him sleep through breakfast. If he didn't start his day with something to eat, washed down with a strong coffee, well, you're best not to get in his way.

He snorted as he came to, thanking the stewardess for doing what he asked her to. She told him that he was welcome with a scowl on her face. As Matthew looked to his right, his dad was still fast asleep. Matthew decided to leave him be as Chris wasn't quite the same hangry – hungry angry – monster as Matthew without a good nosh first thing.

As Chris snored lightly, Matthew wiped the congealed crust from his eyes as he perused what sat upon the tray table in front of him. He knocked back a little carton of water, followed by an even smaller carton of orange juice. What awaited him beneath a little foil package? Ah, a half-decent looking full English breakfast. Well, a half English breakfast really; it was teensy. He polished it off in under two minutes, wiping up any juices with an almost stale roll while thinking about Sarah.

Sarah's cooked breakfasts were amazing, he thought to himself. She always knew exactly how to get the bacon with just the right amount of crisp on the fat, and she daren't let the baked beans sit next to the runny egg. As far as Matthew was concerned, runny egg yolk and beans did not make for good friends with each other. Never the twain shall meet was the motto he went by in that respect. That was the rule. Matthew smiled thinking about her cooking, but not just that. Just about her in general. He was so in love with her. Just as in love with her as when they'd met as teenagers. He wouldn't do anything to upset her on purpose.

"Tea or coffee, sir?" asked a different cabin crew member.

Matthew nodded to the coffee, smiling, and a steaming cup of coffee was poured into the little plastic cup that he held out to her. He recoiled as a splash of boiling hot water hit his skin. The hostess hadn't noticed. The poor bugger must have been worn out after working such a long shift, so he let it fly.

Sarah was a great wife. Always had been to be fair. She'd never stopped believing in Matthew, whatever idea or scheme he threw at her and however hairbrained it might seem to her. Basically, she stuck with him through thick and thin. There wasn't much trouble in their marriage, though, but that was mainly because Matthew would have been daft to cross Sarah.

Just like his mum, his wife was a tough nut not to be crossed. If Matthew promised her something, then be it upon his own bloody head if he didn't stick to it. She always, absolutely always, held him to his word. What about lying? Well, if a word that fell out of Matthew's mouth happened to be close to untrue, then Sarah could sniff it out like a boar hunting for truffles in the Italian countryside. She had a sixth sense for lies, and Matthew was more than aware of that. He'd been caught out by her superpower a few times in their younger years. They had just been a few little lies but they were enough to raise the beast in his wife, so he had quickly learned that honesty was the best policy with her. And that had served him well across the years without a doubt.

Before Matthew had even taken a third sip of his coffee the first stewardess came to collect his tray, not even asking if he was finished with everything. He was though, so it didn't matter. He still had his coffee to wake him the hell up and that was the important thing.

Sarah was all about family. Having a nice family life was something that she had always craved and had always been willing to work hard to establish. Part of such a family life was having a happy home. It was always her biggest dream, and nothing would get in the way of that. When Matthew was out and about working on whatever movie had come the business' way, the days weren't easy. They were long old days, sometimes reaching as much as fourteen hours each day. And as if that wasn't bad enough, much of the time he had to put in seven of these a week for weeks on end. This sometimes carried on for months at a time. Day often turned into night, with Matthew forced to work right through the hours of darkness until he forgot about the unsociable hours he was operating in. It wasn't uncommon for him to find some cosy, hidden corner to take a quick kip in, just to get his batteries recharged and get him raring to go again.

All through this Sarah never uttered a single word of complaint because she knew how important his work was, not only to him but to their family. Matthew was the breadwinner. He was the one who brought home the proverbial bacon that Sarah used to buy the actual bacon that she could crisp up to perfection. This way of life, Matthew gone all the time and coming back home at all hours, was totally the norm for the family.

In total they'd eventually have four children – three boys and one girl – which really is no mean feat. Even though they say that the first is the worst when it comes to having and raising children, anyone who actually has four of the little terrorists will tell you that it's one of the most monumental challenges a person could ever face in their lifetime.

Sarah was a grafter though, not shy of hard work in the slightest and always approaching the care of her children with enthusiasm. She looked after them in the unrelenting way a proper old-fashioned matron would with her charges, but the difference between Sarah and an old battleaxe was that she looked after the kids with unmeasured love. It was the ideal approach to raising kids. A tough but fair approach that made them knew that they were loved, but taught them that if they were planning on fucking with her there would be consequences. It wasn't too far off the standard she'd set in her marriage with Matthew. It's a method that works, so why not?

Matthew took a look at Chris who was still fast asleep. What a machine, Matthew thought. His mouth was hanging open a bit by now, so Matthew gently pushed his flycatcher shut. Nobody needed to see in there. He sat twiddling his thumbs and closed his eyes for a few minutes, continuing his thoughts of his wife.

In 2007 when the steel deal started to come to fruition, Sarah was heavily preggers with their third child. She was a petite woman, but extremely sexy and beautiful with it. She wore her long blonde hair all the way down to her hips and she carried it really well. It always accentuated her gorgeous face, and when you paired that with her exquisite sense of style and fashion, she was the perfect partner and wife in physical terms as well as all the rest.

Whenever she was pregnant was when Matthew really knew to be especially careful around her. This is when he paid close attention to the invisible manual that he'd written in his head. That manual was entitled *How To Deal With The Trouble And Strife Wife*. In the manual, which had become a lifesaver at certain points of their marriage as an unfailing go-to guide, there were five deadly terms used by Sarah that Matthew absolutely could not forget or he would be in a hot mess. When these terms came out of Sarah's mouth, Matthew knew that it was time to replace his shoes with small, fluffy clouds so that he could tread very carefully around her.

As the cabin crew finished off clearing up after the breakfast service, Matthew thought about those five deadly terms, chuckling to himself at the thought of them.

#

The first was "Fine". Matthew had come to learn that's the word that Sarah would use when she wished to bring an argument between them to a close. When Matthew heard this word, he knew that the argument was no longer on the go and that he should shut his mouth without delay. It didn't actually mean that everything was fine or that he'd won. It simply meant that she'd had enough and wasn't willing to listen any longer.

The second was "Nothing". As many men have come to understand, "nothing" absolutely, unequivocally means "something". Huh? Exactly, it makes absolutely no sense to men, but to women it makes all the sense. Because it makes sense to them, the fact that you men don't get it is of no consequence. You simply need to accept that when you ask the question, "what's wrong?" and you're met with a "nothing", oh boy, you are in hot water, my friends. If you hear that you're in trouble, but there's no hard and fast set of rules about how you should tread after you've become sure that you're buggered. Probing further may just enhance the foul temper, but equally, simply accepting that nothing is up could lead to further turmoil. This one is massively subjective. Good luck figuring it out.

The third was "Go ahead". Now, this one isn't anything like you might think it is. It isn't a dare and it doesn't mean that Matthew has been given permission to go ahead and do something. Oh no. Rather, it's a clear statement that if Matthew was actually to be bold enough to go ahead and do the thing in contention his head will be on the chopping block. He'd never been bold enough to accept the fatal challenge, so he had no idea what the consequences were to be exact. He was certain about the fact that they weren't likely to be all fun and games, though.

The fourth was "Whatever". This isn't like Catherine Tate's mouthy character Lauren and her famous "Whatevaaaaaaaaa," uttered by the generation of teens who loved her comedy. Instead, it's another way for Sarah to tell Matthew to go screw himself. With this one, whatever the circumstances, no matter if Matthew is, in fact, right, "whatever" means that Sarah isn't willing to accept it. It means that she's called bullshit and there's no questioning it. Think of it as the same as when a person calls shotgun to reserve the passenger seat in a car next to the driver – the seat with the most legroom and the best view in a motor. You don't ignore it when someone calls shotgun, do you? No, you don't. It's just the unwritten law of car seating space. Well, this is the same. When Sarah called bullshit, Matthew didn't cross call her out on it even if she was in error. Not if he cared to avoid the doghouse. She didn't give a jot.

The fifth was "It's OK". Like "Nothing", this means quite the opposite. It's certainly not OK, whatever it is. It's so far from being OK that Matthew might as well be at the fiery gates of the devil's hangout if he hears these words one after the other. The hidden meaning behind this one is that Sarah is biding her time until she can think of the most twisted way to make Matthew pay for his transgression, whatever it might be, and when that will be. And without fail, she always makes him pay. It might take a while, but it'll come. I know what you're thinking, and no, she never forgets. EVER.

As the cabin crew took their seats for landing in their jump seats – those special little seats that face the wrong way – and as the dulcet tones of Chris's snoring still resonated through the plane, albeit with greater vigour by this time, Matthew was gripped by a fresh fear of Sarah's wrath.

"Christ," he whispered, clenching his teeth, thinking that he'd better be damned sure not to get up to anything in China that would make her kick off. He'd already been warned to behave prior to his departure. That fear of doing anything to enrage Sarah compounded the fear that he already had about the steel deal. While he couldn't foresee any major problems, something made him a tiny bit anxious. It was just a tiny niggle, but it was enough to make him have a word with his pal Chris P – yeah, another Chris just to confuse things – before setting off for China.

Matthew and Chris P had been best friends since they were seven years old and kicking about together at primary school. They'd been totally inseparable since they'd met as kids, both always keen for a world of good times and adventure. They were never done looking for their next escapade, and it was always just around the corner, waiting for them to take charge of it. Text messages, Facebook, WhatsApp, and all that jazz – even MSN Messenger – weren't around back then.

Those were simpler times when kids were more concerned with getting together to communicate and have fun with each other. However, even when Chris P and Matthew weren't out getting into mischief, they'd be sure to call each other on the phone every week without fail.

They'd sit or lie there in their respective bedrooms, long phone cables dragged in from the landing outside, clutching the receiver even if they had absolutely nothing to say to each other. They'd most likely already seen each other that day, so what on earth would there be to talk about? They were thick as thieves, though, so a topic of conversation always found its way to them. The pair were always having a laugh with each other, their senses of humour identical in every way possible.

And they were both fearless, something that got them into a spot of bother on occasion. They fed off each other's fearlessness; it strengthened their confidence and their willingness to push boundaries in all aspects of life.

By the time he was an adult Chris P had become a big guy. Now, Matthew was a big guy too, but nothing compared to his best buddy. Chris's weight sat at a consistent twenty-two stone and his head was as bald as a coot. Everyone made fun of him because he'd gone bald pretty early on – well, earlier than any of their other friends for sure. They'd tell him that he looked like a lightbulb, that he was follically challenged, a barber's dream – all that kind of shit. Because he was a bit heavier he also had those Michelin man-esque rolls of chub at the back of his head, especially when he tilted his noddle back a bit.

Over the years he'd found himself in a string of various jobs, but he'd occasionally also worked with Matthew on a movie or two here and there, helping out in both the workshop and on set.

Chris, Matthew's dad, was happy to have Chris P around. He admired the friendship between the two of them knowing that a bond like that was as rare as they come in friendship terms. Chris never had anything comparable but was sure that Chris P would never turn his back on Matthew, whatever happened. They were unswervingly there for each other and that was never going to change.

Matthew had kept Chris P in the loop throughout the steel deal preparations. In fact, Chris P had encouraged him from the very start from when Matthew had stumbled upon the offer online in the first place. When everything was set for China, Matthew's hint of anxiety had caused him to call his pal and ask to meet for a beer.

Chris P wasn't used to Matthew being deadly serious, but when they met that day in a local boozer called the Nag's Head, he could sense that something was troubling him. He just wasn't quite his usual chirpy, jokey self. When he'd enquired as to whether there was a problem, Matthew spilled.

He was essentially putting in a request for Chris P to step in if anything was to go down in China when he and his dad were there. Always one to be there for his family, Matthew wanted to be absolutely sure that if anything dodgy was to occur, and something awful happened to him, that Chris P would be there for Sarah and the kids in some role. Matthew knew that he needed to ask this of somebody before he set off and there was no man for the job other than Chris P. He could trust him to look after his family without trying to get in there with his hot wife with him six feet under the ground. He'd seen that in plenty of films to know that kind of thing happened.

Matthew hadn't doubted that Chris P would argue with him. He did reassure Matthew telling him not to worry about anything terrible occurring, but simply nodded in response to the request. He didn't need to use any words to state what his role would be in such an instance. Matthew's mind was set at rest allowing him to head off to make his fortune, comfortable in the knowledge that his pregnant wife – now the size of a fairground – would be looked after in the event of his untimely end. Her wellbeing, in general, and her health as a heavily pregnant woman was paramount.

To alleviate Matthew's worries even further Chris P even said that he'd check in on Sarah and the kids every couple of days to make sure that everything was ticking by. Matthew knew that she had a support network around her, but it was still nice to think about her having an extra pillar to prop her up while he was on the other side of the world trying to make them rich.

Sarah's safety had actually been one of Linda's ground rules for the trip going ahead. Over a cup of tea with her husband, her son and Chris P one afternoon, Linda had stated, in no uncertain terms, that under no circumstances was Sarah to feel any stress or worry about what was going on. At six months pregnant that simply wasn't an option. Everyone involved knew it so the agreement was struck. Linda had also pulled Chris P aside and given him a warning that if he found out anything dodgy was going on in China and didn't tell her, she'd cut his balls off. He'd laughed, but her face made it clear that she wasn't altogether joking.

#

It wasn't until the smoking rubber of the hefty 747 kissed the hot tarmac of Beijing Airport with a screech and a thud that Chris finally came back to the land of the living.

"Well hello there, Sleeping Beauty," Matthew greeted his dad. Before he said a word, Chris felt around in his seat for a bottle of water he'd tucked away. He found it under his arse and took a swig.

"Thank fuck. My mouth was dry as a nun's crutch."

They both laughed.

"Gandhi's flip-flop, you mean," Matthew said.

Laughter again.

"We're here by the way, Dad."

Looking out of the small window as the plane pulled into its bay by the terminal, Chris responded.

"It certainly is son. Showtime eh?"

"Fucking aye, showtime. Bring it on."

There was a bit of a wait on the stand, everyone impatiently waiting to disembark. An air hostess came onto the public address system to apologise and explain the delay, but neither of them could make it out. It was a bit scratchy and unclear. The air conditioning seemed to have been turned down too, so Matthew was sweating his tits off even though he was only wearing a T-shirt.

Remembering his mum's warning not to worry Sarah in the slightest, he was chomping at the bit to get off the plane so that he could call Sarah and tell her he'd landed safe and sound. He didn't want to call her there and then, all of the other passengers in such close proximity and able to hear his conversation. He detested that and people who had personal calls on public transport.

Finally, they escaped their tin prison and he got on the blower. She appreciated the call but told him not to fuss about calling every five minutes during the trip. However, she wanted updates at reasonable intervals.

"You understand me, Matt?" she demanded.

Matthew understood perfectly and agreed to her conditions. It was in his best interests. Matthew fully meant this at the time, but he was blissfully ignorant as to the fact that he wouldn't be sticking to his word on this one. He would break his promise to her at the fury of the insistent Linda. He'd get into situations so unbelievable and so gross that it would cause him to start weaving the most convoluted web of lies he ever thought he'd be capable of coming up with. His manual on how to handle the missus would be of no use to him on his return to the UK.

After another lengthy wait, Chris and Matthew collected their luggage from a slow-moving carousel. Matthew wondered if everything was this slow in China, but he'd soon find out that it wasn't.

As is the case in a lot of Asian countries, on exit from the terminal they were met with a sea of men all shouting the same thing: "Taxi, taxi? Sir? Taxi? You want taxi." For the love of God, Matthew thought, as he scanned the twenty-five different Chinese faces in front of him, all jumping in front of them and grabbing at their bags. Matthew refrained from telling them to fuck off, all the while yanking his bags back and looking around. Getting through this mental throng of taxi drivers was daunting.

After a few seconds Chris noticed a strange-looking Chinese man standing in a tidy black uniform in the distance, a far cry from the dirty, scruffy outfits worn by most of the screaming horde of taxi drivers. The guy just stood there calmly beside a large white station wagon, staring at them with zero emotion showing as they struggled through the crowd. Chris thought this was odd but was sick of the onslaught.

Chris turned to Matthew.

"Fuck this lot. Let's go with that calm-looking fella over there."

Matthew caught sight of the driver and almost made a beeline for him. At that point a little sensible character popped up on his shoulder urging him not to do that. Worried that they might be walking into danger by opting for the ominous-looking guy, Matthew set about convincing his dad otherwise.

"No, Dad. Let's just take one of these guys. They seem like they need the money, the poor blokes," he said convincingly.

Chris knew his son was right as he took in the torn clothes and the dirty fingernails of the skinny men. They all seemed to be full to the brim with desperation, so why not give them a bit of cash? He nodded at Matthew in approval of the suggestion. They made the collective decision to go with the rattiest-looking one and were then ushered towards his little banger of a taxi.

This thing was on its last legs and Matthew couldn't even work out what make of car it was as the badges had fallen off. It wasn't one he recognised. The tyres were almost bald, the seats were threadbare, and the windows didn't close properly. They didn't even want to imagine what sort of fumes the exhaust would bellow out once the engine was started.

Matthew looked behind him as the driver settled in, saying something to them in Mandarin through a brown Stonehenge of a grin. The man in black was quickly making his way towards the taxi and blind panic set in for some reason.

"Move. Come on, move. Let's go," Matthew yelled at the confused man.

He was baffled as to the hurry but did what he was told. He might not have spoken much English, but he sure knew how to hurry the fuck up if needs be. A plume of black smoke burst out the back of the car as it backfired, covering the man in black. It reminded

Matthew of *Uncle Buck* when the same thing happens to John Candy's character – the eponymous Uncle Buck. Matthew nearly shat his knickers thinking that the man making his way to the car had fired a shot at them before he realised what had gone on. Chris looked at Matthew like he was starting to unravel, wondering what was going through his son's mind, totally unaware of the supposedly lingering danger.

"What the fuck is wrong with you, Matthew?" he asked through a severe frown as the taxi driver put his foot down.

The taxi peeled off out of the pick-up area of the airport terminal at speed, almost coming away from the road and up into the air as it hurtled down a ramp onto the main road. Matthew, ignoring Chris's question, looked through the back window at the man. He was now just standing there staring after the whizzing taxi, fanning the black smoke away from his face with flapping hands.

Matthew sighed out of relief, his dad looking at him questioningly. Matthew shushed Chris with a half-close of the eyes and a subtle shake of the head. Chris raised his eyebrows in disbelief as if to state that Matthew had lost the plot altogether and decided to probe no further. The driver held his hands up as if to say where am I going? This is a world known hand translation that everybody can decipher. Matt coughs and apologises, "Sorry, sorry," while fumbling with a piece of paper with an email from Arthur with instructions for the hotel they are staying at in Beijing. "It's the Xian pong hotel, no, no, sorry Xianyong Hotel!" The driver smiled revealing brown stained teeth in the rear-view mirror and nodded and spoke something in Chinese in agreement to Matthew's unconfident directions. Both Matthew and Chris looked out of their windows taking in Beijing as it pinged by, both silently hoping that they were being taken to the right hotel and they remained that way until they arrived.

The taxi pulled up at the four-star Xianyong Hotel that Arthur had booked for them. It was right in the centre, just a little down from Beijing's Palace Museum and nestled between three different residential districts – Jianguomen, Donghuashi and Qianmen. He'd never heard of the area before, but Arthur in the emails had said it was nice and safe.

Chris was enjoying looking at the city and was daydreaming when they had arrived. By then he'd forgotten about Matthew's behaviour back at the airport, so he failed to find out what had been going through Matthew's mind. A smartly dressed bellboy hurried towards the taxi in order to take care of their bags, which Matthew thought was pretty impressive for a fairly inexpensive hotel.

"This looks amazing," Matthew declared to Chris, who nodded in agreement as he sized up the joint.

It would turn out to be mutton dressed as lamb, though. As their bags were whisked off inside the hotel by the bellboy, Matthew and Chris stared at each other cluelessly as they tried to figure out the value of the money in their wallets. They'd both bought some Chinese currency – Yuan – at a local travel agency back in London the day before they set off, but neither of them had bothered to do any research as to how much each note was worth when compared with pounds. The cashier had told Chris, but he couldn't recall by now.

Matthew held up a wad of cash in front of the taxi driver who was waiting to be paid for his services. Neither of them used to being screwed over in terms of money, they were sure that they had this covered. In broken English, the taxi driver asked for 1000 Yuan. Taken aback, Chris was sure they were getting stiffed.

As he and Matthew debated it, the taxi driver swiped 1000 Yuen, hopped back in the car as quick as you like and slammed his foot down on the accelerator. It happened so quickly they could barely blink. It wasn't until they got inside the hotel lobby, where there was a currency exchange, that they realised they'd just been had for £120. All that for what was no more than a twenty-five-minute journey. They were raging.

"Ah well," Chris conceded. "What can we do now? He's away."

It was unlike Chris to take being swindled so lightly. Matthew sighed, vowing that it wouldn't happen again.

Chapter 11 – The Xianyong Hotel And Its Treasures

The lobby of the Xianyong Hotel had an impressive and expansive marble floor stretching all the way from the entrance right up to the reception desk and beyond to a large, sweeping staircase to the bar and restaurant.

Once checked in they were accompanied by a porter to room 666. Jesus, Matthew thought, talk about getting an unlucky number. He looked down at the carpet on the floor of the elevator. It was bright red – the unluckiest colour of them all. He couldn't help but worry that things were going to go belly up.

Somewhere in the back of his mind he recalled once hearing that red is a symbol of good luck in China. Yeah, he was right. He'd read that on the internet somewhere. Red, which corresponded with fire, symbolised good fortune and joy, used all over the shop across the country, particularly for special celebrations and family gatherings and banned at funerals. Matthew was impressed with his memory. He didn't usually retain information like that. He perked up a bit thinking that maybe things were looking good after all. Were they, though? Were they?

The elevator pinged when it got to the sixth floor and the porter showed them to the door of 666. It dawned on Matthew that maybe 666 was also a lucky number in China as well as the colour red. He plonked their luggage down in front of one of two large beds and stood grinning with his hands clasped behind his back like a cub scout or a soldier standing at ease. What was he waiting for? Ah, Chris realised, he was hanging around for a tip. After just being swindled out of 120 squid, Chris put his hand on the porter's back and guided him towards the door without giving him a bean. Waving at the porter as the door closed he heard some under the breath mutters, but he couldn't care less. He was done throwing away money.

The porter now gone, Chris and Matthew were able to poke around the twin room that overlooked what appeared to be a vibrant, bustling city. But they'd just be there for one night so they wouldn't get to see much of it.

Matthew made his way into the bathroom, trying the taps. And then room 666 started to show its true colours as one that certainly wasn't lucky. The taps didn't work at first with nothing coming out. After about eight seconds a couple of clunks rang through the taps as they began to judder. Matthew was about to shout to his dad, but before he could say a thing dirty brown water spluttered out of the taps. He grimaced, looking at the water with the expectation that the crap will run through and clear water will make an appearance. No such luck, unfortunately. The sink filled up with the grimy liquid. Matthew realised that the plug was covering the drain. He turned the taps off before being faced with no other choice but to plunge his hand into the black pool that had formed in the sink. The plug was stuck, and no amount of yanking would loosen it. There was another sink to the right of this one, so Matthew moved across to that to try once again. He and Chris may not have paid the porter after learning their lesson with the con man of a taxi driver, but no lesson had been learned here. Matthew repeated his actions but the second sink was soon the same foul mess as the first one.

"For fuck's sake," Matthew shouted to nobody in particular.

"What is it?" Chris replied.

"So, these sinks might look lovely but nothing fucking works. They're shit."

The façade of the nice hotel and the pleasant room 666 was starting to peel away as the gammy accommodation that lay underneath revealed itself.

"Tell me about it," hollered Chris from the bedroom. "This room looks great, but when I tried to turn on the TV it started to smoke more than your mum in a cloud of fag fumes. Then I tried to pull the drawer open and the handle fell off. And then I gave the window a go, but the bastard is rusted shut."

Matthew looked at Chris with dismay thinking that they had two options. One, they could stand here and complain about how shit the room was, or two, they could head off to do something fun.

"Let's destroy this jet lag with the best cure possible – BOOZE." Chris was trying to create a positive out of a negative.

"That, Dad, sounds like a plan. We can hit the lobby bar and try some Chinese liquor." Matt was excited about the prospect of letting his hair down for a bit.

They quickly grabbed what they needed and hit the lobby bar. It was a decent-sized bar located at the rear of the hotel and stuffed full of leather chairs, sofas, and a row of stools in front of a wooden bar. They opted to sit on the stools at the bar first since there's something pleasant about being right up there in front of the action.

The barman, a short Chinese fella, well-dressed with a black, silk waistcoat and white shirt, stood waiting for their order. He said something in Chinese and an educated guess told them he was asking them what they'd like to drink. A discussion commenced even though none of them could understand a word of it.

After a good ten minutes of trying to understand each other, Chris pointed at what he thought looked like whisky.

"That. We will have that."

The barman bowed his head and jumped into action.

"Shi," he announced.

Matthew thought he remembered this as "yes" from the Chinese dictionary. The barman grabbed some highball glasses, which looked to be made of crystal, from a shelf. He then mixed up a concoction comprising of many different spirits. In fact, the only one he didn't include was the one that Chris had actually pointed at. It was a cocktail of sorts, with the obligatory tacky umbrella and a cherry floating on top.

Chris gave the barman the eyeball and Matt could tell his dad was not impressed. He turned to his son.

"Why even ask if you're not going to bother with the customer's choice?"

Both of them were fairly irritable after the long journey and crappy room. Matt, realising his dad was a little upset, sipped the drink.

"Mmmmm. Fa Kin Su Pah," he said while nodding his head in delight at the barman.

Chris burst into laughter and followed Matt's lead.

"Mmmmmm. Yeah, Fa Kin Su Pah."

Matt was lying his tits off. The cocktail tasted like watered-down toothpaste, but Chris realised that his son was just trying to make good of a bad situation. Hopping off the stools, both retreated to the back of the bar in the corner.

"That is fucking rank, Dad. I think we should stick to beer from now on."

"That will probably taste like dishwater going by this cocktail," Chris responded.

They slowly sipped their rancid cocktails while taking in the surroundings and the occasional guest appearance. Matt went back to the bar after about twenty minutes. It was definitely time to take this drinking session to the next level.

"Two beers please, garcon," Matthew said thinking the guy wouldn't understand a word. To his surprise the barman did understand, pulling two pints of lager and sliding them in front of him. Matt picked up the beers in shock at how easy the order was and telling his dad on return.

The beer was OK but it certainly wasn't going to win any prizes. At least they could stomach it and get a bit pissed. About five hours and hell knows how many beers went by and they were both well on their way to drunksville. They reached their limit and headed back up to the room. Of course, the taps were still spewing out brown water and Matt and Chris wanted a wash so badly. Matt had a brainwave.

"Dad, fuck it. Let's go for a jacuzzi."

They made their way down to the basement floor in the lucky red lift armed with a couple of slightly stained towels they'd picked up from the disaster of a bathroom. The Xianyong Hotel had what was advertised on a room pamphlet as a "luxurious spa", but the reality was nothing more than a small area that housed a hot tub and some other stray offerings. The hot tub was to the left in a nice space tiled in slate, while to the right was a tiny dipping pool. Matthew assumed that it would be filled with freezing cold water. There was also a couple of wooden loungers, but they'd seen better days so Matthew doubted he'd be lying on them. The hotel had made an attempt at installing some mood lighting in the room, but half of the coloured bulbs were on the blink and the ones that were working bathed them in a horrible yellow light. It made them look jaundiced like they were just on their way for dialysis treatment at the hospital.

It seemed pretty clean so at least there was that small saving grace. The bubbling water in the hot tub looked really inviting, especially considering the vile mess they'd just abandoned in the bathroom.

"How come this water comes through the pipes in here all right, but that crap's spraying out upstairs?" Chris asked.

Matthew shrugged as he cautiously dipped a foot in the water to test the temperature. It was just right so he threw the rest of his body in there. Chris blindly followed his son, happy with the assessment that all is well enough to get in. The trouble was that the vigorous bubbling had masked what lay beneath the surface of the water.

It didn't take a very long time for them both to realise that the jacuzzi was filled with yellow water that absolutely reeked of piss. Now, that was most likely because it was actually piss. It took them an even shorter space of time to begin scrambling to get out of the hot, pissy pot of soup they had elected to get into. Due diligence had definitely not been done here.

"What the fuck is in here, Matthew?" Chris barked at his son, trying to stand up but slipping and knocking into him.

In turn Matthew fell, his head submerged under the water. While down there he made the mistake of opening his eyes. Although they stung like hell, and not just because of the chlorine in there, he could make out little brown lumps floating around in the water. Chris pulled him up but they both slipped again. By now the penny had dropped. They were swimming in piss and shit deposited there by some dirty fucking bastards. They might as well have stepped straight into a giant toilet.

All of a sudden Matthew was reminded of the scene from *Trainspotting* where Ewan McGregor's character Renton is pulled into that stinking toilet overflowing with excrement, all the while gagging and legs up in the air.

Chris and Matthew had never moved so fast in their lives as they escaped the hell of the hotel's "luxurious spa". What an experience that had been. The hotel really needed to update their listing. They made a dash for the room to get into the shower as quickly as possible, completely failing to take into account that some fresh hell would await them on arrival.

They battled for dibs on the shower, but Chris managed to muscle in there first. Matthew had the last laugh, though, as Chris was covered from head to toe in smelly, discoloured water when he threw on the shower. The magical shower that he'd hoped for had left him filthier than before.

After bickering for five minutes about their next course of action, they settled on attempting to towel themselves down as much as they could before trundling down to the reception desk. In the lift their odour was apparent not only to them but also to everyone who entered on floors 5, 4, 3, 2 and then 1. Of course, the lift stopped on every floor. Why wouldn't it?

Once they finally made it to the reception desk it was at this point that Chris and Matthew were informed that the Xianyong Hotel was experiencing a pretty serious water problem that wouldn't be resolved until the following day. As if it made the whole thing better, they were also told that all other guests were faced with the same problem.

"And you don't think that it would have been fucking pertinent to inform us of this when we checked in? No?"

The hotel staff apologised – albeit insincerely – and the outcome was that the guys would merely have to bide their time for the next twenty-four hours, tainted by the remnants of urine and faeces. The best that they could hope for was that the stench would dissipate, but that really was the best-case scenario. As it turned out it was also a scenario that didn't materialise. In fact, the smell got staler as time went on, the shit and piss really maturing like a nice wine or cheese.

For the remainder of the evening Chris and Matthew lay around on their beds trying not to throw up as they were forced to exist in their current state. After a while, their fury was overcome by tiredness as it pulled them into sleep. It turns out that they wouldn't just be seeing not much of Beijing, but none of it at all. Their smell precluded going out anywhere for the rest of the evening.

Before Chris fell into the land of nod, he joked, "At least you can tick having a shit-uzzi off your bucket list before you leave this world. Or a piss-uzzi. Actually, in our current state, a stink-uzzi."

Matt did not find this funny, unimpressed at their current state of affairs. He just replied with an angry puff.

For him, sleep was not destined to be a deep one. Right through the night he kept waking up and retching at the rancid smell. Jetlagged and disgusted, he couldn't come to terms with what had happened. But he developed a sense of positivity that things could not get any worse from this point onwards. Boy oh boy, was he wrong.

He scratched his armpit discovering some nasty treasure while he was there: a hardened lump of poo that had got stuck to one of his underarm hairs. He felt like crying but he didn't want to wake his dad. At least one of them could get some shuteye under these circumstances.

As he lay there unable to sleep, Matthew thought about their meeting with Arthur Chang in the morning. Well, in a few hours from then really. Arthur had told them that he'd meet them there at the hotel. He had no idea what Arthur was like because he'd never actually met him. He'd heard a fair amount about the guy from Chris, though, and Linda had given him a few titbits too. It wasn't until a couple of years later, in 2009, that Matthew would come to realise that Arthur looked incredibly like Ken Jeong's character Mr. Chow in the film *The Hangover*. The likeness was uncanny, except Arthur's English was even more broken than Mr. Chow's and he might just have been even crazier.

Chapter 12 – Arthur Chang

The atmosphere in the morning was sombre as the unsmiling pair bathed in deodorant and aftershave and donned some fresh clothes. This was the best they could do. Matthew was convinced that they must have smelled like toilet attendants who had got lost in a tart's boudoir. He'd tried the taps once more to no avail. The sinks were still blocked too, but that wasn't their problem anymore.

They barely spoke a word to each other as they found their way to the lobby. Just to get the day started off on the right foot, the lift was out of order. Or it was just taking ages to come. Whatever the case, neither of them could be arsed to hang about for a minute longer to wait for it, opting to try the stairs instead. The stairwell was pungent in its own special way, but foul odours were now part and parcel of the Chinese experience.

"Unless he says anything, keep shtum about all of this to Arthur for now, will you?" Chris asked Matthew.

Matthew signalled agreement with a nod of the head as he pushed open the door between the stairs and the breakfast room. Arthur was waiting at a large table at the back of the dining space. He stood up as Chris and Matthew approached him. He was a tiny man with a face that only a mother could love. You know, one of those faces that you'd never get tired of punching. Even so, his face was always adorned with a smile, but it was an odd smile accompanied by an even odder personality. Arthur truly was an unusual character from beginning to end.

The three of them engaged in some polite chit chat, at least as much as Arthur could manage with his crap English. It was a real struggle to understand what he was saying half of the time, and Matthew had to be really switched on to clock most of it.

He was relieved when the waitress swung by to take their order. Nobody had even looked at the menu yet, but it didn't matter anyhow because Arthur just went ahead to order breakfast for everyone in Cantonese. Christ knows what would arrive at the table, Matthew thought.

While they waited for their food the strained conversation continued. Chris wasn't taking the same approach as Matthew, being somewhat more direct than his son. He asked Arthur to repeat absolutely everything that he said at least two or three times. For some reason this made Matthew feel awkward. He was concerned that it would piss off the little Chinese man, but he didn't seem bothered by it at all. When Chris became aware that Matthew was just listening and nodding, he made the assumption that he wasn't understanding a word that Arthur said.

"Ask him twice, Colin," Chris instructed.

Matthew stared at his dad in puzzlement, thinking that he was just as mad as Chris thought he was back at the airport the day before.

"You know, ask him twice, Colin the farmer. You have to talk to him like that. You get me?"

Matthew was still baffled, just about catching his dad's drift about asking Arthur twice. Why on earth was he banging on about some farmer called Colin? Who the fuck was Colin? Whatever he was going on about it was abundantly clear that Chris was taking it all like a big joke. He was amused at the fact Matthew had no idea what was going on, getting a kick out of that and making fun of Arthur in some way. This was making Matthew feel even more awkward at the whole situation for a couple of reasons.

First, Arthur was unaware that Chris was ripping the piss out of both him and Matthew. Second, they weren't here for hilarity. They were here on business. Things should have been a bit more serious than all of this. It was bad enough that they were sleeping in a hotel where nothing works as it should, but now they were sitting in a restaurant reeking of piss and shit with a supposed translator whose handle on English was direr than that of Manuel from *Fawlty Towers*. It was a sheer farce and it was making Matthew's blood boil. He couldn't fathom how Chris ever thought that this guy was the right one for the job, translating Chinese in a deal worth so much money. It beggared belief.

As his anger simmered, Matthew realised that he was starving. The food arrived just at the right time, stopping him making a snarky comment to Chris. The waitress looked like she winced when she approached, and Matthew was paranoid that it was in response to their smell. Although, he figured it would be better if she hated the cologne scent rather than what it was designed to conceal.

She put down a veritable feast on the table, which Matthew guessed they'd be picking up the tab for. There was a little pot of thick looking cream or milk, accompanied by deep-fried sticks of dough that reminded him of the churros he'd once eaten in a tapas place in Soho. On top of that there were a few other dishes: some steamed buns, but he had no clue as to what they were stuffed with; some bowl of a pudding type thing that smelled like soya milk; some steamed sticky rice; some things that seemed like dumplings, but again he didn't know what was in them; and finally, some pancakes. There was way too much food, but Matthew was up to the challenge.

As they ate Chris and Arthur still struggled on through their attempts at chatting, but after twenty-five minutes Matthew had firmly given up. As he stuffed each Chinese breakfast delicacy into his face, none of which appeared to be of top-notch standard, Matthew nodded and made the right sounds at the right times to delude Arthur into believing that he understood a single thing he was saying. Arthur just kept on rambling on and on and on, but Matthew could only make out about 10% of it all.

In a surprisingly coherent paragraph, Arthur started to chat about Tianjin. Matthew understood what he was saying on this occasion.

"We make good deal, I get respect. Tianjin best port to move goods undercover. Very corrupt. Very dangerous. We get the steel out no problem."

Matthew might not have done any research on the value on the Yuan as compared with the pound sterling before leaving London, but he had certainly read about the benefits and downfalls of Tianjin as a port. He'd come to the conclusion that Tianjin was a great port for their purposes. It was basically the port of choice for anyone looking to move any product illegally due to the lack of supervision from port authorities. On the whole, they generally had a lax approach towards illegal activities, something that they've since cracked down on in recent years.

After every plate on the table was clean the bill came. Chris and Matthew, as predicted, ended up paying. Arthur then announced in perfect English that they should set off. Matthew understood this to mean that they would now make their way to Tianjin, which caused him to fall into a state of panic. There was no fucking way that he was willing to embark on a four-hour journey to another city smelling like the lavatory at a dodgy nightclub. Matthew turned to Chris, speaking under his breath.

"Dad, we're honking. How are we gonna wash?"

Unexpectedly, Chris just chuckles. He pushed Matthew towards the lift which seemed to be operational now. Arthur wandered across the lobby towards the exit of the worst hotel that Matthew had ever had the pleasure of staying in. In the crowded lift they moved upwards, and Matthew urged his dad to answer his question. Chris shushed him.

"Son, calm your baps. Seriously, just chill out."

Matthew rolled his eyes in frustration.

"Listen, I'd love to wash too, but Arthur says his chauffeur is already waiting outside for us. We need to get our shit together and get down there fast."

"Totally missed that. When did he say that?"

"When you were paying for the food. You didn't hear?" Chris didn't wait for an answer. "Anyway, for some reason, Arthur says that we need to get going as soon as possible so that we don't arrive in the dark."

"Arrive in the dark? It's four hours away and it's only 11am."

"Yeah, it makes no sense to me either, but our backs are kind of against the wall with this one, ain't they?"

"Oh, whatever," Matthew found himself saying sulkily as he used one of Sarah's five deadly terms. Shit, Sarah, he thought. He really should check in with her at some point soon. He hadn't even looked at his phone since the previous night, distracted by everything that had been going on.

Back in room 666 they threw anything that had made its way out of their suitcases back in them haphazardly. There had been no order during their stay, so why pack in any kind of sensible way? It took them a mere flash to gather up their stuff and leave the room, bidding their hellhole farewell.

With an uncharacteristic stroke of luck the lift was sitting at their floor, door open and empty. As they dropped floor by floor, Matthew pulled out his aftershave, Issey Miyake's L'Eau D'Issey, which he had stuffed in his pocket for easy access. It was his sole means of improving his smell, but the heady scent of the cologne itself was now so strong in his nasal passages that he felt he had become the cologne.

Chris and Matthew stood at the reception desk, impatiently waiting for the next available receptionist to check them out.

"Can't we just ditch the keys and bolt?" Matthew asked Chris.

"We might still need to pay."

Immediately, it came to Matthew that Arthur might not already have paid for the Xianyong when he'd booked it. If he'd thought of that the day before, when shit was hitting the fan – or his face – then he was pretty sure that he'd have insisted that he and his dad do a runner to locate new accommodation. What was done was done, but damn he was annoyed.

As Chris settled up Matthew could see Arthur outside beckoning to them. The little shit seemed to be calling all the shots here, which is not what Matthew had intended from the arrangement originally. Matthew held his hand up making the peace symbol with his index and middle fingers to indicate that they'd just be a couple more minutes. Arthur was evidently irritated at the lack of expeditiousness and continued to motion with his arm frantically.

Chapter 13 – The Journey To Tianjin

Arthur seemed to have composed himself by the time the guys had got to the car. The more Matthew looked at the white station wagon, the more he was sure that he'd seen it somewhere before. He brushed this off as his imagination. Matthew wondered if the sudden change in nature was something that they'd be seeing again from Arthur and didn't doubt that they would.

As they approached the vehicle Arthur had his back turned to the guys as he chatted with the chauffeur, making lots of hand gestures as if to give him directions. The closer they got Arthur inched out of the way slightly and Matthew could see that the chauffeur was wearing a chauffeur cap that looked like that of a policeman or a bellboy. He'd seen a cap just like that recently, but where was it? He couldn't remember for the life of him.

Then Arthur moved completely and Matthew gained an unobstructed view of the chauffer. Leaning against the car was a creepy-looking Asian fella dressed from top to toe in black. Wait a minute, Matthew thought, I've seen that face before. He was just too familiar for it to be a coincidence. Then it dawned on him like a sunbeam literally burning his face. It was the ominous-looking driver from the airport, the one that Matthew had avoided at all costs.

"Fuck," Matthew muttered under his breath, just loud enough for Chris to hear though. His dad looked at him questioningly, but Matthew ignored his glare. He felt like a right tit. The mystery of the potential airport killer – that darkly dressed assassin that had been sent to off them – was, in fact, their driver. He's obviously been sent by Arthur in the first place to collect them and drop them off at their hotel. Jesus, Matthew was cringing at himself. He told himself that he really must stop watching thriller movies if this was the outcome of them. On arrival back in the UK, no more of that shit. They lead to paranoia central. Nonetheless, he felt it a tad strange that Arthur hadn't mentioned any of this at breakfast.

Matthew and Chris stepped into the car and took their seats, but neither Arthur or the driver said anything about the misunderstanding from the day before. The driver introduced himself as Won. In more broken English, and over some horrific Asian pop song blasting out of the overly loud radio that the driver had switched on, Arthur stated that the drive would only take ninety minutes in total.

Ninety minutes? An hour and a half? Matthew had been convinced that Tianjin was four hours away from Beijing. He couldn't fathom how he'd made such an overestimation of the time it took to drive there. Perhaps, when he'd been researching back at home, he mistakenly looked up the time the journey took by train. Regardless, now it seemed even more bizarre that Arthur had been so anxious to get going to make it before dark.

What made this seem less bizarre was the insanely heavy traffic that they managed to get caught up in while they were trying to get out of Beijing to the motorway. For a long portion of time, they sat there bored out of their skulls as the traffic moved along at a glacial pace. However, every cloud has a silver lining, as they say, because this gave Chris and Matt the chance to take in some truly hilarious Chinese road signs that had been poorly translated into English.

"Having fun prohibited" which they saw on a street post was just the first of these, shortly followed by a large totem lightbox sign that read, "Fu King Chinese Buffet". These were the only two that were in pretty close proximity to each other, but they saw some others later too as the traffic crawled along. The best of these was one that said, "Temporary park only for getting off". That one had been a layby sign, which they'd seen close to a seafood store offering "Fresh Crap". It had been tempting but they passed up that offer. Later, they were instructed by a safety sign on the street to "Carefully slip and fall down", which again was an offer they could and did refuse. "Erection in progress", which they'd seen on the front of some bamboo scaffolding was one of the best.

Matthew lifted his wrist to look at the time after it felt like they'd been in the traffic forever, but his watch wasn't there. Either it was in his suitcase with the other jumble of stuff or he'd left it in the mad dash to get out of there. It wasn't expensive but he'd still be pissed off if that hotel caused yet another problem in his life. He couldn't see the time on the dashboard anywhere.

He was hot and sweaty so pulled his jacket off, remembering that his phone was in his inside pocket. He unlocked the screen to see the time. It was just after twelve by this time, but more importantly there were six missed calls from Sarah. Shit, she'd be absolutely fuming that he hadn't got in touch since landing yesterday. It had now been about twenty-four hours since they last spoke. To Matthew that seemed like a reasonable gap, but Sarah would assess that very differently. He considered calling her there and then, but again he hated the idea of making a personal call like that in front of a car full of people.

He decided just to drop her a short text message to keep her posted about their progress. Well, not the full progress report of everything that had happened thus far, but just a little note to tell her they'd met up with Arthur and were on their way to Tianjin. He accidentally set the phone keyboard to all caps and started to type:

ALRIGHT LOVE. ALL WELL HERE. HAD BREAKFAST WITH ARTHUR THIS MORNING. ODD GUY BUT NEVER MIND. ON OUR WAY TO TIANJIN NOW IN A CAR WITH A DRIVER. GIVE YOU A SHOUT WHEN WE ARRIVE. MATTHEW XXX

He hit send but unbeknown to him the message didn't send properly. He'd hit the send button when they were in an area of low signal, but his phone didn't give him a notification or anything like that. He sat back content that he'd done his husbandly duty. Sarah would be relieved that she'd heard from him.

The journey had been pretty relaxing for the twenty minutes they'd been on the move. Arthur was gabbing away in Chinese with Won. Matthew noticed that they speak so fast to each other. And really loud too. It was a bit like listening to Italians speaking to each other. You know, they're most likely just talking about what they're going to have for dinner that night, but it really sounds like they're giving out to each other about something major. Arthur laughed really loudly, so Matthew knew that they were just having a bit of banter with each other and knew not to let his thriller movie level suspicions kick into action once more.

Even though the faint odour of shit and piss still lingered, Matthew finally began to relax a little in the belief that things were beginning to go right for a change. He looked out of the car window as the Chinese countryside flew past. The air outside looked misty, but it was the humidity that Matthew could see.

Along the roadside, even further outside the city, the grassy banks were covered in litter. People clearly just chucked their crap out of car windows here with little care for the environment or anyone else. Matthew mused on whether the people throwing garbage out of the window were the same people shitting and pissing in hot tubs all over the place. Pondering on the disrespect, an ounce of anger rose in him again, but he managed to subside it before it made a real appearance.

Looking past the rubbish on the roadside Matthew could see a tonne of derelict old houses, some of them huge. They looked like the sort of rundown mansions you'd find in horror flicks. The sort of big wooden houses blackened by dirt that the neighbourhood talks about being haunted, but the local kids just can't keep themselves away from curiosity.

There was the occasional rice paddy too, with workers toiling away in dirty clothes and scruffy, pointed straw hats. Some of them were bent over double doing whatever they do with the rice, while others were walking along upright carrying long sticks. They were just long, thin tree branches as far as Matthew could make out, but they were pretty far away for him to make a more accurate assessment. He guessed that there would be much larger rice fields deeper into the Chinese countryside than these roadside ones where the crop wouldn't be affected by pollution from vehicles.

Matthew had just about been fully lulled into a false sense of security by the quiet passing countryside, lost in his thoughts, when he was torn back to reality with a jolt. The car tyres began screeching as Won frantically attempted to halt the car, screaming something in Chinese that neither Matthew nor Chris could comprehend. The car was filled with gasps coming from every passenger as fear took hold of them. Won had been forced to brake too soon for the car to stop in a straight line, so it began swerving towards another car. He yanked on the steering wheel and narrowly escaped smashing into it, the tyres really being put through their paces.

The vehicle spun at least two times while Arthur screamed like a little girl. Matthew and Chris were terrified too, but they'd both become paralysed by fear to make any screaming sounds, girly or otherwise. Won expertly danced with the steering wheel until he managed to pull the car to a halt. If he hadn't managed to stop at that time, they might have continued up the small grassy knoll and gone flying over into the rice field beyond. That could have killed them.

As the car stood still, the engine hissing and ticking like mad, Matthew looked behind them as car after car ploughed into each other in what eventually became a fifty vehicle pile-up. Thank fuck for Won and his mad skills because they could have been smack bang in the middle of it.

He watched as the less fortunate didn't just slam into the back of each other, but were thrown on top of each other, piled high like little mountains of cars, torn metal jutting out like a multitude of craggy peaks. Passengers hung out of shattered windows dripping with blood, screaming through their now red teeth. Their screams were only halted as new cars smashed into the disaster zone, adding to the carnage.

As he held his hands up to his face, shaking, Matthew went out of himself for a few seconds, aware of the dark symphony of crashing, screaming, screeching, smashing and banging that had engulfed him. He had that intense ringing in his ears that you get when you hear gunfire at close range.

He came back to himself with a whoosh as Won's skills kicked into action again. Matthew felt like he was in a car driven by Kato, the masked driver from the Green Hornet series, able to operate a vehicle just the way any vigilante needs on their adventures. That's all Matthew saw now: Kato but without a mask.

Before any cars could career into them Won reverse spun the car like an absolute pro, miraculously weaving in and out of all the oncoming traffic despite the unpredictability of where those cars are heading. He did this across four entire lanes, all the while beeping and screaming – presumably at other cars to get out of the way – in Cantonese: in, out, in, out, stop, start, slow, fast, slow, in, out, fast, spin, brake, slide sideways, start, in, out. It seemed to go on forever, but it probably took just a few minutes in total.

By this point, Matthew had found his voice and joined Arthur in a shrieking contest. After his initial shock Chris has started to find some hilarity in all of it and was roaring with laughter. Maybe it was hysterical laughter, but Matthew was stunned by it as if the entire thing was one big game. They were quite literally zigzagging in and out of crashing cars like they'd just been hired to replace Daniel Craig in the James Bond movies.

The car eventually came to an abrupt stop on the polar opposite side of the motorway from where they'd started off. Matthew looked over at the ongoing pile-up. The two sides of the motorway were divided by a large metal barrier. How the fuck had they managed to make it across to the other side without colliding into that?

He bent his head around Arthur's headrest to get a clearer view and saw that, in his utterly surprising display of driving prowess, Won had somehow succeeded in aiming perfectly for a tiny gap in the barrier. It looked as if it was barely large enough to squeeze a small hatchback through it, so hats off to the guy for his spot on aim. That, on top of the fact that they'd missed so much oncoming traffic going the wrong way – forwards, backwards and sideways – up a stretch of motorway that went for miles.

Who the hell was this legend who was driving them? He needed to ditch his job and get a new one as a stunt man in the film industry. Chris and Matthew did, after all, have the right connections to actually make that happen.

The entire experience was more terrifying than anything that Matthew had ever encountered in his entire life. Now that they were at a standstill, Chris's laughter had ceased, and Matthew figured that it had been hysterical after all. The four men sat in silence for a few seconds gathering their thoughts and their composure.

Matthew heard a loud scratching sound and glanced down towards his dad's hand. He was gripping the handle on the car door, petrified. Although he was scared himself, Matthew had the wherewithal to put his hand on Chris's arm in a gesture that told him that everything was now OK.

"What the fucking fuck just happened?" Matthew burst out. Arthur shrugged.

"I ask driver," he stated.

I think you mean Kato the fucking hero, Matthew said in his head, his mouth hanging open in disbelief. Arthur and Won calmly discussed something, but neither of them explained anything to

Matthew or Chris. They didn't really need an explanation, to be honest. It was a car accident. It was as simple as that.

Won took a nearby exit from the motorway and wound around a few side roads before returning to the motorway a few miles past the scene of the destruction. They remained in silence for a while, all requiring a bit of time to process what had just happened. The drive to Tianjin had returned to normal even though a solemn atmosphere lingered in the car.

It was when they were back on the motorway, heading in the right direction once more, that Arthur finally turned around to speak to the guys.

"You OK?"

OK was not the word that Matthew would have used to accurately describe his state of being at that moment in time, but he wasn't not OK so he just nodded. Chris did the exact same thing too before looking at his son. They just stared at each other blankly for a few seconds before simultaneously looking away out of their respective windows. Arthur then turned around, grabbing hold of his headrest for support, to deliver a real corker.

"The driver, he tell me that car on loan. It not his car. He say, it get stolen, they kill him. It get scratch, they cut off his leg. Not back on time, they cut his finger off. He sleep in car. He stay with car. His life depend on car being return."

Right, thought Matthew, then that explains why Won the nutty superhero went to the most extreme lengths to stop the car from being totalled in the crash. He really must have been sure of his driving skills to be confident that he could pull off that extensive catalogue of exploits back there.

Matthew was sitting there baffled at what they'd got themselves into. They had planned to go to China and got this guy on board to translate and help them get around. He was the local, the one in the know. Matthew had trusted that he'd give them what they needed and in an above the board way. But no, here they were still covered in the residue of bodily excretions – through no fault of Arthur to be fair – and sitting in a borrowed car after the most insane car crash known to man that must be returned or the driver's fucking fingers will be lopped off. And that's the best-case scenario. WHAT THE

FUCK? Matthew screamed internally. WHAT THE ACTUAL FUCK?

Matthew and Chris looked at each other, stupefied by what Arthur had just announced. Then Chris came out with something that took Matthew aback.

"Wow, that's incredible. This guy has a hell of a lot to lose, so we'd better make sure that he gets this car back in one piece and on time."

Matthew couldn't understand why his dad wasn't questioning any of this; questioning the situation that Arthur, this joke of a human, had engineered. All his dad was concerned about was getting the bloody car back when they shouldn't have a god damned thing to do with getting a car back to stop someone being terminated by the Chinese mafioso, whatever the hell they were called.

Matthew let it wash over him, though. Whatever, as Sarah would say. Whatever. He looked at his phone but there was no reply to his text message. He put it down to the eight-hour time difference and the fact that she'd likely be in the land of nod. Now thinking about Won's situation, and so far out of his comfort zone that it was almost unreal, Matthew began to look back at the early days of the business in East London and Soho. All of a sudden arguing over money with clients wasn't a patch on how business is conducted in this part of the world. It all seemed more brutal than anything he'd ever heard of in London or anywhere else come to think of it. It was like a post-apocalyptic civilisation, where everyone is out for themselves in the most savage way possible. More specifically, it was reminiscent of Mos Eisley, the fictional spaceport town on the planet Tatooine in the *Star Wars* universe. In the first film of the original trilogy in the franchise, Alec Guinness's character Obi-Wan Kenobi calls Mos Eisley "a wretched hive of scum and villainy". Just like Tianjin, Mos Eisley was a busy port city. Both were lawless, although probably more Mos Eisley than Tianjin attracting those looking to engage in illegal trade activities. By the sound of the way things are done in Tianjin, the similarities were striking.

The remainder of the drive between Beijing and Tianjin went without fault, aside from the fact that the stress of the journey and all the sweating it had caused, made Chris and Matthew smell even worse than when they'd started out. The fresh perspiration had reactivated their old bathhouse aroma, adding to the Eau de Stale body odour scent they now had going on.

Matthew was sure that there was no way the smell had escaped the attention of Arthur and Won. They had now both unrolled their windows – even though the car was air-conditioned – after exchanging a couple of surreptitious glances. They thought they were being discreet, but Matthew had clocked them and even saw Arthur motion towards his nose. Subtlety at its finest, Matthew mused. Matthew's insecurity relating to his smell was at an all-time high, and a shower – or a wash of some kind at last – could not come fast enough.

By the time they reached Tianjin it was already getting dark. After all the drama of the crash and getting back on the motorway, it transpired that Won had managed to find his way onto the wrong road. They'd been heading in the wrong direction for over an hour.

Once he found his way back he'd succeeded in getting lost a further two times, adding another couple of hours to the journey. Arthur's suggestion that they ran the risk of not getting into Tianjin before nightfall didn't seem so outrageous now. The fact that they'd lost so much time that day aroused Matthew's anxiety again. Considering the events that had unfolded since their arrival in the country of the red dragon, Matthew was most assuredly being followed by his bad luck shadow once more.

Matthew remained observant as they made their way into the city. The third most populous city in China, it was absolutely huge, far bigger than Matthew had imagined. However, it made perfect sense given its nature as a popular port city. The thing that struck Matthew the most was not the number of buildings or the swell of the city itself, but the sheer volume of people. There were people everywhere, hundreds of them, thousands of them, millions of them. And there was zero order.

Barely bathed in poor street lighting, crowds of people attempted to cross roads with no traffic lights, dodging cars that couldn't be arsed to stop, bicycles and rickshaws weaving in and out where they could. In such a bustling city, it was crazy that the physical infrastructure was so poor.

Matthew thought about all the stuff people say about China becoming the most powerful nation in the world someday then looked around him. The likelihood of that was low in his opinion. It was total pandemonium, and the hordes of people were making it nigh impossible to move along the road at anything faster than a snail's pace.

Won, the one who supposedly knew what he was doing, had no clue where to go. He had no sat nav fitted in the car to direct him and had to figure it out by himself. Obviously, Matthew and Chris were more useless than an ashtray on a motorbike sat navigating their way around Tianjin.

Any signage that existed was in Chinese symbols that were little more than gammon to them. Won struggled to take the right streets as the sky became increasingly darker, and making his way through so many people proved to be a greater challenge than speeding several miles the wrong way down a motorway through oncoming traffic.

Stuck with vehicles and people all around, some even leaning on their car while they waited to push past, Won pipes up in shoddy English.

"I no been Tianjin before. First driver job."

But of course. He had no fucking clue where he was going in a city he was in for the first time ever. Hiring this novice was just the next cross against Arthur's name on his rapidly growing rap sheet. Buffoon was the word that came to Matthew's mind as the car turned into a dead-end road. It was pitch black by this time. Matthew gazed down to the end of the road where he could just about make out some roadworks. Again, it was like a scene from some dystopian film, the creepiest, darkest place Matthew had ever set eyes on.

It was no wonder that Arthur's priority was to get them to this hell hole of a city before darkness fell and brought all the terrors of the night out to haunt them. If only Sarah knew about all of this. She'd have him back on a flight before you could shake a plane ticket at an air hostess. If only Linda knew about it. The boss would go ballistic.

The car sat still with the engine running. Matthew noticed a few groups of dodgy men loitering up and down the street. It's incredible how different people, from the same family, can interpret situations in such a disparate way. There was Matthew looking at these guys with trepidation, and then Chris speaks up.

"Here, Arthur, tell the driver to ask for directions."

Matthew grunted at Chris. "Dad, that is one bad fucking idea."

It was too late, though, as Arthur was already putting in the request with Won. The driver let out a snort and Matthew knew exactly what it signified. Thank god someone else had sense. Won said something sternly to Arthur, who then turned around to fill the guys in with the calmest, coolest tone.

"He say that we can't ask anybody for direction, because if anyone think we lost we be in tomorrow's dinner."

How casual, Matthew stated with irony to himself. Let's not ask for directions then. Chris and Matthew looked at each other.

"Right, let's reverse out of here then, eh? Come on, go," he barked at Won.

The driver understood exactly what Chris was asking of him, starting to roll the vehicle back down the street to the next junction. Once again, fear began to set in as one group of men started to make their way towards the car. At first they were walking, but as Won realised that they were being pursued he sped up the car. At this the group picked up their pace to a run and Won slammed his foot down. He backed the car up as fast as he could, tapping into the same skills he demonstrated earlier that day on the motorway, and spun the car around in the main road. Won the stunt driver was back with a vengeance, near missing both a bus and a rickshaw by mere inches. Dear god, this man was such a lucky son of a bitch.

They were out of yet another sticky situation. In the words of Blackadder, it was "the stickiest situation since sticky the stick insect got stuck on a sticky bun". They carried on driving around for another twenty-five minutes trying to work out where the hell they were and how on earth they could get to their next hotel. Won was still driving pretty glacially thanks to the bustling crowds and repeatedly checked the rear-view mirror. Matthew was curious as to what he was looking at.

"Arthur, is there a problem?" he asked.

Arthur started to repeat the question to Won, but he had understood and began to answer in English himself.

"We have visitor," he stated, nodding his head towards the mirror.

Chris and Matthew both glanced up at the mirror, noticing the glare of headlights reflecting in it. They turned around, but as they did the headlights got brighter. They both shielded their eyes then turned around. They had managed to pick up a tail which was a terrifying prospect. Matthew questioned who it could be, coming to the conclusion that it had to be the guys from back in that shifty little side street. They didn't appear to have a car with them, so that wasn't plausible. Perhaps it was the fuzz or the Chinese government or even the British government. Na, it couldn't be. Why would it be any of those? Maybe it was the carjackers or the Chinese mafia for some reason. Those ideas were more credible. Matthew was annoyed that he couldn't recall the name of the Chinese mafia so asked Arthur.

"They used to be called Triad."

That was it, Triad. They had been one of many different branches of transnational organised crime syndicates based in China and other Asian countries like Hong Kong, Macau and Taiwan, as well as in other countries with large Chinese populations. However, they'd been wiped out when the People's Republic of China had been established. There were newly organised crime groups, but they're not Triad proper. Rather, they're dark forces – which are loosely organised groups – and black societies – more mature criminal organisations. Essentially, though, these groups were the Chinese version of the mafia.

"Do you think it could be them?"

Arthur shook his head but offered no alternative explanation. Whoever they were, none of the potential options sounded ideal. Eventually, the supposed tail vanished. Whoever it had been, they'd lost interest for some reason. Matthew and Chris didn't think about it much more after that.

Won continued to drive around ramshackle, less-developed parts of the city seemingly aimlessly until, like a wobbly mirage in the burning hot sands of the desert, appeared a giant cluster of skyscrapers with brightly lit screens atop them. The brightness was a reminder of the neon signs of their business. With this sight they felt a sense of familiarity and security, knowing that they were heading in the right direction for Tianjin city centre.

Arthur was gleeful.

"Ding dong," he shouted.

This assured Chris and Matthew that they would now be able to find the hotel with ease. For once the strange little Chinese man was telling the truth, as a short while later they approached the Fuk Mi Business Hotel. It didn't look like much from the outside, but the last place had a nice exterior and it was filled with nightmares. Matthew hoped that it would be vice versa with this hotel.

They drove down into the hotel car park in the basement and everyone stepped out of the car. Looking at the shiny paintwork in the fluorescent lighting of the car park, you'd never know what this car and its passengers had gone through since it departed from Beijing earlier that day. Won popped the boot and dropped their suitcases on the ground. Chris grabbed Won's hands once they were free from baggage and offered him a heartfelt thanks for everything he'd done for them that day.

"Honestly, thank you so much. Would you like to come in for a drink?" he asked, his voice echoing around the concrete clad car park.

Matthew was a bit surprised by how thankful his dad was. However, he quickly nodded in agreement. The guy had done a great job at saving their bacon on a couple of occasions that day, and he supposed that it wasn't Won's fault that Arthur had hired someone who had never been to Tianjin before. Any annoyance he felt about the mishaps he should direct at Arthur, not Won.

"Yeah, come in for a drink on us," Matthew added.

Won hesitated, opening his mouth, closing it and then turning to Arthur to provide an answer in Chinese. He obviously wasn't sure of the words in English.

"He no want leave car," Arthur informed Chris and Matthew.

Ah, yeah, they'd forgotten his desperate need to protect the car – and his life. In spite of the fact that the car was safely nestled in the underground car park, with an entrance covered by metal security shutters, he was still reluctant to abandon the vehicle. Fair dos, thought Matthew. He wouldn't be willing to risk it for a biscuit – or a drink. Won gave a traditional bow. It was the first one that Matthew had seen since they'd arrived in China. He enjoyed the gesture, getting a taste of a different culture. Simultaneously, Won uttered something in Chinese and nodded his head towards the car.

"Sleep car," Arthur translated.

As they left Won to kip in the car, Matthew felt guilty thinking that they should have offered him a hotel room. Then he surmised that Won would have turned down the offer anyhow, as he'd already stated that he had to sleep in the car to keep an eye on it. Matthew looked back and waved at Won as he climbed under a blanket in the back seat and pulled on a sleeping mask. Matthew chuckled. Well, now this guy really was Kato, the masked driver.

Chapter 14 –
The Tianjin Hotel

In the lobby of the Fuk Mi Business Hotel, Arthur dealt with the check-in process. Matthew was thankful for this as he was exhausted from the day's events. He surveyed the decent lobby, filled mostly with Chinese businessmen, and then checked his phone to see if Sarah had responded to his text message yet. It was early hours of the afternoon in the UK by then so she should have received it. There was no text message from her, but he did have three missed calls from her as well as two from his mum. He tapped Chris on the shoulder and held up the phone to him.

"Better give them a call when we get up to the room, eh?" Matthew suggested.

Chris nodded and winked. True relaxation was setting in for the first time that day. They were just minutes away from a warm shower, soap and cleanliness. They both had a dry, thin layer of shit and urine across their bodies, now mixed with copious amounts of dried deodorant and aftershave. It was like the layer of skin a snake would shed. Every time Matthew picked up his suitcase he could feel the tiny crumbs of turd in his armpit hair.

"Matt, do you notice how your skin feels so tight with this dry shit smeared across it? My skin feels like it's not breathing now, like my body is about to hibernate or cocoon."

Matt nodded. "I have never felt so disgusting in all my life. You nailed it in that word right there, Dad, a cocoon of shit!"

All the while Matt was moving his arms and legs and readjusting his underwear to try to get comfortable.

"All done," said Arthur as he ushered Chris and Matthew towards the lifts, handing them two separate keys. They were attached to giant wooden keyrings with the number 3245 carved into them. 3245? How many rooms did this place have? Once in the lift they were met by a huge panel of buttons. Arthur pressed button number 32. The thirty-second floor it was then. Matthew couldn't wait to see the view from that high. Then he pressed button number 27 and turned to the guys.

"You on thirty-two. Me on twenty-seven." He opened his mouth to say something else and then paused, looking Chris in the eye with a look of concern. "Listen to me. This very important. You go to room. You barricade door. Those men that follow, they outside."

"WHAT?" inquired Matthew, furious. So they hadn't lost the tail after all. He then mimicked a Chinese accent. "Why you no tell us before?"

Arthur didn't get that Matthew was making fun of him, but Chris did, smirking before remembering what Arthur had just told them.

"Sorry, I hope they go away, but when I check in I see them park outside hotel. They many men and they watching us. I don't know who they are, but they bad men."

Both Matthew and Chris were stuck to the floor with fear as Arthur went on.

"If they come in through back door, nobody know they here. They take you and nobody know."

Chris and Matthew looked at each other, shaking their heads.

"And then what?" Chris asked Arthur.

"I will keep look out. I ask for front room. I watch them and come for you when safe."

Because Arthur had pressed 27 too, the lift stopped there first. Nobody got it. He ignored it and accompanied Chris and Matthew to the thirty-second floor and saw them to the door.

"Remember, block door with heavy thing," he reminded them before disappearing.

Chris and Matthew slammed the door behind them, checking that the lock was secure and setting about sweeping the room to make sure there were no unwanted guests already lurking anywhere in there. They did all the usual stuff a child would do to make sure the bogeyman isn't in their bedroom. There was nobody under the bed or behind the curtains. The bathroom and the wardrobe were free. It got ridiculous, with Matthew checking behind a chair in the corner and rechecking every space that they'd already gone over. He just wanted to be totally certain that they were alone in there.

They were, and on top of that there was no interconnecting door to worry about. The only way in or out was using the door that they'd just walked through, and that was locked. On one hand this made them feel safe, but on the other it meant that there was no means of escape should any unsavoury characters come knocking at the door.

Matthew pulled the curtains back, peering out of the window at the view he'd been looking forward to before Arthur delivered his latest terrible news. He could barely see a thing through the dark, thick smog outside, but one thing shone through the filthy haze: an enormous LED screen on the side of the building closest to the hotel displaying an advert for the Bank of China. Again, the sign reminded Matthew of home, somewhere he really wished that he was at that particular moment. It also brought Ridley Scott's *Blade Runner* to mind, which was set in a dystopian 2019 Los Angeles and which Chris had worked on. Chris and Matthew both saw it at the same time.

"BLADE RUNNER," they shouted simultaneously at each other, Matthew thinking that the movie was before its time and that so were they.

A dystopian LA. The gritty Mos Eisley. Where. The. Fuck. Were. They? This place, so far from home and so detached from everything they know, was crazy dangerous. Alas, there was no time to waste reminiscing about home, Hollywood, and the past. The guys turned in synchronisation, gathering every item they could see to erect a protective blockade in front of the door. Prevent entry they shall.

Chris slowly heaved a mammoth cabinet across the wooden floor, screeching and scratching the varnish as it went. He was a strong guy, but even he'd met a worthy opponent in this beast. While he grappled with the cabinet, Matthew pulled a significantly lighter desk across the floor. It didn't scratch the floor because it had little rubber feet attached to the bottom, but he wouldn't have given a shit even if it had torn a hole in the floor. Together, they shifted a sofa and then two smaller chairs in front of the door. For now that was the best they could accomplish, but as far as barricades go this one appeared to be pretty decent.

The room had been fortified to the best of their ability and resources leaving them free to accept their next mission: SHOWER!

Chris and Matthew were at that level of tiredness that everything seems a bit too real, and they stank to the high heavens. Without thinking about it they stripped off every item of clothing that had been in contact with their body all day, stuffing them into a black plastic bag that Matthew found in the bin. As they pulled off their clothes they disturbed their stench, and they both recoiled in disgust at themselves.

Hoping that they weren't living in a pipedream of the shower working just fine, they hopefully made their way towards the bathroom without deciding who was calling shotgun on the first session. Chris almost didn't want to try the water, afraid at what might await them.

Chris placed his hand over the shower lever while Matthew wrapped his hand around the hot water tap in the sink.

"One," Matthew said, raising his eyebrows. Chris joined in. "Two, three."

Low and behold, clean water flowed from the taps. Their elation was as plain as the shite they were covered in.

"YASSSSSSSSSSSSSSSSSS," they screamed, smashing each other's hands in a painful high five. A Chinese gang might very well be hunting them down to eliminate them for reasons unbeknown to them, but they would die clean and smelling of the ginseng and rice shower gel left in the bathroom. Chris hopped in the shower as

Matt retreated to the bedroom to wait his turn. He sat back onto the bed gently as not to cover it in his present shit-covered condition, the ding ding ding of a slot machine rattling around his head as he thought about the jackpot they'd finally hit. Aside from the fact that all the furniture other than the bed was pinned against the door, the room was pleasant. More importantly, everything in it bloody worked. There was a god and he'd finally graced them with his presence.

Once he was done Chris was like a new man. He pointed towards the bathroom.

"Heaven awaits you, Matthew. Off you go."

Matthew didn't need to be told. He was in there faster than the speed of light. He didn't surface from his watery, soapy paradise for half an hour, revelling in the fact that he was no longer forced to languish in a miasma of poo, piss and stale sweat any longer. If ever there was a turning point on the trip, that had to be it – minus the brutes who were apparently after them that is.

Getting clean had been Matt's first port of call, but he figured it would be a good time to give Sarah a quick shout after the shower. The second he picked up his phone to call her the phone rang. It was Chris P. Matt filled him in on everything, telling him that they had been followed, that the hotel was surrounded, that they were blockaded in the room, and that shit was getting dangerous. He made it perfectly clear that Chris P wasn't to breathe a word of this to Sarah or his mum. The call was brief as Matt was keen to call Sarah. He said bye to Chris P promising to keep him updated and went out into the room.

Chris and Matt lay on the bed in their pants, relishing the freshness but worried about their fortune. The room was adorned by several red items, so perhaps good fortune was on their side and Arthur's last words were a load of tosh. Maybe the impenetrable fort that they'd created was totally unnecessary? They decided to leave it where it was for the time being – just in case.

They lay in silence, the quietude disrupted by an almighty grumble emanating from Matt's stomach. Chris laughed but it acted as the springboard for overwhelming thoughts of hunger and food. As Matthew reached for his phone to finally call Sarah, Chris began to ask a very pertinent question.

"When do you think we'll be able to…"

Before he could utter the word "eat" there was a loud knock at the door. Matthew dropped the phone. They both stood up quietly, the bed making a slight squeaking sound as they lifted their arses off it. Matthew was about to say something when Chris raised his index finger to his mouth.

"Shhhhh."

Chris's "shhhhh" was probably louder than anything that Matthew was about to say, but he shut up regardless. They waited for what seemed like an eternity, and after a few minutes of silence another three knocks resonated around the door. These knocks were louder and more aggressive than the last ones, which was mildly worrying.

After the second round of knocks Matthew points to their suitcases and, like he was playing charades, mimes getting dressed. They both tiptoed across to their clothes, each pulling on a pair of linen trousers, a T-shirt, socks and shoes. Matthew realised that his socks were mismatching which bothered him, but this was no time for a fashion parade.

Another ten minutes went by as they stood in front of their makeshift blockade, the pair of them hunched over holding their heads out as if that would actually help them hear better. There was no further knocking. Like it was now his turn in the game of charades, Chris mimes the removal of the furniture from the doorway. Matthew just about shits his heart out of his arsehole, violently shaking his head and mouthing "no" over and over again. He couldn't believe his dad's terrible judgement. What was he thinking?

Chris ignored Matthew's consternation about what might happen if they undo all their good work with the barricade, removing the furniture piece by piece. Despite it being against his better judgement, Matthew helped his dad. He had no clue what the plan was, but it must be a good one to dismantle their security system. He hoped so anyhow. When they were moving the cabinet one door fell open and Matthew spied a half-empty box of Trojan condoms sitting on the bottom. At least the last guests had a better time in this room than he and his dad were having, he thought.

Before going in gung ho with guns blazing, Chris and Matthew cautiously placed their ears against the now liberated door. It took them a couple of minutes to realise that there was a peephole concealed behind a little wooden disc. Chris pushed the disc out of the way but it was stiff and made a loud scraping sound. Matthew raised a hand and moved his fingers up and down slowly to get Chris to push more gently. They took turns looking out the peephole, but there was nobody out there. The hallway appeared to be clear, at least as far as the peephole permitted them to see.

Chris unlocked the door and softly pushed the door handle down. It clicked when he couldn't push down any further, so if there had been anybody hiding outside, this would be the best time for them to charge the door and knock Chris and Matthew on their backsides. No such thing happened.

Before Chris pulled the door open Matthew ran back into the room, frantically searching around for any type of makeshift weapons that he could source. The best he could do was a flimsy table lamp and a rolled-up copy of *National Geographic* that had been left on the bedside table. Oh, what damage that would do. He returned to the door, grasping the lamp and handing his dad the magazine. Matthew clenched his teeth in apology to his dad at the fruits of his efforts, holding his lamp up ready for battle.

In so many different horror films that he'd seen, the dumb protagonists always pick up something ineffective like a lamp. He'd shouted at the screen so many times for them to arm themselves a real weapon, something that would actually do some damage to whatever villain was after them, and here he was doing the exact same thing in reality. He felt like a total chump but understood that, under pressure, you do the best that you can with what you have to work with. He'd remember that the next time he was watching a horror flick.

For the first time that day, even following the mental pile-up on the motorway, Matthew considered that this might be where he meets his maker. He might die right here in this hotel room, wielding nothing more than a fucking table lamp. His thoughts were shelved as Chris hauled the heavy door back. There was nobody immediately in front of the door. In formation, their weapons held up, they advance forwards like a tactical unit of poorly equipped troops. As they proceeded with stealth, a voice came from down the hallway.

"Aha, I wondered where you were. Why you no answer door?"

Chris and Matthew jumped out of their skins, both letting out a thundering yelp of fear. It was only bloody Arthur knocking on the door the whole god damned time. Arthur, causing yet another problem. This guy, Matthew cursed internally.

"Erm, and what the fuck happened about letting us know when it's safe to come out?"

Completely sidestepping the question, as well as his responsibility to let them know when they could come out of their room, Arthur simply stated that it's never safe in China and that they are still not safe.

"What the fuck does that even mean?" whispers Matthew to his dad. Chris just shrugs in wonderment at the little Chinese odd bod.

"Now we go eat. They not expect us to leave hotel. If they come to get us, they come in first thirty minute. They not come, so they not come at all."

Matthew was in a muddle as to who "they" were and why they might want to "come" at all. Half of him was convinced that Arthur was a paranoid freak talking utter bullshit, while the other half of him wanted to keep a guard up just in case the little nutter was right all along. But he decided it was best they were as safe as they could be in the circumstances. Chris sighed in relief at Arthur's words, clearly content with the answer.

"We're all good now, son."

"Yeah, seems so, doesn't it? My arse was going big time there."

Arthur announced that he was taking Chris and Matthew to dinner, which was a big surprise to Matthew. He had simply assumed that Arthur was planning to take them for a ride when it came to paying for anything during the trip. However, he explained that it would be his honour to buy dinner on their first night seeing as he was the host. They overlooked that it was actually their second night and that their first night had been shitty – literally. They accepted Arthur's generous offer, grabbing their room keys and leaving any dread they may have had back in the room.

Dread wasn't the only thing that Matthew left in the room. His phone remained there too. Just as the room door was slammed shut, Sarah's name popped up on the backlit phone screen. The phone had been set to silent the entire time, which is why he hadn't heard her calls and why he didn't hear it as he made his way for the lift.

The evening's "you couldn't write the script" level of drama had, once again, led to him conveniently forgetting about his wife and the promise that he'd made her. Even more trouble was just around the corner.

Chapter 15 – The Dinner

For once on the trip Arthur seemed to be doing some right, as he'd sourced a pukka restaurant just down the road from the hotel. Both Chris and Matthew were glad not to have to wander too far from the hotel for a bit of grub. The restaurant was renowned in Tianjin for serving the best crispy duck known to mankind. Matthew was almost salivating at the thought. Duck was one of his favourite dishes, cooked in Chinese style or not. They walked down past a little fountain outside the hotel. Matthew looked through the water across the road, trying to locate the car that had supposedly been stalking them earlier like deer in the Scottish Highlands. There was nothing there as far as he could see. There was an old Volkswagen Jetta and an even older, more battered, Lada Riva.

During the short walk to the restaurant Arthur was talking about China quietly. He was explaining that there are ears and eyes everywhere, that around 40% of the country work for the government and that you have to be very careful about what you say in public. He said that many of his friends and family had been dragged out of their houses and places of work by the police without explanation never to be seen again. Anyone asking questions would, at times, also go missing. Arthur spoke about it like it was the norm, that it was accepted by everyone. The Beijing Olympics was looming, and Arthur reported that many people's homes were destroyed to build the arenas and stadiums. Any homes and shops that were in the way of construction would be bulldozed, and if the inhabitants refused to leave then they would be bulldozed too. He even regaled one story about a man of nearly 100 years old, who was dragged out of his home and killed in the street for refusing to leave when ordered to. This was some of the darkest stuff that Matt had ever heard about.

As they passed a shoe shop Chris pulled Matt over and pointed in the window where there was a sign that said, "Know dis cunt", which they both giggled at. Obviously, it was meant to read, "No discount".

Both Matt and Chris could not stop laughing until they approached the door of the restaurant, where Matthew could see through a small gap in the steamed-up window. It was chock-a-block with Chinese people, which made sense given that they were in China and all. Back in the UK the fact that a Chinese restaurant was filled with Chinese people – or that any cuisine-specific eatery was full of people from the country the cuisine originated from – was a sign that the food must be excellent. Here though it wasn't Chinese food, it was just – erm, well – food. Anyway, Arthur promised that it was good, and he ALWAYS came through on his promises, right?

They were seated right in the middle of the restaurant which seemed all good as the evening kicked off. Hanging from the ceiling were huge, multicoloured paper dragons and typical Chinese lanterns. Matthew wondered if this was common or for the benefit of tourists. Arthur had been pretty legible throughout the entire day's shenanigans, but perhaps panic had led to a heightened level of understanding in Matthew, or maybe it had even caused him to be a little clearer. By now Matthew was back to being barely able to comprehend a word he said.

The loud din that roared across the restaurant didn't help. They got their order in pretty quickly. Neither Chris nor Matthew could understand the menu despite the small pictures that accompanied each menu entry. How the fuck were they supposed to ascertain what the hell these little blurry photographs represented? Arthur was taking charge of the ordering once again, so it was of no consequence.

Once the waiter had been dispatched with their order some potent rice wine arrived at the table. It was like drinking paint stripper – or what Matthew imagined paint stripper to taste like. It reminded him of a party that he'd been to in his teens where some idiots were filtering methylated spirits through baguettes. Their goal had been to remove the purple dye, leaving just the ethanol for recreational consumption. The whole point of the dye was to discourage that, and Matthew had been pretty sure there was other crap in there other than the dye that made the stuff unsuitable for human consumption.

Matthew and Chris raised their glasses with Arthur, repeating his toast: "Genbei." This was pronounced "gon bay". As they knocked back the vile libation Matthew heard some strange noises coming from the tables around them. He was trying his hardest not to laugh at the cacophony of burps, but whenever he was forced into a situation where he can't laugh at something he finds hilarious he finds it funnier and funnier until he eventually releases little tittering bursts. Tonight was no exception, and the quick looks of amusement he was getting from his dad in response to the burps weren't helping much at all.

The more of the strong booze they threw down their thrapples, the more difficult it was to understand Arthur, but the easier it was getting to ignore the belching symphony around them. Some of the food came after fifteen minutes. As it was plonked down on top of the paper tablecloth with a small Aztec style pattern all over it, Matthew realised that he hadn't even thought to ask Arthur what it was that he'd ordered them. He soon found out as a wide array of dishes were laid out in front of them; a veritable banquet. Chris asked Arthur what they were dealing with, and he informed them that there was everything they could ask for.

"Ah, so we have all the delicatessens you could want."

Matthew almost spat out a mouthful of rice wine at Arthur's use of "delicatessens" instead of "delicacies" and this was noticed. Chris scowled at Matthew. To cover his transgression Matthew started to cough, pretending that he had choked on his drink. It seemed to work because Arthur proceeded to explain the food to them. The names of the dishes went in one ear and right out the other, but basically, on the table thus far was pigeon, chicken feet, pig knuckles, cat meat and dog meat. Still to come was donkey dick and, as if that wasn't enough, monkey brains. Yum yum in my tum, Matthew thought with a huge dose of sarcasm. He'd just almost completely shamed himself by laughing at Arthur's mistake, so he didn't want to cause further embarrassment by showing his disgust at the offerings. He sat there for a second or two wondering how he was going to get this stuff down without projectile vomiting all over the table. As Arthur began to serve himself his attention focused on the food. Chris scowled at Matthew once more, only this time elbowing him too.

"Son, it's so rude to not eat the food of your host and show you are enjoying it. Just eat it and make it seem like you're loving every bit of it," Chris whispered encouragingly.

Although there wasn't a bit of duck in sight, which Matthew had been really looking forward to, he obeyed his dad's instructions. Matthew looked over to Arthur smiling. He smiled back at him.

"Eat, eat. Please eat my lovely food," he said with enthusiasm as if Matthew was waiting for the host to start eating, when he was really just stalling for as long as he could.

Oh lord, Matthew thought, here goes. He picked up his chopsticks, eating implements that he'd never been able to master. He'd never fully understood why Asian people don't use forks. Yeah, he got that chopsticks were more traditional, but why continue to using them when a better utensil had been invented. It boggled the mind.

Although Chris looked at the food with disgust too, he was enjoying Matthew's torment, and Matthew could see that from his dad's grin. As all fathers would, he thought it would be a good life lesson for his son to learn how to respond appropriately to unfamiliar social situations. He figured that it would serve Matthew well in the long run to do something that he didn't enjoy for the sake of sticking to the social conventions of a new culture and respecting the people involved. That was the furthest thing from Matthew's mind at that time, though.

Chopsticks at the ready, Matthew perused the options forgetting which was which. He scanned the dishes attempting to the best of his ability to evaluate which of them looked the most palatable. As he did so his face was plastered with the fakest smile he could muster under the circumstances, and he hoped that it wasn't coming off as disingenuous. He dipped his chopsticks into one of the bowls and pulled out what he hoped was the pigeon. He'd had that before at some swanky restaurant in London that Sarah had taken him for his birthday one year, and it hadn't been half bad. He raised it to his mouth, popped it in and chewed away.

"Mmm. Yum. Thank you," he said, totally mendaciously. The tough, fatty meat most certainly wasn't the pigeon. Whatever it was, it was repulsive. Matthew conjured thoughts of KFC, imagining it was a tasty fillet tower burger that he was pushing around in his mouth. Just swallow, he told himself. Just swallow. Hesitantly, Matthew went in for the kill again, this time desperate to avoid putting something mysterious into his mouth. Fuck it, he'd go for the chicken feet. Maybe, just maybe, they'd taste like KFC chicken. He wasn't optimistic.

As Matthew forced the mouthful down his throat realising that it did not, in fact, taste like KFC chicken, Arthur let out a deafening, rip-roaring burp. Matthew nearly choked on the chicken foot then politely smiled at Arthur. Matthew questioned whether the little Chinese weirdo was just a bit of a creature or whether it was customary there to burp during food. He prayed to God that it was the latter. As he smiled at Arthur he gets a look of confusion back.

"Matthew, you not enjoy food?"

Matthew responded in the affirmative and Arthur repeated the question to Chris who also states that he's enjoying it. The look of confusion remained on Arthur's face.

"Well, then, why you not show your appreciation?"

Showing their appreciation? Matthew was nonplussed. What was he on about? He looked at his dad who also clearly hadn't understood the question either.

"What do you mean, Arthur?" asked Chris.

"When you enjoy your food, it tradition to burp. And very loudly too."

"Ohhhhhh," said Chris and Matthew in tandem. "I see," added Matthew.

"You see? Yes? You burp when eating your food to show your host that you appreciate it."

All of the wind being brought up around them at other tables all made perfect sense now. It was just everybody stating that they love their food. So, Arthur wasn't rude after all. Chris and Matthew were actually the ones being impolite. From then on in both Matthew and Chris made a distinct point of burping as loud as they could every few mouthfuls. Matthew found it to be quite cathartic and enjoyable. It was refreshing to be in a public space where burping was usually frowned upon, and be encouraged to do it. He felt like Mel Gibson in *Braveheart*.

FREEEEEEDOOOOOOM, he screamed in his head. It went a bit too far, though, when Matthew almost tore his seat with a booming fart by accident. Matthew's face went a dark shade of red as mortification took hold of him. He quickly realised that there was nothing to be embarrassed by when Arthur turned to him with a pleased look.

"Yeeessss. This is very gooooood," he practically shouted.

Chris glared at Matthew, unamused and with a completely straight face. "Behave, son."

Even though his host seemed to appreciate the fart, Matthew made sure that it didn't happen again. He didn't want to cause his dad any shame. The evening continued and they tried each dish one by one. Each was more disgusting than the last, and getting to the end of the meal was true torture. Matthew wondered if he was dead and in hell because, if there was a hell, this must be pretty close to what it's like.

In general Matthew had a weak stomach. He'd heard horror stories from pals who'd been to far-flung lands and ended up throwing up in the sink while simultaneously giving the toilet a doing. The worst stories seemed to come from India where most British tourists – with their weak stomachs – ended up with the famous Delhi belly. That was usually down to the quality of the water being used in cooking.

One friend had told him that he avoided eating in a Varanasi restaurant while visiting India's most holy city after seeing the cook fill up a bucket of water for cooking from the Ganges river. Matthew hadn't understood why that was quite so bad until his friend informed him that locals used the river for everything you could imagine: drinking, laundry, bathing, pissing, shitting, brushing their teeth, floating dead bodies after burning them.

Matthew had never heard anything like that about eating food in China, so fingers crossed that everything would be grand in that respect. Chris had a stronger stomach, one that seemed to be made from iron.

As the evening went on the worst dishes came. Matthew thought he was getting to the end of his own personal torment, but unfortunately not. He became a master at pretending he was loving the food. He even developed a special method of getting the food down. He'd take a mouthful before immediately taking a big swig of booze to fill up his mouth, then he'd let it all fall down his throat. It wasn't perfect but it minimised the degree to which he was forced to chew and taste the food.

He switched from rice wine to beer at some point because he figured that a carbonated beverage would heighten his ability to burp. It took a lot of brainpower for Matthew not to throw up through the meal – a lot.

Speaking of brains, the arrival of the monkey brains presented Matthew with real trouble. At least everything else was just about indiscernible and he could pretend that it was something else. Things were different with the monkey brain. He'd heard about this before but had laughed it off as an urban legend. It seemed like such an extreme thing to eat that it couldn't possibly be real. The truth was grimmer than he could ever have imagined. Not only did they eat monkey brains, but they ate it directly from the head of the monkey.

A stony-faced waitress brought a large spinning plate to the table. Atop it was a whole monkey head garnished with bunches of beautiful plants and leaves. Matthew could not believe what he was looking at, or rather what was looking at him. The monkey's eyes were staring right at him. Matthew knew that the animal was dead, but it was all just a bit too much. It might have been the most barbaric thing he'd ever been faced with.

Arthur looked at Chris, motioning at the animal.

"You must try first," he declared, bowing his head respectfully. Was the respect for the dead animal or was it for Chris? Matthew wasn't sure.

Matthew daren't even look at his dad at this point. While he was still dreading having to eat the bastard, he was grateful that he wouldn't be the first one to have to tear a strip of brain from its head. He had no idea if the brain had even been cooked and put back into the head. Even if that was the case, the prospect wasn't one he relished.

At this point Matthew clocked his dad's face. Chris and the monkey were staring each other out, the monkey looking deep into the soul of the man who was about to chomp on his thoughts. Chris looked at Arthur for reassurance as he reached out towards the monkey's head. All around the top there was a small line where an incision had been made. Chris grabbed hold on the top part – the lid if you will – and tugged on it. Nothing happened at first.

"Harder," encouraged Arthur.

Chris strengthened his grip and yanked at it harder, as commanded to. As he lifted his arm upwards the lid came away from the remainder of the head with an ear-splitting, sickening pop. Matthew's face was chalk white like a thousand evil spirits had just wandered in front of him. He winced, clenching his teeth so hard that it was painful, and squinting slightly to mask what horrors were revealed. Luck was not on their side as it turned out.

The top of the skull now gone, Matthew and Chris could see clearly that the brains had not been cooked and placed back in there. The top had been lopped off and a bloody mangle of uncooked brains was waiting to be gobbled down. The kitchen had the decency to chop it up for them, though. How kind of them, Matthew thought.

Chris reached in with his chopsticks, tearing a piece of the chopped brain and, with a teensy moment of hesitation, throwing it into his mouth. Matthew, looking through his half-shut eyes, watched his dad's face that looked to be in a state of shock at the horrifying scene playing out in front of him. To his credit Chris chewed the lump of brains and swallowed it without fault. He pulled it off with finesse and Matthew was massively impressed by this.

The smile that had developed on his face soon disappeared as his turn came around. Arthur nodded at Matthew, indicating that he should eat some. Matthew picks up his piece with the ineffective eating tools and makes the foolish decision to sniff it before putting it into his mouth. It reeked of rotten eggs which made the entire experience worse than it needed to be. Unable to control his gag reflex, Matthew let out a substantial dry-heave but continued to place the chunk in his mouth. He was out of beer by this time, he couldn't employ the special methods of getting food down that he'd developed across the meal. Forced to chew it properly to be able to swallow, Matthew sinks his teeth into the brain.

"Mmmm. Tastes just like chicken."

It did not. As he spoke bits of the food scattered all across the table, and Chris could see it all over the front of his teeth. Like an angel before him, a waiter dropped off a few more beers to the table. Matthew grabbed one without haste and washed down every foul morsel, swigging again and again to get rid of the taste. Like the good guest he'd learned to be, he burped loudly and sat there looking as pleased as punch.

"EASY," he announced as if he was in some sort of competition with his dad.

The monkey brains were topped by the donkey dick. It was mostly just the concept of eating a cock that Matthew found so challenging, irrespective of which animal it came from. The mere thought of it made his own dick tingle with sadness and called to mind that German killer, Armin Meiwes, who ate a voluntary victim's severed penis in 2001 for what they both felt to be the ultimate sexual gratification. Matthew had experienced the same feelings in his dick when he'd seen a documentary about the cannibalistic manslaughter.

When the donkey dick had come Arthur was distracted by a small child screaming on the other side of the restaurant. Matthew took the opportunity to speak to Chris.

"Dad," he whispered quietly, "how can I eat that? I'll hurl everywhere."

Holding back the laughter that he so desperately wanted to let out, Chris replied,

"You've got to, son. You've just got to."

Matthew knew that if he didn't try it, it wouldn't be an end of the world sort of scenario, but it would come across as seriously bad for both of them. Matthew had never had any draw to penises in the slightest, other than his own of course. However, now he was in this situation it occurred to him that he would rather eat an attractive penis rather than the thing that lay on the plate in front of him.

It was really long, so congratulations to the well-hung donkey that had been slaughtered to provide them with this dish. It was brown in colour which was off-putting to say the least. And it had a giant bell end. In human terms this would have been called a mushroom dick, which is basically just a long, thin penis with a disproportionately large end.

Arthur was now watching him as he prodded the cock with a chopstick. Matthew thought back to the cannibal documentary which reported that both parties had trouble eating the dick because it was too tough and chewy. It had been raw, though, so perhaps that was why. He hoped that this cooked cock would be a more pleasant texture to eat. Yet, his exploration with the chopstick told a different tale altogether; it definitely felt tough.

"Eat, eat," Arthur willed him on.

Fuck it, thought Matthew, and went for it. Also fuck the chopsticks too. He was sick of struggling with the bloody things. He dived straight in with his hands, unsure if this was a grave faux pas in Chinese dining culture. The floppy dick now in his right palm, he pulled it towards his plate from the centre of the table.

Matthew was surprised by how heavy this thing was. It made his own dick feel as light as a feather in comparison with this bad boy. Thinking that he's speaking to himself in his head, Matthew word vomits everywhere.

"But I can handle it."

Chris laughs as Matthew recognises his mistake. Looking at nothing else, he gripped the cock at its base as the rest of it flopped around from side to side. He assessed that this was his second biggest mistake of the evening, next to sniffing the monkey brain before eating it. It would have been a far better idea to hold the large head and put the smaller end in his mouth first, but now he'd have to stuff the mushroom bell end in his mouth like he was blowing the thing.

Christ, did life get any worse than this? He pushed the head of the cock past his terrified, quivering lips and attempted to bite into the thing. As anticipated it was way too tough, and he couldn't manage to bite even the smallest piece from it.

Both Chris and Arthur's mouths hung open aghast at Matthew grabbing the dick and going for it like that. This wasn't the way things were done and Matthew was making a wanker of himself. By now he couldn't have given a single flying fuck about doing things the way they're done in China. His primary goal was to get this dick dish over and done with. Too tough? Not a problem for Matthew. He started to chew as hard as he could, but the end result was a load of slurping sounds like he was fellating the dick instead of eating it. Matthew struggled on trying to make all the right sounds as he fought with this thing.

"Mmmm," he mouthed as he nodded at Arthur, whose gob was still catching flies. The more noises he made, the more he bobbed his head, the more it seemed like Matthew and this donkey dick were engaged in a private, elicit evening of pleasure. Matthew, head down, had no idea about the look of shock painted across the faces of his dad and Arthur, so proceeded.

He was blissfully unaware of the fact that the restaurant around him had fallen almost totally silent, every other diner transfixed by what the hell was going on over at their table. A good minute had passed with everyone enjoying the ridiculous show that they were being treated to. Matthew was dripping with sweat, his efforts having exhausted him. Eventually Chris stepped in, unable to continue watching this shitshow for a minute longer. He raised his hand.

"That's enough, son. I don't think that's how it's done."

Matthew looked up at Arthur, seeing the look on his face, and then around the restaurant. Realising that a crowd of diners were staring at him with disbelief, he wanted the ground to open up and swallow him whole. Instead, he'd been swallowing the giant mushroom dick of a dead donkey. It gave a whole new meaning to *Drop The Dead Donkey*. This used to be one of Matthew's favourite television series, but not any longer.

He caught sight of an old Chinese woman at the next table who was mirroring his actions. Jesus, she must have thought that's how they do it wherever Matthew was from. He quickly stopped dead in his tracks, pulling the dick away from his face slowly and returning it to its original plate. He looked down at his T-shirt which was covered with dick juices and saliva. He looked a real fright. Then his eyes moved back to the dick that he'd just placed on the plate. It was mangled and deformed beyond recognition after he'd chomped away at it, all limp and lifeless.

In an effort to remain as cool as a cucumber and redeem some sense of dignity, Matthew took a casual sip of beer, gurgled for a while and then swallowed. He turned to Arthur.

"Mmm. Not bad. Not bad at all," he lied. "It is a little bit tough, slightly overcooked, but the seasoning on it is really nice."

Arthur's open mouth quickly turned into a beaming smile and erupts into a cackle as he jumps up. Now in a standing position Arthur begins to clap outrageously like a frantic standing ovation. He was a lone ranger in this standing ovation, though. Matthew had already worked out that Arthur was quite a character; a couple of sandwiches short of a picnic. By now, Matthew had come to the understanding that Arthur was as mad as a hatter.

Arthur took his seat. Matthew, laughing at Arthur's display, looked around the room. Everyone was now back at their own food, some smirking, some with raised eyebrows and some still in utter disbelief at what they'd just witnessed. In a delayed reaction, Chris burst out laughing.

"Oh, you crack me up. That's the funniest thing I've ever seen." He was in pieces, struggling to catch his breath and tears streaming down his face. "I wish I had a camera."

Arthur mimed taking a picture, pointing an imaginary camera at Matthew.

"At least the balls aren't chewy," Chris added as he munched down on a spicy fried testicle in capsicum.

They finally got to the end of the dinner and it couldn't have come any sooner. Matthew's weak stomach couldn't handle any more. The rest of the meal ticked by without a hiccup – well, just one or two from Matthew, who was full of food he'd rather not be full of. As they rounded off their time in the restaurant, Chris and Matthew watched with curiosity as Arthur added an unknown spice to their drinks. They wondered if it was star anise or cassia bark or something else they hadn't heard of. He looked back and forth between the two of them at their puzzled faces.

"Chinese herb. Make you very strong. Make you confident."

Chris and Matt knock their drinks back seeing no problem in consuming something that'll improve their strength and confidence. Why not?

"Bottoms up," said Chris.

"Genbei," replied Arthur and Matthew.

By the end of the meal, paid by Arthur as promised, Chris and Matthew were keen to get back to their room for a decent sleep, smelling nice and fresh. Matthew thought about treating himself to a second shower to wash away any monkey brain and donkey dick residue on him.

They got out onto the street and Matthew checked the other side of the road once again for the car that had been tailing them earlier. The Lada and the VW were still parked there joined by no other vehicles. Matthew was relieved. The worst thing to happen to him that night would be sucking off a severed donkey dick rather than being taken out by hitmen.

As they strolled slowly between the restaurant and the Fuk Mi Business Hotel, Arthur explained that nothing goes to waste in China;

that Chinese people aren't afraid to eat any part of any animal. He added that with such a large population – just over 1.3 billion people – this was the only way forward.

"You will see no cats or dogs or birds in China," he said. "Look around you. Nothing. We eat them all."

At first Matthew thought Arthur might be joking with them, but he wasn't. Matthew was a bit disturbed by the fact that the Chinese will eat anything, thinking about the animals commonly seen in the Western world. The more thought he gave to it, the more sense it made to eat any animal. Why had it become acceptable to consume certain animals in the UK but not others? Why was it OK to eat pigs, sheep, cows and so on, but not cats and dogs? It was a bit ridiculous. They'd become domestic animals, ones that people want to have for company, not ones that people wanted to serve with roast potatoes and carrots. Matthew figured that this would, no doubt, be part of the vegan rhetoric in trying to make meat eaters see that no living thing should be eaten.

Matthew looked around but he couldn't see any animals on the street. He hadn't given that any thought before the night's dinner. However, was he really surprised at any of this? Considering how the whole trip had been so far, was the slaughter of cute little cats and dogs for the purposes of food really that shocking? A resounding no bounced around his thoughts.

As a group of drunk white men in suits went by, Matthew reflected on the fact that the social side of the trip was supposed to be the simplest part. The difficult shit wasn't meant to come until the business dealings began. It hadn't worked out that way. What the hell would the business side of the trip offer them? Surely to buggery things couldn't get any more awful, could they? Matthew and Chris wandered ahead a little as Arthur struggled to get a cigarette lit.

"I wouldn't mind about all the animals, Dad, but what about the fucking duck? We went to a famous duck restaurant and there wasn't a bit of duck in sight. Is there a shortage or something?"

Chris and Matthew both chuckled as Arthur caught up with them. They all made their way up the stairs to the entrance and across the lobby of the hotel. Finally, sweet rest awaited Chris and Matthew up in their room.

Chapter 16 – Too Much Dick

As Chris and Matthew waited patiently in the hotel lobby for Arthur to walk across and meet them, every minute seemed to go by like a migraine. Matthew was absolutely exhausted by this time and his bed was calling him like a sexy siren from the sea.

Why on earth did this little Chinese man have to be so fricking weird? Why were they having to put up with all his little eccentricities when he and his dad were so bloody tired? Wasn't it bad enough that they'd just been forced to endure that massive onslaught of the vilest food Matthew had ever been faced with in his entire life? Did he really feel the need to punish them even more than they had already been punished across the entire evening? Clearly so.

Chris wasn't really up for saying very much at this point, just leaning against a stair railing waiting for Arthur. Matt just looked around the hotel lobby as Arthur moved across it glacially. Before he could even think of sleep that night he absolutely had to call Sarah before she actually got on a plane, came to China, and hunted his arse down to give him the biggest rollicking of his existence.

He patted his trouser pockets on both sides to make sure he didn't have his phone with him there and then to give her a quick text to say he'd be calling in a minute. A horrible feeling of anxiety was creeping over him now that the impending phone call had come to mind. Sadly, his phone wasn't in his pockets. Where was it, though? Ah yeah, he'd left it up in the room on the bed. If this was a movie it would be the part where the scene cuts to the phone sitting all on its own on the bed looking like not very much at all, but secretly harbouring the trouble that Matthew was in with his ballsy wife.

Chris and Matthew were still waiting for Arthur who'd now stopped to chat, in what looked like a bit of a clandestine meeting, with a guy dressed in the uniform of the hotel.

"What are they chatting about, Dad?" Matt asked Chris.

"How the fuck would I know? First, we ain't close enough to hear them, and second, even if we were, how the fuck would I be able to decipher what the two of them are saying? You are a pillock sometimes, son."

They both laughed.

"It was more of a..."

He was about to announce that it was more of a rhetorical question, when Arthur finished his convo with the man and made it to the home stretch across the lobby to meet them. Matthew wondered if Chris P had contacted his wife yet. What was it that he'd asked his pal to tell her? He couldn't for the life of him remember after all the beer and rice wine they'd been drinking all evening to wash down Arthur's delights.

Arthur finally reached a bored and sleepy Chris and Matthew who were ready for bed and curious about what his little chat with the hotel employee was about. And Matthew was so anxious to get to his phone.

"Shall we?" Arthur said to them, motioning towards the lift with his arm and nodding for them to make a move. The three of them made their way across to the lift, Matthew thinking thank fuck they were finally on their way to slumber, possibly via the toilet to retch before putting his head down.

Standing at the lift Arthur patted them on the back at the same time – a hand for each of them. They both turned to look at him, a wide grin plastered across his face. "So, boys, next on the itinerary."

Matthew's heart sank as he made eyes at his dad, whose facial expression was currently feigning interest in what Arthur was about to suggest. They were so close to rest. What the fuck could they possibly be doing now? They were already at the lift after all. Did this have something to do with that sly little chat Arthur was having in the lobby? There was no doubt about it.

"Massage, massage," Arthur said in a high-pitched voice, before roaring with laughter. He was enjoying this, the little bastard.

"Massage? What do you mean? Tomorrow?"

"No, don't be silly. Massage now, not tomorrow. Tomorrow we have no time for massage."

To protest Matthew was about to pipe up that they were too exhausted to do anything else that night, but as he opened his mouth Chris pinched his arm. Never one for discretion, Matthew let out a little yelp. It was the equivalent of "Why did you just kick me?"

when someone nudges you under the table to keep shtum about something. Chris rolled his eyes but luckily Arthur didn't respond to Matthew's little whimper. Arthur went on.

"Massage in China. It very good. It the best there is. I promise. Come on. I host, so you must. You come with me. Come come."

After his dad's response Matthew knew that they'd just have to acquiesce on this one as they'd had to do for the entire duration of this trip so far. Still gagging to get to his phone and his wife – a long-lost one by this time it seemed – Matthew was reluctant, but he softened to the idea of a massage as he thought about the comfy bed he'd be on with some hot Chinese bird working his back over. It sounded OK actually.

Simultaneously Chris and Matthew agreed, to Arthur's excitement. "Yesssss. English men get massage in China. You like it for sure."

The lift arrived with a ding. Matthew hadn't noticed it before now, but the resonation of the ding gave it an eerie sound as if it was the lift in the hotel featured in *The Shining*. The doors opened as aggressively as Sarah would no doubt welcome him when he finally got in contact with her. The three of them got in there with no other guests, and Matthew looked on in confusion when he noticed Arthur pressing the bottom-most button with a huge B on it. B? Basement? Why would they be going down there?

"Arthur, don't we have to go up to get to the sauna? Yeah, I'm sure we do," Matthew asked.

He looked at his dad who was also clearly baffled as to what was happening. Arthur had a little smirk which told them both something was amiss here.

"Yes, the sauna is up. We not going up, though."

Chris and Matthew continued staring at each other. Chris mouthed, "What the fuck?" at Matthew who just shrugged and mouthed back, "I don't fucking know."

"You in China now. You need proper massage. And when you in China, you must enjoy the best sort of massage we have to offer."

Matthew knew it, that the guy in the lobby had a part to play in this. Arthur was obviously getting the lowdown on exactly where to go for these fabulous, must-have massages. What the hell sort of massage was this gonna be? Jesus, Matthew thought, more fresh hell.

When the lift reached the basement level it came to a shuddering halt. Matthew half expected the doors to open to a dingy, dank basement with some rusty iron door in the distance guarded by a giant Chinese goon. The doors opened. He wasn't far off. They were facing a long, dark corridor with concrete walls and an array of pipes running from one end to the other, some clunking, some with steam coming out of small cracks, and others dripping on the floor. It was a scene straight out of a horror film, and Matthew wondered at what point the creepy doll riding a tricycle would turn a corner and come to kill them? Chris muttered, "Fuck me," under his breath.

Matthew looked down through the darkness to the end of the corridor. And there it was, the big door with a giant Chinese man standing in front of it. Matthew was gobsmacked that this shit actually happened in real life, and not just the make-believe of films, television series and books.

The guys followed Arthur's lead who'd already started to make his way towards the door. They kept a little distance, allowing Arthur to speak to the doorman alone. Chris looked around taking in the sinister surroundings, while Matthew looked over Arthur's shoulder. A drip of water fell from one of the pipes and bounced off the shoulder Matthew was looking over. Arthur said something to the doorman in Chinese, holding up three fingers. Matthew had never noticed before, but one of the fingernails on Arthur's right hand was missing.

The burly guy tilted his head, looking past Arthur at Matthew and his dad. Chris was still gazing around furtively, but Matthew caught the guy's eyes and smiled. He got no smile in return as he put out his hand and said something in response to Arthur. A wad of cash was exchanged – around $150 worth of Chinese currency it seemed. Matthew had now got a decent handle on what the currency was worth in China after being ripped off on arrival by the taxi driver.

Muscled arms yank the heavy door open, which creaks as it leaves a clear path for the three of them to go through. Before stepping through, Matthew got a little whiff of something perfumed and a glimpse of something red on the floor. Seconds later, the door closing behind them, they were in a completely different setting.

They found themselves in a large lounge-style room, covered wall to wall in a plush red carpet. The heady scent or something familiar yet simultaneously unfamiliar filled the room. What was it? It didn't take Matthew long to come to the conclusion that it was the same scent as in the sauna of their shit-filled nightmares, only this time it wasn't marred by the smell of excrement.

"What's that perfume, Arthur?" Matthew asked their host.

Arthur stood there for a few seconds looking into the air with real concentration. He looked puzzled, closed his eyes, and took a deep sniff. Then, without hesitation, he announced that it was sandalwood and jasmine.

Soft carpet underfoot and a beautiful scent filling the air, things didn't seem so bad. It might have been the fanciest place they'd been since they'd landed in China. Matthew glanced at Chris and they nodded at each other in surprised approval. As the mystical tones of Chinese flute music played gently, Matthew looked around the room to take it all in properly.

Sturdy-looking massage beds were positioned across the room evenly, each upholstered in what appeared to be brown faux leather. They were all made from an indistinct wood that had been varnished in a mahogany colour. Behind them, at the end of the room they stood in, sat small chairs.

Arthur took a seat on one and Chris did the exact same. It took Matthew a while to see that they were sitting down, but when he did he went to plonk himself down next to his dad. As he made a move for the chair, Arthur swiftly put his hand up in protest.

"No sit, Matthew. You first. Take clothes off and towel yourself behind there."

Arthur pointed at something across the lounge, and Matthew turned his head to see what. He was indicating towards an area closed off by a large screen. A bag of nerves, Matthew decided not to bother asking what was behind the screen. It was pretty obvious at this stage of the game anyhow. He made his way over, his heart beating so hard it felt like it would burst out of his rib cage. Sod it, he thought, what could go wrong? Not much really, he decided.

Matthew popped his head around the side of the screen cautiously, his body quickly following. There was nothing there other than some clothing hooks and a small bench at one side with some towels on top of it. On one wall was a garish painting depicting some snow tigers wandering around snow-covered mountains. On the other a picture of an ornately dressed woman with a giant headdress and some Chinese symbols to the side of her. Realising that he had spent too much time in there appreciating the artwork fully-clothed, he whipped everything off fast.

He grabbed one of the towels and wrapped it around himself. It could have been a little larger to fit around him comfortably, but he was sure that this was a moot point as the towel would likely be coming off soon. Matthew stood there, his hands on his hips, took a few deep breaths, and stepped out from behind the screen.

As he came back into the room six women had appeared as if by magic. In his state of nerves, he hadn't heard them come through a door or anything. Either that or they're as light as feathers, he thought. He looked down at his hands which were a bit jittery, and then back up. There were actually seven of them. One was so small that he hadn't initially seen her behind one of the taller ones. Matthew scanned their faces deciding that each was prettier than the last. He'd never been with an Asian woman before, casually or otherwise, but he'd always thought their delicate features made them really easy on the eye.

Once he'd registered all of their faces, Matthew's eyes were free to wander south a little. The girls were clad in even smaller towels than the one wrapped around his own waist, covering only their lower half. On top, they were wearing tight boob tubes. None of them had particularly large breasts, which was probably a godsend. It might mean he wouldn't get a hard-on during his massage.

As Matthew stood there, his eyes dancing between the girls' faces, their smallish breasts and some nice bums, he felt like a bit of a spare part. What now? Once they'd noticed him standing there two of the girls approached him with enormous smiles, albeit fake ones. They were so slim that their stomachs were actually concave. Matthew wondered how that was even possible and all of a sudden felt body-conscious.

The girls took his arms, saying something in Chinese in a coquettish manner, batting their eyelids at him and pouting their plump lips. It was becoming clearer and clearer as the minutes past what kind of massage this was. He knew it already, but confirmation was being delivered in small chunks.

The girls ushered Matthew to the centre massage table near the seating area that Arthur and Chris were still waiting in. Red-faced, he lay down on his front, placing his face in the hole in front of him. He was now thankful to be face down on the bed, his tummy no longer hanging out in front of these sexy, slight women. He supposed he shouldn't really care, after all, they were being paid for the pleasure. Matthew reached under him to loosen the towel, pulling it out so that it was hanging down each side of the massage table and covering his arse. He could hear the girls speaking softly, his dad and their host giggling.

Now unable to see Chris and Arthur, he relaxed into the whole thing a bit more, blocking out any sounds around him. As he lay there he felt a sense of relaxation come over him, but at the same time he couldn't quite fully relax. Something was holding him back, but what was it? Fuck, he was excited, and not just in the enthusiastic and eager kind of way. He was properly sexually aroused, but it felt different than usual. It was the sort of sexual arousal that totally consumes your thoughts. A lot of guys talk about the hangover horn, where they get so turned on it's almost unbearable. Well, that's what this felt like.

Matthew's heart was racing and his breathing erratic. He attempted to get his breathing under control by taking in large gulps of air, and eventually it petered out. It all felt more than he could handle, but he was here now and there wasn't much he could do about it. He glanced up to catch his dad's attention, although he wasn't sure what for. However, Chris was focused on the masseurs seductively approaching him and Arthur.

Matthew put his face back in the hole, able to see nothing but the red carpet below. Before long, with the appearance of four delicate, pedicured feet, two each side of the table, Matthew knew the massage was about to commence. The two girls who ushered him over there were the same ones now standing beside him.

He was surprised to feel four hands on his back, even though he could see the same number of feet. It was just a strange sensation, that's all. It led him to think about all the threesomes he hadn't been having across his life and made him chuckle. The smile on his face was quickly wiped off when the thought of threesomes brought Sarah to mind. Oh boy, she could never find out about this. No thinking about Sarah just now, though, he instructed himself. Enjoy this while you can.

The sensation of four hands ceased being the strangest thing going on when he began to hear the girls speaking softly in Chinese. Were they speaking to him or each other? He tried to look up to work it out, but one of them firmly pushed his head back down. Then the soft-spoken tones of their voices transformed into gentle whispers spoken directly into Matthew's ears.

He could see four lovely feet, feel four soft hands on his skin, and now he has two hot women breathily speaking into his ears. He had bugger-all idea what they were saying to him, every word of it in Chinese, but it didn't matter because it felt so damn good. His whole body was tingling from top to toe in a real-life ASMR experience.

Matthew was able to turn his head slightly, still half in the hole on the bed, but allowing him to see what was going on with Arthur and Chris. They were now accompanied by the remainder of the women who'd been there when he came out from behind the screen. They were all laughing and chatting together, but he couldn't make out what was being said or if it was in Chinese or English. The fact these girls weren't speaking to him in English suggested it was the latter. At this time, Chris and Arthur were still seated on the chairs, and Matthew wondered why they hadn't gone to strip and get on massage tables just yet. Why was it just him lying there?

A couple of the girls disappeared behind another screen and returned some five minutes later with a tray full of drinks, still giggling and chatting. Matthew had lost all sense of time, but if he had to guess he'd say around thirty minutes had passed and he could certainly do with one of those drinks soon.

Although he was turned on by the whole experience, something kept him from getting a boner. It might have been some sense of decency, or it might just have been fear of embarrassment. Whatever the case, he was able to flip over onto his back when asked to without displaying a giant tent pole for the girls.

He was now so unwound that turning over felt like a task of giant proportions. He somehow conjured up the strength to do so and the girls carried on with their task of bringing him pleasure. As he'd flipped around he'd done it with enough care that the towel covered his tackle, but he was back to feeling a little self-conscious about his body once more. He'd never really been bothered about being a bigger guy, but there were few occasions where he had to be half-naked in front of strangers.

Now that he was on his back, the girls looked at Matthew and both gave him a warm smile. Sarah's smile was warm like that. No, Matthew, he told himself, do not think about Sarah right now. The girls repositioned themselves, moving towards the lower half of his body. Matthew's face felt bizarrely hot even though the rest of him felt perfectly temperate, and he wondered why that would be. They started with his feet, working their arches and balls before playing with each toe individually for what seemed like a lifetime. Who knew that foot massages felt so good? They'd definitely be something he'd invest in on his return to the UK, even if they weren't given by gorgeous Chinese girls. The masseurs worked their way up, concentrating on his ankles, then the calves and upwards.

Matthew's face was getting even hotter and it was incredibly overwhelming. He was so close to asking the girls to stop, but at the same time he was enjoying what they were doing so much. Every ounce of pressure they placed on his body felt better than the last, and every look they gave him drove him wild. Hot blood was coursing through his veins at the fastest speed like some hypnotic drug was pumping through his entire body. And he felt all that blood moving straight for his penis which was destined for an erection at any moment.

Fuck, fuck, fuck, he screamed in his head. Oh my god, DO NOT GET AN ERECTION. Do you understand me? While his shoulder angel and devil battled it out, Matthew's cock got stiffer and stiffer. No amount of willing it to fuck off was going to do the trick. Whenever he'd found himself getting close to a boner in the past he was usually able to persuade it to back off. The standard thought of naked grandmas, world poverty, famine, and all those sorts of awful things usually worked. He pictured his gran naked. Nope, hard-on is still there. Starving African kids? Nope, still there. Dead people? Argh, what is wrong with me, he asked himself. He's certainly not aroused by any of these things and these girls aren't that bloody sexy that he can't control himself. What the hell was happening?

It was then, like a million moments of realisation hitting him all at the same time, that he understood that he wasn't just being a horndog of epic proportions. His body had been offered a little unanticipated help along the way. What is a hot, red face a side effect of? Fucking Viagra, that's what. He was certain of it. That, plus his inability to get rid of this raging boner, equalled the consumption of Viagra.

This was no accident, though, his mind shooting back to the dinner earlier. The mysterious spices that Arthur had added to their drinks, supposedly in aid of making them strong and confident, was only Chinese fucking Viagra. The sneaky little shit. Matthew was absolutely livid. He should have questioned exactly what it was before he'd thrown it back without question. What a plonker. Anyway, this wasn't going to solve anything right at that moment.

Matthew had never taken an erection enhancer before now, there was absolutely no need. But he'd heard about what it feels like, giving you a hard dick that doesn't subside for hours sometimes to the point of agony. Strong his cock certainly was, but confident he may not be. Panic stricken, he desperately tried to get his dad's attention, but Chris was still otherwise engaged. He looked up at one of the girls apologetically, but her smile suggested that she wasn't giving a single flying fuck about his big, swollen dick right there in front of her. Matthew looked at the other girl too, who was licking her lips and moaning gently. Jesus, they were enjoying this. This was definitely a sex massage. No two ways about it.

Both girls continue to rub Matthew's upper legs, working their way up to his nutsack and gooch.

"Ohhh, you like? Yes? You strong. You big. We liiiiiike."

The way they were talking was driving him wild. He looked down at his dick just to check that it was still ridiculously hard. It was. In fact, it was harder than he'd ever seen it. And bigger too? No, it couldn't be. It really looked like that, though, about an inch bigger than it usually did. It was the most abnormal thing he'd ever seen looking at any part of his body. If only it looked like that every day. He'd really be onto a winner there.

The size and stiffness weren't the only abnormal features about it. It was throbbing in a way Matthew had never felt before as if he was overcome by the desire of all virile men ever to have existed at once. He felt every beat of his heart push more and more blood into it, making it pulsate. *American Pie* references abound, but he could have shoved his dick in that apple pie right about then. These special herbs, whatever the hell they were exactly, was compelling him to bang any sort of hole. It was as if there was nothing less natural than that dick not being permitted a hole to fuck. He didn't know what to do with himself.

Again, he swung his head around to catch his dad's attention. Chris and Arthur were still in the seated area with their clothes on unlike Matthew. Only now the women on their laps were starkers. Seeing that certainly didn't do Matthew any favours, their tight bodies making his cock throb even more. Chris and Arthur were hysterical with laughter, though. What on earth would they have been laughing at? It was so childish, the two of them snickering away like a pair of schoolgirls. Matthew assessed their line of vision and figured that they couldn't possibly see his erection. So, it couldn't be that, but they were definitely looking in the direction of his table.

Matthew looked up at his two girls again. They were also giggling, but much more demurely than his dad and Arthur. What was this big joke that everyone seemed to be in on apart from him? Chris now had tears rolling down his cheeks, barely unable to control his laughter and pointing at Matthew's masseurs. Matthew simply couldn't see whatever the fuck it was that he and Arthur were able to see and it was driving him nuts. He was absolutely mortified at his dad's behaviour. It was all just too much, every bit of it, and all he could think of was getting out of there. There was zero chance of that with this third leg attached to him.

Why didn't Chris have the same problem? He'd taken the spices too. And then time played its part, Chris getting his own Chinese Viagra experience as the spices kick in for him. His cock jumped to attention without warning, and just like Matthew he was unable to control it at all. Chris was still ending himself with laughter, and this just made it all the worse.

As his dad desperately and fruitlessly tried to cover up his own raging boner with both his hand and his arm, Matthew suddenly realised something. The girls cavorting on his dad and Arthur's laps are only bloody ladyboys. The girls had their backs turned to the guys so they were unable to see that the women actually had giant erect cocks underneath their towels, the tents they'd formed now staring Matthew right in the face. They looked like bigger dicks than he'd ever seen before.

Still unsure about what Chris was finding so funny Matthew started to laugh uncontrollably too, assuming that the hotel employee up in the lobby hadn't mentioned this to Arthur earlier. Still lying down on his massage table, Matthew was guffawing so hard that he almost choked, pointing at the girls. He felt mean but it was too good that his dad had no idea what was happening.

In a huge explosion of sudden comprehension among the men, the laughter fell away and silence took hold of the room. Chris and Arthur threw a quick look of bewilderment at each other, discerning that if Matthew is tickled by the same thing they've been laughing at, then that means…Oh god, their girls are ladyboys too. Sure enough, as they look around the girls' midriffs there it was – a veritable banquet of Asian cock just about covered by skimpy towels. At the same time Matthew bolts up seeing what the other guys found hilarious. His own girls had big ten-inchers under their towels.

The three of them look repeatedly back and forth between themselves, then to the enormous knobs of the supposed girls in front of them, and then at each other again. Each other, the dicks, each other, the dicks. Not one of them knew what to do. It was as if they were put under a spell by these big magic wands. Harry Potter would have a field day here. The laughter fully put to bed, terror set in with Chris, Matthew and Arthur as they wondered how the hell they'd escape the circus they'd found themselves in.

All the while this hilarity was going on, the girls had just been chuckling along. Matthew had no idea if they knew they were having the piss ripped out of them or whether this was a regular occurrence, guys turning up here clueless as to the product that awaits them. Was this some awful kind of deception or should Arthur have known what would go down?

Now was not the time for these questions clearly, as Matthew felt a hand running up his erection from bottom to top.

"You want special massage?" one of his masseurs asked. "I give you special massage. You like?"

Matthew certainly didn't have to put any thought into his response. "Erm, no, no," he said spiritedly. "Please, no. Stop, please. No, just stop now. STOP. THANK YOU."

The masseur wouldn't take no for an answer. Either that or she had no idea what no meant. Perhaps she was under the mistaken belief than no meant yes, and not just in a lost in translation kind of way, but also a rapey sort of way. You know, the lack of understanding that leads so many guys to sexually assault women?

Realising that she wasn't going to accept his refusal of her very generous offer of a "special massage" which most definitely meant a hand job to completion, Matthew started to pull away. He loved his wife and liked to think he'd have said no regardless of the discovery. As he tried to get up off the table, covering his still raging boner with the towel, both of the girls start to tug at it, trying to get it off him. What the fuck was wrong with these girls? Matthew stood his ground, firmly holding the towel in place. They were really strong, far stronger than they looked, but he managed to keep it in place for a while.

Every single one of the ladyboys in the room, now standing, let their towels fall to the floor. Chris, Matt, and Arthur didn't know where to look as seven huge cocks stood to attention before them. Stunned and off his guard, one of the girls manages to whip Matthew's towel away from him leaving him as bollock naked as them. He then jumped up, frantically trying to decide what to do. Suddenly aware that he was standing erect in front of his dad, Matthew spun around with the aim of hot-footing it back to his clothes behind the screen.

Unfortunately for Matthew there was a 5 foot 4, dick-swinging, Chinese obstacle in his path. As he turned to shield his erection from Chris, he found himself face to face and cock to cock with one of his masseurs, the one who hadn't pulled off his towel. Their dicks knocking against each other as if they were in a porn version of *Star Wars* called *Chicks with Tentacles* or *Sex Wars Episode IV: A New Hole*, battling it out with their sexy light sabres, Matthew tried to back away to get around her. The force couldn't have been any less with him if it tried, as the other dirty Jedi came up from the rear blocking him in and swinging her own light sabre against his arse cheek.

"Oh my god, get the fuck off me," he shouted at them. "Get the fuck off right now."

He desperately struggled to slip out from between them, trying not to end up being the reluctant meat in a less than ideal ladyboy sandwich. But he found out the hardest way possible that escaping two ravenous ladyboys with a penchant for British guys is a lot more difficult than a person might think. It's made all the more challenging when you're trying to avoid your boner being spotted by your dad when one of those ladyboys is trying to penetrate your arsehole – without even the decency to lube it up first – and the other one is mostly concerned with entering into some bizarre little cock-tangled dance. There's only so much defence you can offer your arse while also trying to cover your privates unless you do actually have multiple tentacles that is.

After accidentally ending up with their cocks in his hands again and again, in the end Matthew had no choice but to resign himself to the only viable deterrent on offer: simply grabbing them to keep them away from his own dick and arse.

It certainly allowed him to retain his anal virginity, which he'd proudly kept throughout his life, but it wasn't a happy sensation by any stretch of the imagination. It took everything that Matthew had in him not to hurl everywhere as he dry heaved. Suddenly, the donkey dick consumed at dinner didn't seem so horrific after all. He'd swap these dicks for that one anytime. As he gagged, making as many sounds as he could think of that would demonstrate how unhappy he was in the situation, he continued writhing to get away.

"Oh my god, no. Noooo. Yuk. Definitely not. Please move. Move now. Out of the way, please. Can you take your cock off me immediately?"

No matter what Matthew said to them, no matter how many noises of disgust he made, and no matter how much he pulled away, they just wouldn't listen to him. Christ, how had he found himself here begging two ladyboys not to whack him with their giant cocks? Of all the things that had gone down on the trip, this one might have been the least expected.

Finally, Matthew manages to wriggle free from his tormentors, doing a runner past the two girls and making a swift beeline for his clothes behind the screen. He pulled on his clothes as fast as he could. If only Sarah could see him now she'd never have a go at him to get ready fast again. She'd see that, with the right motivation, her husband was able to get dressed as fast as lightning.

Even though their prey had made an escape and was now out of their clutches, the masseurs were still hungry for further nonsense. Unhappy being abandoned, they turned instantly towards Chris and Arthur, darting over to them. By this time Matthew hadn't been the only victim. As Matthew saved himself, Chris was left fending off these enormous cocks left, right and centre. He felt like he was stuck in the epic movie *Zulu*, one of the British soldiers, Zulus hurling their spears at him during the Anglo-Zulu war. Would the British come up trumps as the dicks are thrown at them? Would he be defeated by cock? It was anyone's game at this point who the victor would be in this heroic, phallic struggle.

Arthur's situation? Well, that's a whole different ball game. As Matthew and Chris fought against their enemy, Arthur was absolutely fucking loving every bloody minute of it. When Matthew and Chris both saw and heard Arthur continuing to giggle at it all, it suddenly became apparent that he'd been in on everything the whole time. He wasn't a bit surprised when Chris realised the girls on their laps had dicks. His supposed look of shock, now that Chris and Matthew thought about it, was really one assessing Chris's reaction.

By the time Matthew was fully dressed he reappeared from behind the screen and went to his dad's rescue. Chris, never gladder to see his son than ever before, had a terrified, pleading look on his face. Matthew shuffled across the room, stopping briefly to throw back a half glass of whisky that was sitting on one of the tables. Fuck, it was not whisky. Christ knows what it was that he'd just knocked back, but it burned and it took the edge off the hell he was in.

He grabbed Chris by the arms and yanked him, but the girls were just as stubborn as when they'd had Matthew stuck between them.

"Get the fuck up, Dad. Come on."

"I'm trying, son. These fuckers won't let go of me."

"Right, enough is enough. For Christ's sake."

With full force Matthew heaved at his dad's arm, hearing a pop as he did.

"Shit, Matthew. You almost pulled my arm out of its socket."

"What would you rather? A gammy shoulder or to be left here to be gobbled up by these man eaters? Your choice."

"Point taken. Let's make a move."

At that the two of them made for the door they'd come through. Was the bouncer, doorman, or whatever he was going to let them through? Or was it gonna be like that horror film *Hostel* where you're only allowed to leave once you've finished what you came to do? Matthew was freaking out.

They threw the door open leaving Arthur to enjoy his carnal pleasures alone. The door belted the Chinese guy on his left arm. He yelped in pain, grabbed hold of it, and shouted something angrily in Chinese to Chris and Matt as they headed for the lift, speed walking and not stopping to look back. Whereas he'd been nervous entering that grimy basement corridor earlier, Matthew was pleased to be back in it. That dank smell was like sweet relief compared to the floral scent of that house of horrors back there.

Chris pressed the lift button again and again, but the light wasn't coming on. As he tried it repeatedly, Matthew just stared at his dad, shaking his head in disbelief.

"What the actual fuck, Dad? I mean, what the fucking fuck just happened there? Where do you find these people? Really?"

The lift button had lit up and they could hear its mechanism going sending it down for them. Matthew looked up above the lift doors. It was still six floors away. Damn.

Chris was over the impending terror and started to laugh again.

"Right, so you're saying that you're not into man cock then? I had no idea, son."

Matthew let out a slight chuckle, but he wasn't quite ready to erupt with laughter about his experience just yet.

"Just donkey cock for you is it, Matt?" Chris added.

Matthew grimaced, repulsed by his dad's humour and the fact that he was able to make jokes about it this quick when they could still hear the "oohs" and "aahs" coming from the other side of that door at the end of the corridor, Arthur no doubt knee-deep in dicks by now.

The lift landed at the basement level with a ding and they got in and pressed the button for their floor. As they made their way up to the sound of some music that was eerily close to the music they'd just been listening to in that massage parlour from hell, Matthew had the vilest thought. Does Arthur like to fuck them or does he like to take it up the arse? He shuddered instantly. The image of the little Chinese man with them would feature in his nightmares for years to come. Buddhist my arse, Matthew said to himself quietly.

The lift stopped at the lobby and the doors opened. It was surprisingly busy for that time of night, and as they stood there two old men and two old women stepped in followed by three young ladies. It was at this point that both Chris and Matthew looked at each other in panic. They were standing there fully erect, both of them wearing thin linen trousers that barely concealed a thing. Their dicks were at full mast, pushing the waistband of their trousers out and plain for all to see.

They hadn't registered if any of the people who'd got in had actually seen their erections, but they absolutely must have done unless all seven of them were as blind as bats. And it was so cramped in the lift their dicks were almost poking the men in front of them in the back. It was horrifying. The journey between the lobby area and the second floor, where the older couple were heading, seemed like the longest time imaginable, every second feeling like an excruciating lifetime.

When the lift hit the second floor the old men and women alighted and moved down the corridor without looking back. Phew, Matthew thought, they hadn't seen anything untoward. They had narrowly escaped any embarrassment there. The door closed and the lift continued up to the floor below theirs, where the young ladies were getting out. All three of the women began to giggle at this point, it now clear that even if the older crew hadn't seen their erect penises this lot most certainly had. This stretch of the journey was feeling even more infinite than the one to the second floor had.

Two of the women looked back and down at the trouser tents. Then one of them, a pretty twenty-something with large nerdy glasses, looks Chris square in the face.

"You Barracuda?" she asked him.

As you know Chris is a solidly built guy, handsome, and with a long ponytail. Matthew glanced at his dad baffled, looking him up and down and wondering what the girls might have meant. He noticed his dad's watch which was an expensive American silver and turquoise watch. Did it have something to do with that? Matt didn't think it was made by a brand called Barracuda, or was it? Then he clocked the signet ring on Chris's finger sitting not far from a chunky silver bracelet he'd worn for yonkers. If it's got nothing to do with the erect cock then it dawned on Matthew that these girls might think his dad was some kind of mafia boss with all the heavy jewellery. Maybe that could be it?

Chris didn't answer the girls; just raising one eyebrow and shaking his head in wonderment. It was then that Chris came to the same realisation as Matthew and laughed, but it had nothing to do with his watch, ring and bracelet. The girls were probably referring to Barracuda Frank, the name of Frank Sindone, a loan shark and soldier in the Bruno crime family who helped to plot the 1980 murder of family mobster Angelo Bruno. Or they might have meant Barracuda, the giant Marvel Comics villain.

"No, no. Not the Barracuda," he said while still chuckling.

Despite the joke the whole situation didn't cease to be massively uncomfortable, and the remainder of the journey was sent from higher powers to punish them for their sins. It was so awkward, the two of them stuck in a confined space with these three young ladies continuing to giggle at their misfortune, looking at them unashamedly. Did they have no bloody decency at all, Matthew thought to himself. They didn't let up after that either.

"Are you from USA?" the tallest one asked Matthew, equally as pretty as her friend who'd just spoken. She wasn't looking at his face while she asked, though. Three guesses as to where she was looking. As if she was consumed by the spirit of sexual arousal, she moved towards Matthew as she posed her question. They'd literally jumped from the frying pan into the fireplace here, from one terrible set of circumstances to another. Hadn't that been the case the entire trip, though? Pretty much, Matthew thought.

By this time he felt like a raging bull in a china shop.

"No," he said assertively. "London. UK. You know it?"

He wanted to regain control of the situation, but there was only so indignant a man could be stuck in a lift with his dad, both of them with painful stiffies and being questioned by a group of hot women.

Raising her eyebrows, pleased with his answer, she giggled. "Oh, you are English." She placed her hand on Matthew's arm. It was really cold, he noticed. She stood inches away from his erect penis, staring him in the eyes, waiting for his answer to her last question. Matthew was forced to tap into what little inner strength he had left to hold it together. He told himself that he and Chris would be getting out of the lift soon and not to lose his cool.

As she stood there he felt increasingly nervous and fidgety, little beads of sweat running down his brow, dropping off and running down his cheeks. He was both annoyed at what was going on and still overcome by the horn, the special spices coursing through his veins even more than they had been down in the basement. His heart was pumping blood through his body like a formula one racing track and his cock was pulsating.

After what seemed like an eternity, the lift stopped at their floor with a welcome ding.

"This is us," the tallest one said, turning her lips down in sadness.

She turned away from Matthew, running her hand all the way up his cock from the balls to the tip, tightening her grip as she got near the top. She tugged at it, slowly stepping backwards out of the lift doors. Eventually, she released her grip, Matthew pulling back all the while saying nothing and shaking his head anxiously at her.

Now standing outside of the lift, staring at Matthew as her friends giggle beside her, she winked at him. In a coquettish way, she pursed her lips to blow him a kiss and beckoned him with her finger to come hither. Matthew turned to Chris with a look that almost asked permission. He was in two minds about whether to go with her or not, still feeling guilty about what had just happened, but still so turned on he felt like he was going to explode. Chris was stunned that his son was even thinking about it at all.

"Matt, really?"

His dad was right. He shouldn't even be thinking about this with a pregnant wife at home. Then he understood that wasn't his dad's primary concern after what they'd just gone through.

"Matt, for all you know she's got a huge donkey cock under there. Would it really surprise you at this juncture in time if that was the case?" he said to his son as quietly as possible with the girls just feet away from them.

But Chris's comment had helped Matthew make up his mind. He shouldn't be considering fucking about regardless of his insatiable appetite for a fuck right now, and more to the point, he certainly wasn't going to risk coming across – not literally – another ladyboy cock or three. He squirmed and launched at the lift button fast. The doors would have closed of their own accord shortly, but Matthew didn't want the choice in front of him any longer. The concoction that Arthur had spiked Matt with was giving him the wrong erotic thoughts. This was a powerful substance that was getting the better of him. He pressed the "doors closed" button, but they didn't shut immediately, or perhaps they did. Time was just moving slower for the lads that night.

"Hurry up. Hurry up. Come on," Matthew muttered under his breath while coyly looking around the lift and avoiding eye contact with the girl. Chris just gave the girls a quick pitying smile that informed them they weren't getting lucky tonight.

As the doors finally closed, Matthew caught a short glance of the girl rolling her eyes and shrugging at the rejection. He imagined that didn't happen to her very often because she was really gorgeous. Then again, so had those girls downstairs. Matthew had no idea that ladyboys could be quite so convincing. Whenever he'd seen any trans girls or women in the past they were always huge ex-rugby players called Mike with broad shoulders, a five o'clock shadow and a voice that was just that bit too deep to be a biological woman.

Finally, in the safety of their own company, Matt turned to Chris.

"Fucking hell, Dad. This place is worse than the Titty Twister in *From Dusk till Dawn*."

Chris roared with laughter. The Titty Twister was a Mexican desert strip club in the film and he remembered it well.

"Yeah, son, only instead of vampires it's ladyblokes with massive cocks."

After quite a journey the lift drops them off at their floor. Were there any more surprises awaiting them between the short space separating the lift and the door of their room? Thankfully not. Once the key card was in the door and they could see before them the refuge their room offered them Chris turned to the corridor, and in a snarly, loud voice bellows out into the corridor.

"All right, people, cock, cock, cock. Come on in, cock lovers. Here at the Cock Twister we're slashing cock in half all night! Make us an offer on our vast selection of cocks, ladies and gents. This is our biggest cock blowout yet! All right now, we've got white cock, black cock, Spanish cock, yellow cock. We've got hot cock, cold cock, wet cock, smelly cock, hairy cock, bloody cock. We've got steel cock, hard cock, stiff cock, bang bang cock. We've even got donkey cock, dog cock, chicken cock, erect cock. Come on, you know you want it. You know you want cock, so come on in, cock lovers. If we don't got it, you don't want it! Come on in, cock lovers, this is the Cock Twister!"

Matthew was ending himself laughing in the room as he started to reshuffle the furniture they'd been using as a barricade earlier in the night. Just as some doors in the hallways started to twitch, guests curious to see why some loud English bloke sounded like a cock stallholder at an East London market, Chris shouted, "Peace out, cock lovers!" and slammed the door shut.

Once the room was in decent order, Matthew threw the duvet back as he collapsed in bed. Not seeing his phone between folds in the sheets, he knocked it on the floor as the scraping noise of Chris moving the wardrobe at the same time muffled the sound of the fall. Once again, Matthew would forget to call his worried wife and the phone would run out of battery during the night. Chris fell into bed and the two of them, cocks still stiff as posts, nodded off to block out yet another horrific day in China.

Chapter 17 – The Day Of The Deal

Chris and Matthew slept better than they'd done since they'd landed in China, give or take a few cocks that flashed through Matthew's dreams. At one point during the night he'd dreamed about an army of walking cocks coming at him, like a moving version of the Terracotta Army in Qin Shi Huang. He'd snorted awake, and unlike a lot of dreams he had, fortunately, didn't go back into it.

Regardless of the stressful events of the day and night before, Chris remained true to his early-bird style and had the pair of them up at 7.30am. He rarely needed an alarm clock these days with the power of his own body clock. He was now simply used to waking up at the same time every day, which sometimes annoyed Linda who had always liked a bit of a lie-in. And today it annoyed Matthew a bit too, who would have welcomed an extra couple of hours in bed. Chris hopped straight in the shower, though, giving Matthew an extra ten minutes or so to come to properly.

He only used five minutes of that time to sit up, wipe the crust from his eyes, and get out of the bed. But to his shock horror the erection was still there, still as big and hard as the night before. Shit, Matt thought, this is so fucking annoying. How can I walk around like this in public? This thing attracts all the wrong people. He took the other five to search for his phone. He knew it was in here somewhere because he'd taken a call from Chris P from it the night before. It wasn't on the bed. It wasn't on the bedside table. It wasn't on the chair in the corner, or even down the back of it for that matter. Where on earth was it? Blissfully unaware that his mobile phone had actually found itself wedged in a small gap between the floor and the skirting board after it had fallen on the floor the night before, Matthew went about his search until Chris was finished with his shower.

"What are you doing crawling around on the floor like that, Matt?"

"Phone, Dad. I'm looking for my phone. Have you seen it?"

"I haven't, mate, but go get ready. Arthur's expecting us to meet him downstairs pretty sharpish."

Matt didn't recall his dad and Arthur making any specific plan to meet for breakfast, but he was sure they had and it just slipped his own mind.

"Alright, but…"

"No buts. Just get in the shower. You can call her from my phone later in the day, OK?"

"Yeah, OK, that'll do I suppose."

Fuck, Matthew thought, as he was stepping into the (functioning) shower. She would be absolutely livid by this time, as he washed away the previous day and night's sweat. He peered out of the small window in the hotel bathroom. Things were a little clearer. Still very smoggy but not so humid he guessed. He could see the hustle and bustle of a busy city going about its business in the distance as the water tumbled over him.

Once he was dressed, a little more leisurely than he'd been forced to dress to escape the massage parlour the night before, his dad was waiting impatiently.

"You finished tarting yourself up now, sweetheart?"

Matthew laughed but Chris didn't.

"Hot to trot, Dad. Let's hit the road."

They left, locked up and waited for the lift. It reminded him of the three girls from last night. Matthew had a new pair of linen trousers on, still as thin as the other ones though. And his crotch area still wasn't back to normal. He tried to hide his erection from his dad, panicking about what to do with it.

"Jesus, Matt. You've still got a bloody boner."

"Yeah, well, it's harder than it was last night, and I have no way of masking it. I have tried everything in the shower, but this thing just won't budge. I even tried knocking one out, but it's like having a strap on attached to me. It's big and looks like a penis, but the damn thing won't ejaculate or give any sensation,"

"Arthur, the cheeky bugger, must have given you a hell of a lot more of that spice stuff than he gave me then. Or himself, now that I think about it."

"Yeah, that's what I was thinking. About you anyway. Not sure he needed that much to get hard for that lot."

They both laughed as the lift arrived.

"Either he gave me too much or I'm slimmer than you."

They laughed again as the lift started moving down with that same music. It was everywhere. Matt's erection was so obvious now. He'd brought a jumper with him, no intentions of wearing it, just to hold in front of him to cover it up.

"I am absolutely Hank Marvin, son. You?"

"Erm, I wouldn't say that, no."

"No? Still not over the donkey dick? And all the other dicks?"

As he was about to answer Matt's belly started to grumble really loudly.

"See, son. There you go. Knew your appetite would make its way back to you post-cock," Chris said as he howled with laughter.

As the lift arrived at the breakfast area, Matthew knew that the rumble wasn't anything to do with hunger. That was definitely the sound of a tummy that's not happy at all, the sound of something in the works down there. The sounds were accompanied by a horrible, tight cramping sensation, and he was a bit sweatier than usual. They hadn't even made it to the heat outside the air-conditioned hotel yet and he was already sweating like a pig, which wasn't a good sign.

Walking into the restaurant behind his dad, Matt went to tap Chris on the shoulder to tell him his stomach sounds were bound to be something more sinister than a spot of hunger. He held back, though, worrying about having a dicky tummy during the deal later in the day. Chris wouldn't be best pleased that his son was turning up for these negotiations dripping with sweat, tummy roaring like a lion, and his dick still at full mast like the flag above Bucky palace letting everyone know the crown jewels are at home.

Matthew, thinking that this was the latest in the long series of unfortunate events that had plagued him and Chris on the trip, was so hoping that today would be the day he'd feel fresh, revived, confident, happy, and raring to go. He needed to be as clear-headed as possible for what was coming that day. Being sick wasn't part of the plan, and it was something that he didn't need right now on top of still being a bit hard, to say the least. The hours ahead of him were the most important on this whole trip. It was this day that would get things rolling on making them that fortune from the deal.

While he'd been in the shower upstairs, Matthew had been toing and froing between saying something to Arthur about the stunt he'd pulled on them the night before and just letting sleeping dogs lie. Now that he could sense some sort of food poisoning or tummy bug at work in his mid-region, he'd decided just to keep his thoughts on what had happened to himself. He knew if he'd asked his dad about it Chris would have told him just to keep his mouth shut and not to offend their host right before the paramount section of the trip.

Across the other side of the room Chris spotted Arthur sitting by himself. The little Chinese man was on his phone as they approached the table. Matthew looked around to see if he could spot any of the people from the lift the night before, the old couple or any of the three frisky young ladies. Fortunately, none of them were in sight. A small glory it had to be said.

Matthew was dreading how he'd navigate avoiding breakfast without telling his dad that he wasn't feeling so well. They had a look at the menu and Matthew really felt like someone was looking out for him when Arthur suggested that they opt for the continental breakfast that day. Praise the lord, thought Matthew. He didn't really need any food at all, but if he was going to have to force something down then at least it would be something palatable.

It was a DIY buffet sort of affair for the continental fare, so he could get away with just taking a small nibble. He brought back some toast and jam to the table as the waitress delivered a few coffees. By now, though, there was nothing Matthew would do to hide the fact that he was getting sicker by the minute.

Sweat was literally pouring off him and his movements were a bit off. He was feeling a bit woozy and starting to get a temperature.

"Oh god, Matt, it looks like the tummy rumbles weren't hunger after all. You feeling OK?" his dad asked.

When Matthew opened his mouth to answer, he was trying to grab a glass of water but knocked it over.

"Dad, I feel so dizzy. Like I might pass out kinda dizzy."

Chris, assuming that it might just be the effect of the spices kicking about in his bloodstream, turned to face Arthur. "Right, we need to get the boy better before the meeting or we're all gonna be walking away potless, aren't we?"

"Potless, Chris?" asked Arthur.

"I mean without money. Never mind. What are we going to do to fix him up a bit before we head off?"

Arthur now understood that money was at stake and went in for the kill with some affirmative action.

"We need a needle, right now. I am a monk and I know what I'm doing. I can cure him temporarily if I can just get hold of a needle fast."

A needle? Matthew was thinking. Christ, what's he planning to do with a needle?

"Dad? What's he gonna do with that?"

Arthur looked around the dining room frantically. He stood up to find a waitress, and one walked out of a small utility closet nearby. In Chinese he asked her something, but she didn't seem to have what he was looking for, shaking her head and walking away. Shocker that, isn't it, that a waitress doesn't just have a box of needles lying around?

"Dad, I don't like the sound of this," Matthew whispered.

"It's fine, Matt, he seems to know what he's talking about."

"Really, Dad. Really? Know what he's talk…"

Matthew shut up when Arthur came back to the table.

"She doesn't have a needle," Arthur announced.

Matthew was grateful for that.

"But she does have a cocktail stick," Arthur added.

"A cocktail stick? What for?" Matthew asked, terrified.

"I must pierce your ear."

"What? Why would you do that?"

"Old Chinese remedy."

Yeah, right, just like the herbs you drugged us with last night, Matthew said in his head, looking at his dad.

"This will have to do for now," Arthur said, grabbing Matthew's ear lobe and stretching it pretty far. "Hold still while I do this. Once it's done it will relieve your dizziness. I promise. Age-old method used by monks throughout years."

Once more the little Chinese man had roped Matt into something bizarre and he was just sitting back and taking it. What was wrong with him? On a normal day this would seem a bit fucking weird at best, having a little Chinese Buddhist monk pierce your ear with a cocktail stick in the middle of a restaurant, while you're still erect from the herbal Viagra he gave you the night before to fuck a bunch of ladyboy masseuses. Oh yeah, all totally normal, Matt thought. Normal as fuck. Just your average day to be honest, eh?

There was no way that Matthew would let anyone do this to him back in East London or any part of London for that matter. It was such a messed up situation that it was definitely one of those moments where something had to give. Arthur, still stretching Matt's ear with one hand, leant into him, putting most of his weight on the table and slowly pushed the very sharp cocktail stick into Matt's ear. Bit by bit Arthur increased the pressure, pushing the cocktail stick hard enough to pierce the skin, the areolar and the soft adipose connective tissues that together comprise the earlobe.

Matthew flinched in pain and recoiled. The cocktail stick wasn't going in very well, so Arthur knew he'd have to change tactics. No longer using it to stretch the earlobe, he put his free hand behind the ear to offer the lobe more support and continued to push through. As he pushed harder, it still hadn't gone through the other side. With a little popping sound, blood sprayed out of Matthew's ear onto the white tablecloth in front of him. People at the other tables were beginning to stare in amazement at what was going on. A couple of waitresses stood gobsmacked too. Matthew's display eating the donkey cock the night before was repeating itself all over again, him at the centre of attention in a restaurant full of people. Why did it always have to be him?

When the blood sprayed out Matthew couldn't keep his thoughts to himself any longer.

"Argh. Fuck. Pull it out, you nutter," he shouted at Arthur.

Arthur ignored his wishes, instead responding calmly, "No, no. We must leave in there, otherwise we won't be able to stop the bleeding."

Matt supposed he was right. They always say in movies that if someone gets a foreign object stuck in them somehow to leave it in there otherwise too much blood could come out and they could die. He was sure the blood loss in this instance wouldn't be quite so bad, but he'd better do as he was told.

"Anyway, you are not dizzy anymore, are you?" Arthur asked him.

He hadn't thought about it until that moment, but to Matthew's amazement the dizziness had actually stopped. Arthur's nutso plan had actually worked. What were the chances of that? And all for the meagre price of a painful, bleeding ear. The thing is, Matthew pondered, would something less extreme, also acting as a distraction, have worked just as well to get rid of his dizziness? You know, like when you distract someone and their hiccups disappear. Supposedly that works in one of two ways. One, because you divert the brain's resources away from the nerves responsible for the hiccups, like asking them what they had for breakfast the day before or scaring them. Essentially, it could really be anything that takes their mind elsewhere. Or two, because you directly interfere with or stimulate the parts of the body involved in the hiccup, for instance by eating or drinking something.

Anyway, the point is that there were probably plenty of things that Arthur could have done to take Matt's mind off the dizziness that didn't entail wedging a cocktail stick in there.

So, the situation was now that Matthew was sitting there, not only still a bit hard and his penis now aching, but also with a cocktail stick hanging out of his earlobe. Excellent state of affairs for sure, he mused. What else was there that could go more wrong that day? Sadly, for the lot of them, a fair bit.

Matt's dumb luck hadn't finished screwing with him just yet, and this was just another day and yet another problem to contend with. Matthew hadn't really given much brain space to the bad luck he'd encountered at regular intervals throughout his life, instead focusing on all the good things that had happened to him, but this trip was testing his resolve not to feel like karma, the nasty little bitch that she was, was absolutely tormenting him. And for what? What had he ever done to deserve all this? It was either karma screwing with him or the chief architect of all this was the devil himself. Was he down there in the fiery depths of hell, sitting at his command centre, stroking his evil-looking sphynx cat?

Casually sporting his erection and cocktail stick, Matthew went back up to the room with Chris, his trusty jumper covering his modesty once more. He had nothing to cover his ear, unfortunately. The plan was to get changed into more formal clothing to make the best impression at the meeting, which Matt was pleased about to be honest. The prospect of wearing slightly heavier trousers was one that would work to his advantage, helping to mask his erection. Once they had separated from Arthur, Chris turned to Matt with some amazing reassurance.

"Well, at least you can be thankful for one thing, son. He didn't try to pierce your dick with the cocktail stick."

Chris laughed at his own joke. Matthew would usually have laughed at that too, but Arthur had proven himself to be capable of anything by now.

"Well, I wouldn't put it past him, Dad. The idea isn't altogether impossible knowing him."

Matthew prayed to god that his erection would disappear very soon and that putting holes in his dick wouldn't become a viable option anyone would consider. Now that was something he definitely couldn't handle. The mere thought of other men getting their own dicks pierced by professionals who have been doing the procedure for years made him tremble, never mind the prospect of the little Chinese MacGyver having a go at it.

Back in their room Matt looked around for his phone, but he still couldn't locate it.

"Dad, can you do me a favour and call my phone?"

"Matt, I already told you to use my phone later. Just focus on getting shipshape for the meeting," Chris said as he rushed to get ready.

"Dad, it'll just take one or two minutes," Matt pleaded.

"My phone's been dead since yesterday and I need to charge it," replied Chris.

The filthy look his dad was throwing him suggested a hefty amount of shade telling him to shut the fuck up and get ready immediately. So Matthew did.

They both pulled on almost matching suits, nicely cut and expensive to boot. They were navy blue pinstripe numbers. Although the suits were nearly identical which gave them some uniformity, everything else differed which gave them a bit of individuality. Chris wore a crisp white shirt, a burgundy tie with a silver diamond checked pattern on it, navy socks, and a pair of highly polished brown Oxford shoes.

With his get-up, Matt wore a dark green tie without a pattern, matching socks, a slightly off-white shirt and highly polished Oxford shoes that were a darker brown than his dad's. Both of them were wearing silver cufflinks that Linda had given them for Christmas one year, each with one of their initials – each set being CB and MB.

They had always intended to be suited and booted for the meeting, but it was on Linda and Sarah's suggestion that they made their way down to Savile Row in London's Mayfair to get themselves some bespoke suits made up. It was a pricey business but she was right, they had to make the best impression they could.

The day they went down to get measured up Linda had also suggested they pick up some expensive items in Knightsbridge. She thought it seemed like a good idea to offer the guys they'd be doing business with some classy gifts, things like nice loose-leaf tea from the tea counter at F&M and fancy Swiss chocolates from Harrods' chocolate counter. It would all be part of the impression they'd be making with these big shots in China. Before they'd left the country, Chris had organised the gifts into nice, neat packages. They were in mini baskets covered in thick, good quality cellophane and wrapped up with understated ribbons. As he was finishing getting ready, Chris asked Matt to take a look at the gifts.

"Matt, just check that they're still intact and gather them all together in a bag. How many are there again?"

"Four, Dad. That about right? And yeah, they're all good."

"Perfect. Almost done. And the laptop?"

"It's ready to rock n' roll. Don't worry, it's all going to go well."

Matthew put the gifts in a bag as requested, along with the laptop they'd use to prepare the contract when they were at the company and the parts they'd need to show the company for the purposes of tooling. Most of it, the contract and the plans, were in place on a file there on the computer, but there were a lot of details that would need ironing out before they could be put down formally in the contract.

Finally, after all the shenanigans of the past few days, Chris and Matt were ready for the deal – the one that was going to make them very rich men. As expected, the material of the suit trousers was heavy enough to mask Matt's boner substantially, which gave him a bit more confidence. They sat on the bed waiting, Chris twiddling his thumbs and Matthew darting his head left and right, up and down, still looking for his phone. He was about to use the phone in the room to call Sarah when it made the most god awful screeching sound. It was like the broken buzzer in an old Victorian flat in London. Chris jumped to attention quicker than their dicks had jumped up on the Chinese Viagra the night before and answered the phone before it could make any more of that hideous sound. Once again Matthew had missed another opportunity to call his wife.

"You ready? Come downstairs. Showtime, motherfuckas."

As Chris hung up Matt was chuckling as he'd heard what Arthur said.

"What a little nutter, eh?"

Chris offered a little smile and nod of agreement as he patted Matt hard on the back.

"Let's do this, son. Let's do this."

"Dad, I feel a bit reluctant."

"Gordon Gekko once said 'money never sleeps,' pal."

It reminded Matt of his swim meets when he was younger, Chris always there to give him a bit of a pep talk before he went out, and *Wall Street* was one movie his dad would reference now and then.

Down in the lobby Arthur was nowhere to be seen, but Matt spotted his familiar little frame out front. He was out there waiting for the driver to bring the car up from the garage. The whole time they'd been fannying about at dinner and the massage parlour, dicks ahoy, neither Matt nor Chris had given a second thought as to where Kato, the superhero driver, had been. Arthur greeted them with a smile as Won drove around a couple of taxis waiting to pick people up and met them at the bottom of the entrance stairs. The driver got out of the car. He looked tired, Matt thought. He mustn't have slept all that great in the car. Matt felt a bit guilty.

Won gave a warm smile, picked up their luggage and placed them in the back of the car.

"Oh, be careful with that one," Chris said as the driver was picking up the bag filled with the gift packages. Won froze, not understanding what Chris said, but Arthur translated and he placed the bag in the car gently.

They plonked themselves in the car, Arthur in the passenger's seat in the front again, and the boys in the back. Arthur turned to them.

"Buckle up, boys. We have another funfair ride of a journey for you."

They all laughed except Won who probably didn't understand again.

Arthur said something to the driver in Chinese which Chris and Matt assumed meant "Let's go" or words to that effect. He pulled off the forecourt of the hotel and out onto the road, which was much busier than it had been the night before. Still no sign of the car that had been parked over the road when they'd arrived.

They drove in silence, Matt still enjoying the feeling of dizziness being gone but certainly not enjoying having a cocktail stick hanging out of his ear. It wasn't painful anymore, so that was good. Won hadn't blinked at the sight of him with the cocktail stick right there. Maybe he knew exactly what it was for. The only sound that penetrated the silence was the occasional aggressive stomach growl emanating from Matthew. The guys in the front ignored these, but Chris kept looking at Matt with sympathy.

Chapter 18 – The Teahouse

After driving for around thirty minutes, which wasn't very far given the amount of traffic blocking up the roads that morning, they pulled up at the side of a dual carriageway. They drove through giant ornate gates and into a little car park that sat beside a beautiful building.

"What's this?" asked Chris.

"Traditional Chinese teahouse," responded Arthur.

It really was magnificent from the outside. It was on stilts over a little lake with a small bridge to get to it. It was completely clad in wood it seemed, painted in red and light blue, with a veranda running around the entire top floor as far as Matt could see.

As they stepped out of the car onto the gravel of the car park, Matthew looked back in but Won wasn't making a move to go anywhere. He'd be staying there, Matthew guessed. He didn't feel comfortable with this sort of thing.

A waitress met them at the main entrance and led them to a small courtyard where a large number of people were seated. As they turned the corner harp music began to play. It was literal music to Matt's ears. It was intoxicating. The garden was dressed in an abundance of exotic plants which gave it a really lush, tropical atmosphere. The harpist sat on a throne-like construction in the corner, some guests watching as she played, others engaged in conversations. The heat was picking up already, and Matt was glad when the waitress led them to a shaded table. He was also still feeling sweatier than usual with this dicky tummy of his.

Matt loved the feel of the place but it was a bit of a juxtaposition, an incredible building like this, peaceful and serene, sitting smack bang next to a busy, dirty motorway full of noise and pollution. The two things were in direct contrast with each other. Chris was clearly thinking the same thing.

"Mad, isn't it? This place right here. You wouldn't expect it at all."

Matt was glad that his dad had noticed it too and gave it a bit more thought as Chris turned to look around the place again. Matt supposed it hadn't always been sat there next to a busy road. At one point that road wouldn't have been there, and this gorgeous teahouse would have been surrounded by nature and the tranquillity such a place deserves as a setting. Matthew pictured what that would have looked like. It was a pleasing thought, just like thinking back to what it must have been like to go to Ibiza back in the days it was a hippy hangout and before it got all commercial and stuffed full of drunk Brits looking for a heavy dose of hedonism.

They sat for a while listening to the harpist. Thankfully, it wasn't similar to the music in the massage parlour or the lift evoking no unpleasant memories. It was almost entrancing, like a massage but in the form of sound. They had been there listening to her gentle strums for around fifteen minutes when a different waitress came to collect them. Matthew and Chris had no clue where they were going looking at each other questioningly and shrugging. This was all so pleasant compared to everything else but Matthew could not help but wonder if something was about to go tits up. He thought to himself: don't count your chickens before they hatch, Matt.

Once inside the main chamber, Matt and Chris let their mouths drop open. So much money must have gone into the decoration of this place. It was so extravagant but retained a simple sort of elegance at the same time, which was quite something. The floor was a light grey marble, and so were the walls apart from wooden panels painted red and gold. Dotted around the place there were Chinese lanterns that looked exactly like the ones from the restaurant last night. The room was filled with chunky wooden furniture stained dark, with detailed carvings of Chinese dragons as the legs. The chairs had the same carvings to match.

There weren't so many people there. For that reason it felt very tranquil, especially as Matt was able to hear the gentle trickling of a couple of little water features in the corners of the room. Trickling water had always been a sound that made Matthew feel really relaxed, and the harp music he could still hear from the courtyard complemented it really nicely.

In the main room they found a young lady kneeling in front of a bamboo box, and to their surprise Arthur kneeled in front of her. He motioned with his hands that the guys should follow his lead. Once they were all kneeling in front of the woman Matt looked at his dad's face, full of concentration. Arthur's face was the same too. Matt then looked at the woman who looked awfully solemn. When she made eye contact with him, her straight, calm demeanour fell away when she caught sight of the cocktail stick hanging from his earlobe. Fuck, Matthew thought, he'd forgotten that thing was still in there by this time, especially after being so chilled out since they arrived. She then looked down at Matt's crotch. Clearly, the thickness of the new trousers wasn't quite enough to keep his erection completely masked. It looked even worse now that he was kneeling, the front of his trousers stretched to reveal what lay beneath.

Oh, for fuck's sake, he thought, as the young lady began to giggle. What was it with Chinese women and giggling? First, those girls in the lift the night before, and now this one who'd been totally professional until this point. Most people in the UK would be too embarrassed to giggle at something like that so boldly, instead opting to ignore it out of embarrassment. Matt smiled at her as if to tell her to get over the cocktail stick and boner and just get on with whatever was about to happen here.

The woman returned to her business and placed her hands on the bamboo box, undoing some little fastenings on the side and opening the lid. The box was filled with a cornucopia of various teas. Her hands hovered there for a while, her eyes darting between the varieties before she made her mind up. She pulled out three or four different types of tea and then began brewing them in a number of little flat iron teapots with bamboo handles. She allowed the tea to stew for a few minutes, the teapots hanging from little stands at the side of the arrangement.

As they waited for the tea to brew in time to the harp music they could hear from outside, the woman started some display with a little ornate gold fan, holding it from side to side and eventually folding it back up and resting it on the floor. She smiled at them intensely throughout the whole thing. It was a bit awkward.

The woman then took one of the pots and removed the lid, checking inside. For some reason she then poured the tea into a smaller brown jug before arranging tiny willow patterned china cups in front of them. It was at this point Matthew wondered if china, as in china plates and cups, were called that because they originated in China. It was food for thought anyway.

She poured the tea into the cups and said something to them in Chinese. Matthew thought this was all fascinating but quite different to just having a cup of builder's tea back in England. Milk and two sugars please, love. Arthur tried to translate what she was saying to them, but it was all fast and neither Chris nor Matt could decipher a word of it, both her and Arthur speaking at the same time.

In fact, the only thing that Matt had deduced by this point was that the tea smelled like a steaming pile of shit straight out of a rhino's arsehole. Great, more stuff that stinks of shit. Matthew knew it had been too early to count his blessings with this place. He thought to himself that there should be some ancient English proverb that is a bit more extreme than the whole counting chickens or blessings ones – something along the lines of when things are going too well, don't be foolish enough to trust that it'll continue that way, because some shit will inevitably go down very soon and BOOM, there it is, The Fuckening!

The tea they'd been served undoubtedly smelled like shit, but it was a bit familiar. It took Matt a little while to think why, but he eventually remembered going to a fancy place for afternoon tea with his family once where he'd picked Lapsang Souchong. He'd had no clue what he was ordering but thought that it was tea and that much couldn't go wrong. But that type of tea is a smoked one that tastes and smells more like sausages than the black tea he was accustomed to. When it finally came to him that this was the same type of tea, he shot his head around to look at Chris who was mouthing "Oh my god, again". Chris had been there that day with the sausage tea and had come to the same realisation as Matt.

The two of them held their cups reluctantly in front of their faces, the shitty steam crawling up their noses millimetre by millimetre until it was inescapable. Arthur smiles and urges them along.

"Come on, drink," he said while pointing at Matthew's belly.

"Ah," Matthew replied. "This will help my stomach?"

"Yes, yes. Drink. Good for digestion."

Whatever it smelled like Matt was keen to get rid of these pains and cramps because they would distract them throughout the meeting. He sipped the tea as quickly as he could for a drink that was steaming hot and stank like excrement. After two cups of the stuff, Matt perceived a noticeable decrease in the pains and cramps. Miracle man comes up trumps once more, he thought, with a touch of irony. However, after the tea ceremony was finished and they had said farewell to the young lady, Arthur settling the bill behind them, Matt started to fart. And not just little farts, the long, airy, hot ones that tell you something is really not great downstairs.

Just before stepping back in the car he let one drop. It was one of the grossest farts he'd ever produced. The last time he smelled flatulence that bad was at the hands – or arse more appropriately – of a lactose intolerant pal. Now those guys truly are capable of the farts that smell like burst septic tanks.

When they were seated in the back of the car and on the move Matt turned to Chris.

"Dad, I don't know about you, but I feel a bit strange if I'm honest."

"Jesus, son, your breath smells like actual shit. I thought you smelled terrible yesterday, but fuck me you are absolutely honking today."

"Oh, shit. Really? That bad?"

"Yeah, really bad. These people are going to think you're talking a load of shit in this meeting."

Chris erupted with laughter and both Arthur and Won looked in the rear-view mirror. They said nothing though.

"Oh, very fucking funny, Dad. Well done," Matt responded with biting sarcasm.

Matt turned to stare out of the window. Once again things were going from bad to worse. He now had an erection that just wouldn't bugger off, a bloody cocktail stick hanging out of his ear like some nutjob, a stomach that sounded like a day out in a lion's den, and to top it all off his breath smelled like a dog's backside.

It was the day before all over again. Different day, different shit. What is it that Indian people say? Ah yeah, same, same, but different. Inside his head Matt was screaming, absolutely furious, but he managed to keep his cool outwardly, even though inside he was shouting at nobody or somebody. Just lay off me. Honestly. Whoever you are, enough now, OK? I can't take any more of this crap you're throwing at me. Matt was really trying his hardest to hold it together.

The car was in silence once again apart from Matt's stomach noises. His stomach was no longer in pain, but he was really gassy and keeping the farts in was a noisy business. They drove back into the city centre and Matt noticed that they were headed straight past their hotel. He considered asking Won to stop the car for a couple of minutes so he could run up to the room, brush his teeth quickly, and fart too. He didn't, though, knowing that Chris would just tell him to suck it up. By the time he'd thought about it they were already quite a distance past the hotel, the road now clearer than it had been earlier. Anyway, it would have been a quick fix given that the scent of the tea was coming from the depths of his digestive system and not just his mouth.

Within a few minutes they ended up in a really rundown area of the city that looked a lot like the area they'd found themselves facing a load of Chinese thugs. Matt had lost his bearings given that it had been pitch black, but it might have been the same area. Either that or a lot of this city was as rough as a badger's arse. Little basic shacks made from corrugated iron and planks of wood adorned the street on either side. The roads were all wonky and dangerous here, and there was drying laundry everywhere. It was like a sea of clothes flapping around in the wind. There were barely any cars on the streets and when there were they were old bangers. Instead, the place was strewn with bicycles, which Matt figured was all the people who lived here could afford.

As they drove down one street, it felt like everyone they passed was looking into the car and at them. Some people were very obvious about it just outright staring, while others gave the sort of surreptitious stares you'd find in horror films. You know the ones, where villagers continue going about their business, one eye on their task and one on the protagonists. They fix their bicycles while noticing what's going on. They chop chickens while aware of the presence of strangers. They want to make it clear that this is a local place for local people and that there's nothing for you here.

Matthew was already gutted about his multiple misfortunes, but his paranoia was ramped up to the next level by this place. What the hell was this tea that Arthur had given him and why the hell wasn't his dad feeling as strange as he was? Ah shit, of course, because

Chris hadn't drunk the shitty tea, he'd just smelled it and opted for another one – some delicious, sweet-smelling jasmine infusion.

Matt recognised these feelings from his days of smoking a joint here and there or dropping an acid tab. He had that ridiculous feeling that everyone and everything is out to get him. It was a horrible sensation that he hadn't come across for quite some time, not quite as bad as a full-blown acid trip, but definitely close to the freaking out caused by smoking really strong weed after one too many drinks and under the wrong atmospheric circumstances.

Matt's stomach was now in full swing once again. If he'd been by himself he'd have let out a fart so loud it would sound like tearing into another dimension. The grumbling sounds were now joined by a horrible cacophony of gurgles like some evil soup was boiling away in his stomach. Something was working its dark magic down there, for sure. He was dripping in sweat by now. He had to make it his mission to get to a toilet before they went into the meeting otherwise he wouldn't last long in there.

Chapter 19 – The Meeting

"Ah look, we here. Business building. Look, big building here."

The little Chinese monk was pointing at a semi-modern, five-storey building. Matt had been expecting something a little larger, but there would be a toilet in there he could use. The building seemed really out of place, nestled among all these little shacks and towering above them. What was a business like this doing locating itself in a Tianjin slum? Was the rent here irresistibly cheap? Were they trying to fly under the radar or something like that?

As they got closer to the building Matt sized it up. It was absolutely filthy. Clearly it was supposed to be white in colour, but the pollution of the city and the particular dirtiness of this area had made it closer to a grimy shade of slate grey. Its paintwork was peeling off, no doubt due to both age and the temperature. Matthew wondered if they used different paint formulas in hotter countries so that it could withstand higher temperatures better. If they didn't get inside the awful-looking building it would soon be painted a dirtier shade of shit brown.

Matthew had also been expecting that they would roll up to a really corporate setting, like a big glass skyscraper with a shiny interior and businessmen in suits all over the show. That's not what it was like here at all. There were loads of people standing outside the front of the building, not a single one of them wearing a suit or even business casual clothing. They were all wearing scruffy clothes – dirty T-shirts with holes in them, baggy shorts stained at the back, hopefully from dirt and nothing more sinister, and beaten sneakers. Who were these scruffs? The service staff? Cleaners or something along those lines? Matthew looked among them and noticed a woman in the male-dominated group. She was wearing half-decent jeans with a tidy tight top to go with them and a pair of leather sandals.

They pulled up in front of the building finding a parking space without any trouble. Not another car could be seen anywhere, but again there were plenty of bikes leaning against various walls and posts. Matt wondered if nobody had cars or perhaps they just didn't bring them to work for fear they'd be nicked. Maybe their car would be gone by the time the meeting was concluded. Poor Won would be absolutely bereft if that happened.

Won got out of the car first coming around to open the door for Chris first. Matthew waited, not because he couldn't be arsed to open the door himself, but because he thought it might appear rude not to allow the chauffeur to do his job. He didn't want to make him feel useless or anything like that. As he opened the door for Matt, Arthur let himself out and Matt felt like a chump. Ah well, he'd know next time.

As they stood there, between the car and the building, they were welcomed by a swarm of eyes, all of which were fixed firmly on them. Chris turned to Arthur.

"Why are they looking at us?" he asked.

"Oh, they're not looking at me and Won, just you and Matt."

"But why?"

"They've probably never seen white man before. Not in real life. Only on television and film."

Matthew, humbled to some extent but mostly just feeling like some circus attraction that had just rolled into town for the next few weeks, smiled at the stares as he passed them. The woman he'd seen on arrival fought her way through the crowd, and with difficulty at that as the ignorant men refused to make way for her.

"Welcome to Tianjin," she said in English while bowing at the group of men. "Me Chink, Nice meet you."

Matt was astounded. Had she just called herself "Chink"? He figured it must be an actual Chinese name rather than just the pretty racist colloquial term for Chinese people used by a lot of folks back in England. While Matt was still thinking about this, Chris was the only one to respond to her.

"Hello," he said, offering a half bow, unaware if that was even what he was meant to do. Matt hadn't noticed though, distracted by and uncomfortable with being the centre of attention. He caught the gaze of one guy, a young guy in his mid-twenties, and tried a little experiment – just staring back. That usually did the trick back at home to divert a stranger's gaze, people in the UK normally too polite to continue staring once they know they've been observed. But the result of the experiment wasn't what Matt had expected. The guy entered into a game of stare-off and Matthew was the loser. It was just too uncomfortable to go on any longer than about fifteen seconds.

Won hung back by the car as Chink led them into the building. She was about thirty and not so attractive. That was good for Matthew given he wasn't quite over arousal from the special Chinese herbs. He was one step closer to the toilet he so desperately needed.

As they walked through the entrance, a couple of glass doors that looked like they had seen better days, Matt's senses were slapped with the strong scent of mould. If ever there was a building that needed a good airing, this was the one. The interior was just as poorly maintained as the exterior, paint peeling off the walls, dirty stains everywhere, a torn sofa and a scratched coffee table in the foyer. There were a few spaces where windows once were, or just should have been, every one of them boarded up instead. A few cracks in the boards let in little rays of light that acted like the spotlight on a stage, drawing attention to the dust and dirt swirling around the musty air in the room.

The four of them were led past a lift, presumably a broken one, and they ascended a flight of stairs, and then another one, and another, and then just one more, until they had finally reached the top floor. Matt and Chris were out of breath, but Arthur seemed fine and Chink's breathing rate was just as normal. Obviously, she was used to the trek up there.

They made their way down a long corridor, which wasn't the nicest, but nothing compared to the basement corridor of the hotel that led to the massage parlour of nightmares. On each side of the corridor sat a few doors, and as they walked down anyone who began stepping out would see them and instantly scarper back into whatever room they'd come from. It was very odd. Matthew and Chris looked at each other, screwing their faces up. Why were these employees so scared to encounter them? It was hardly like they were CEOs coming to meet the little people at a company outpost one day, with all the little worker ants scuttling back into their nests to avoid being seen. Very odd indeed.

When they had reached the midpoint of the corridor, Chink turned right into a large but sparse meeting room and they followed her in there. The room was taken up entirely by a giant oval-shaped boardroom table surrounded by faux leather chairs, many of them ripped.

Matthew panicked for a split second thinking they might have left the bag of gifts in the car or the laptop for that matter, but Chris had both with him. He half hoped his dad had left them in the car as this would give him a good opportunity to go back and use the loo on the way there or back. He'd forgotten to ask when they came in, distracted by the Satis House style surroundings. Where had Miss Havisham herself been? He'd just have to ask if he can be excused for a few minutes before the meeting begins.

"Please, gentlemen, take a seat on the other side of the table," Chink said as she pointed to the farthest side of the table by windows, only one of which was boarded up.

They shuffled over and put down their things. Matt could now see a side of the room that had been shielded before. It was as sparse as he'd thought initially. Opposite the table a wall was covered with glass-fronted cabinets, jam packed with trophies of all sorts. Perhaps they were business awards, but what would a company that gets so many accolades for their business dealings be doing with such ramshackle premises like this? It didn't compute. Anyway, Arthur seemed to think the trophies was a signal of something positive, nodding at them and smiling.

"See, good, huh?"

Chris made a subtle phew sound, reassured that the trophies represented the fact they were about to deal with reputable people. Matthew was less convinced, but maybe that was the paranoia from his tea trip still lingering? It was then that Matthew noticed a look on Arthur's face that he hadn't seen until now. What did that look mean? Ah, it was one of certainty. It became clear that all the times before that Arthur supposedly had a look of certainty painted across his face was something else altogether. Had it been blaggery of the highest order? Matt was in no doubt that Arthur was fully at ease here, and among his own people. Any worry he had about the businessmen was put to bed by Arthur's expression.

Regrettably, there was still a significant amount of worry to be had about this toilet situation. He turned to his dad who was busy figuring out the dynamics of the seating arrangement. He had a look of concentration on his face and Matthew knew what he was thinking. How should they position themselves to come across in the best way possible? In the end he opted to sit with Matt in between him and Arthur. The business deal had been Matt's baby from the beginning, and even though Chinese businesspeople might respect age more he didn't want to step on Matt's toes. Matt agreed with the arrangement and took his seat.

"I'm really gonna need to find a toilet, Dad."

"Not a good time, son."

"But..."

"Matt, just wait. It's time to make a million quid."

Christ, why did he always have to listen to his dad? Matt kept his mouth zipped, trying to distract his desperation to fart and possibly release a bucket of shit too – he wasn't sure what would come out by this time. He amped himself up. Come on, Matt. There's a million quid at stake here. A million smackeroos. You can hold off a little longer.

Ten minutes passed, each more agonising than the last for Matt. Each minute that passed, he thought, he could be in a toilet getting what he needed to do out of the way, but with each minute also came the fear that the men would come in while he was away, making a terrible impression for them all.

Chink, who had shown them in, sat at the end of the table the whole time, going over some papers she'd pulled out of a docket. She suddenly said something to Arthur in Chinese. Arthur seemed baffled and responded to her very slowly. There was a short gap between almost every word he uttered, like a Brit trying to speak Spanish or French or any foreign language they only learned at school. Chris and Matt looked at each other suspiciously.

After Arthur and Chink finished their weird exchange, Arthur turned to the guys with a concerned look across his face.

"Erm, we might have a problem here?"

Oh, here we go, Matt thought.

"A problem?" Chris asked. "What sort of problem?"

"They only speak Mandarin," Arthur replied.

"Mandarin? As in Chinese?" Matt asked, baffled as to why the Chinese man couldn't speak Chinese.

"Yeah, I speak Cantonese."

It dawned upon Matthew that, like in other countries like India, there were also different dialects here. Shit.

"So, you speak no Mandarin at all?" Chris asked Arthur, panic lacing his voice.

"Only a little. We speak different languages in different parts of China."

Chris and Matt both nodded at him, fully understanding the situation they were about to be faced with, then looking at each other.

Matt whispered to his dad, "What the fuck are we going to do now?"

There they were, the pair of them. Two Englishmen, who struggled to understand a word of Arthur's Chinese at the best of times, and they were about to begin a meeting with Christ knows how many Chinese businessmen that speak a different bloody language than the one their translator speaks. Great. Once again, Arthur proving himself to be the chocolate teapot he'd shown himself to be so many times before. How much had they agreed to pay this clown?

Eyes wide, shaking his head slowly, Chris whispered back to Matt, "Run?"

He was joking, of course, but that's all Matt wanted to do right at that minute, via the bog. Matthew heard multiple footsteps moving down the corridor towards the boardroom. Ah well, there was no more time to panic about it now. Here they came. They'd just have to get by with a combination of Mandarin and Cantonese and hope that they weren't completely dissimilar.

The door swung open and one by one eight young Chinese men filed into the room dressed in smart trousers and shirts. They took their seats on the opposite side of the table which Matt had figured they'd do, but it felt a shave more intimidating than he'd expected it would. It felt like a job interview or a court hearing. Once they were all seated, Matt noticed that they'd left a seat in the middle of the table empty, either on purpose or by chance.

Then another heavier set of footsteps moving down the hallway told him that the spare seat in the middle was no accident. It awaited whoever those footsteps belonged to – the head honcho. The door opened once more and the fattest Chinese human stepped across the threshold. Matt was convinced that a sumo wrestler had just walked in, although he was totally aware that was a Japanese sport. It was more just the body size and shape of the guy. He could imagine the giant tyre-like rolls of fat under there. Their Chinese Michelin man. A walking Chinese pillsbury doughboy after a night on the cakes. How on earth it was possible for a man to defy science and become this large was a fact that evaded Matthew. And who actually makes clothes for people that big? All of a sudden he felt like a Slim Jim compared to this guy.

The fat man sat on his seat which made sounds that suggested it was struggling under the weight placed on it. He stared at a smiling Chris and Matt. Well, it wasn't so much staring. One eye certainly was looking at them, but the other was off in another direction altogether. It was like he was a gecko, one eye off to the shops to buy groceries and the other one coming back with the change. Matt ascertained that the fat man was staring at him in particular with his one properly functioning eye and at Chris with the wonky one. Matt had a teacher like this guy at school who would always pose questions to someone in the class. "What do you think? Yes, you," he'd say, but the problem was that nobody had a scooby who he was looking at to answer the question.

Chris shuffled about in his seat which Matt knew meant he was feeling uneasy. And that just wasn't like his dad, to be rattled by any situation like this. Matt looked back at the guy who was shuffling some papers without breaking eye contact with them, completely unsmiling the entire time. Chris and Matt might have dealt with some gangster types back in London, but this dude made that lot look like the Teletubbies. This was proper Godfather material right here, a plump Don Corleone looking at them like they'd just taken a dump on his grandmother. His look was one that commanded respect. It was one that betrayed a man with no real soul. It was one that said, "You come into my house on the day my daughter's to be married." It was one that meant business.

The fat guy eyed the lot of them, sizing them up. With glares that would give children the worst nightmares of their life, he moved his gaze between their faces, their clothes, Chris's jewellery, the cocktail stick in Matt's ear, and the little Chinese man beside them.

Chris sat there thinking that this isn't what he had anticipated when Matt arranged the deal, but he had confidence in his son nonetheless. Whatever Matt was thinking at this moment, he'd simply just have to step up to be the man Chris had taught him to be, to be able to walk into scenarios like this with the confidence and balls of a man in charge. This would be the first true test of what Matt had taken from these lessons Chris gave him in his younger years.

Matt had no idea that his dad was sitting there thinking all this, but he did know his dad had faith in him. The issue was that Matt felt quite the opposite. He was now in really bad shape, wishing that he'd just had the guts to insist on going to the toilet before the meeting commenced. His belly was croaking like an army of abnormally large, angry bullfrogs. The magical powers of his cocktail stick earring had worn off and he was overcome by dizziness once again. On top of this, the shitty tea that Arthur had fed him was also losing its potency, which was good for his levels of paranoia but didn't help much with the noises emanating from his digestive system.

The fat man's assessment of them, which seemed to have gone on forever, finally ceased as the introductions began. Chink, still at the end of the table, stood up and introduced the fat man in English.

"This is company CEO, Mr. Hwong," she said smiling.

When Chink turned to Mr. Hwong, indicating towards him with a swoop of her hand, Matthew extended his right hand to offer the customary handshake. Very awkwardly, Hwong failed to extend his own hand, instead maintaining a completely straight and stern face. He should have withdrawn his arm immediately, but something told him to keep it hanging there like a fart in a colander for a while in case a pause was common before a handshake for some bizarre reason. After a very uneasy fifteen seconds, he finally made the choice to pull his arm back feeling like a complete tool.

Matt expected Chink to introduce the other men in the room, but she didn't. After the botched handshake the other men simply sat up straight in their chairs, eyes forward but making zero eye contact. It was all very tense and very strange. Matt obviously knew they conducted business differently here, but if these were customs then they were super uncomfortable ones. Chink looked at Arthur, nodding without smiling, and then resumed her seat.

This was obviously Arthur's cue to introduce Matt and Chris, so he got up from his chair, and in Chinese – Matt and Chris didn't know if it was Cantonese or Mandarin – he introduced the pair of them as the CEO of Electro Signs Ltd and the Deputy CEO of the company. Matt thought this would perhaps be the time the cold, icy stares would stop and some level of human warmth would kick in. But no, nothing.

Once again Hwong just sat in intimidating silence. Once Arthur had stopped talking you'd have been able to cut the atmosphere in there with a blunt spoon, never mind a knife. It was so strained and hideously quiet that you'd be able to hear a pin drop. This wasn't good news for Matt whose stomach was now a full orchestral arrangement of roars and internal farts. It didn't need to be said, but everybody in that room could tell that Matt had something to expel. It was as if he had been possessed by an evil spirit, in there to wreak as much havoc as it could. No person hasn't been there at some point in their life, so there was no doubt they knew.

Matt couldn't bear it, on display like that. He felt so exposed and trying to mask the sounds coming from inside him spluttered a nervous, obviously fake cough while patting his stomach. Jesus, why had he done that? All it had achieved was to draw their attention to his stomach even more. What else could he do to wriggle out of this? He looked at his dad, really feeling for his son, but also consumed by the awkwardness of the situation. He then looks at Arthur who was pointing down at the bag of gifts on the floor. Excellent, Matt thought, time to get these packages out and present them to this mobster.

As Matthew bent down to pick up the bag he'd inadvertently set up the exact conditions his body needed to expel at least some of what needed to come out. Facing the floor, arse up in the air towards Hwong and the other businessmen, Matthew released a belter of a fart that might have just about reached somewhere between 2.0 and 3.0 on the Richter scale, causing a minor to light earthquake across the region of China they were in. Matthew scrunched up his face feeling the blood pumping to it and turning him a bright shade of red. He remained hunched over for a few seconds, afraid to come back up. When he was back at the same level as the others Matthew looked around the room at their faces, but their expressions hadn't changed a bit. These people were unshakeable, it seemed. Matt daren't even look at his dad whose gaze he could feel burning into the side of his head like a death ray from the eyes of the Grand High Witch in Roald Dahl's *The Witches*.

The catastrophe had created an even worse atmosphere in the room, even though the Chinese were pretending nothing had happened. Was it a politeness thing? People in the UK would have been ending themselves at a fuck up like that.

Matthew took the opportunity to put the bag on the table, looking down and allowing the redness to clear from his face. He brought the gifts from the bag, one at a time, and placed them on the table in front of him. When he was sure that his face had returned to a normal colour, he looked up. Still nothing. After he turned around to drop the bag on the floor, although he couldn't see their faces, he was sure that all eyes were fixed on his arse. Like the burn of his dad's glare, he could just sense it. What if he had followed through? He hadn't shat himself, had he? Surely it would feel a bit wet if that was the case? One thing was for sure, he wasn't going to put his hand down there to check.

As Matthew pushed the packages across the table, he made an announcement.

"We have gifts, all the way from London. From Harrods and Fortnum & Mason, tea and expensive chocolates."

He was sure that they would recognise these big name stores and be impressed. It would have been better if the faces of the men had been as blank as before, even if it was intimidating. Instead, they looked horrified and furious. Matthew was unsure of why they appeared to be upset, so pushed the gifts further towards the men, nodding at them to encourage acceptance. Damn, he thought, they didn't want to accept their gifts after the fart he'd just done. He'd really offended them.

He felt in over his head here and turned to Arthur for some support. He knew the little Chinese monk didn't speak Mandarin, but surely he could have tried to intervene in some way? What use was he? Why had they even bothered with him? Arthur refused to make eye contact with Matthew, continuing to stare straight ahead. The little fucker, Matt thought. The absolute fucker, just leaving him out to dry here like this. Unable to think of anything else to do or say, Matt resumed his seat, assuming – or at least hoping – that the reaction of the businessmen to the gifts was par for the course in China.

Breaking the tricky situation, Chink came back to her feet speaking in Mandarin to Hwong and spreading her arms towards him. For the first time in what seemed like an age, the fat man decided to say something. But he was barking at them. Matt had been looking across at Chink when Hwong started to speak, so it took him by surprise and he almost jumped out of his skin. Staring at them, Hwong spoke so loudly that Matt was sure every office on that floor, and possibly the one below, could hear every word of what was being said. Was he shouting at Matt about the fart? The look on his face suggested not. The fat man continued to deliver a twenty-five-minute long speech without stopping for even a minute to let Arthur translate. Not that the men even knew that Arthur probably wasn't understanding much of what he was saying either.

Whatever the hell Hwong was saying, it sounded very important, very serious, and very official. Afraid to offend the man, Matthew and Chris nodded along politely, as if they had a clue what was being said. It was just an instinctive response, but Matt thought it must have come across a bit odd and fake.

As Hwong rambled on and on, Matthew grimaced at the movement in his stomach. It felt like a couple of lively animals had found their way in there and were jumping about playfully. It wasn't good.

The speech finally came to an end with Hwong staring at Chris and Matt. They looked at Arthur. They really needn't have bothered, though.

"Right, boys, I find it hard to understand him. I have been listening to him but I think he need to say it twice! I did get a slight drift of it, but if you want the full information I will need to ask him to repeat. OK?"

Chris laughed scornfully, and Matt knew that meant it most definitely wasn't OK. He spoke softly.

"Arthur, fuck that. Just spit out what you think you heard and then we'll try to fill in the gaps after that."

Matthew was insanely relieved when his dad stepped in assertively like that. That's exactly what he needed at that moment in time. He wasn't fit for any of this and needed to get to a toilet badly. Another twenty-five minutes listening to the fat man just wasn't going to work for him in any shape or form. Arthur began sharing his take on what was said.

"Mr. Hwong, CEO of this company has, erm...has said something about it is good to see you. The trophies in this room are for good business. The company give 87% of all profits to Chinese government. They can provide the steel we need but must see the tooling. I am pleased they say this as this shows they are legitimate company."

Arthur smiled, seemingly pleased with everything he'd heard from Hwong and chuffed with himself for picking up the thrust of the message in another language altogether. He seemed much more relaxed after conveying the message.

Chris leaned into Matt.

"Right, boy, get the laptop out so we can go over the tooling and plans."

Matthew bent down again, confident that he couldn't possibly make the same faux pas twice. Oh, how wrong some people can be. Completely underestimating his body's desperation to expel gas, Matt was now doubled over. And then it came. Another fart that would have registered even higher on the Richter scale, maybe this time somewhere between 3.0 and 4.0, causing a light to moderate earthquake this time. Fuck it, he thought, they didn't react before and they likely wouldn't react again.

He could feel his dad's glare burning once more as he opened up the laptop which had been left on sleep. It fired up fast and Matt opened the necessary files, pushing them across the table. He'd forgotten that Chris had also printed out hard copies of the plans. He pulled those out of the laptop case and pushed them across the table towards Hwong. He noticed a couple of sweat beads drop from his forehead onto the table. One of the Chinese men noticed too. Matthew couldn't believe it – they won't react to farts like that but a couple of drips of sweat gets their attention. Finally, he laid out a series of parts on the table.

None of the men reached out for any of the items. Instead, Chink stood up, walking round to Hwong's side of the table, leans into the middle and pulls them both across in front of the CEO. The men all jump to life suddenly, sniffing around the parts and the papers. Matthew decided that there's no more waiting. He absolutely must take this time while they're distracted to nip to the loo and get rid of these demons.

"I'm afraid that you will need to excuse me while I attend the restroom," Matthew said very politely with a half bow.

Every one of the men stopped, looking up at Matthew, and watching as he walked quickly around the boardroom table, gradually making for the door. Matthew was unsure what sort of reaction this would illicit, but he didn't care right now. Then he heard a slight gasp from the other side of the room before Chink piped up in horror.

"No, no, you must stay," she said assuredly.

Matthew now realised that his exit was a mistake and would be making a terrible impression like he'd hoped to avoid. There was no stopping him, though. Whatever had been cooking down below was now fully done and ready to come out. Unless they wanted him to serve it there and then, he was leaving and that was that. His guts felt like they were about to explode like Mount Vesuvius back in the day. He briefly patted his arse. It was dry. He may not have followed through on either of the two farts he'd let out in the boardroom, but he couldn't guarantee that a third wouldn't be accompanied by a sea of diarrhoea.

Almost at the door, a man appeared in front of Matthew as if he'd come from nowhere like a gust of wind. Who was he? Did this guy just teleport here from the Starship Enterprise? Did Scotty just beam him the fuck up? Matthew stopped with such a fright, the man holding his hand out at him. He was literally mid-step, one leg up in the air ready to land back on the floor. As you know Matt isn't a small guy at six foot two and weighing somewhere around nineteen stone, but this tiny five foot five Chinese guy was able to hold him back. Oh my god, he really just needed to get to the toilet now. Why was the world fighting him on this?

Matthew looked the man up and down seeing that he was wearing different clothes from the rest of the guys. He was dressed in more traditional Chinese clothing. His head was bent to one side, his ear touching his shoulder at a forty-five-degree angle. He spoke English very sternly.

"No leave, no leave!" he declared.

Matt still wasn't for being stopped, though.

"Please, I need the restroom right now."

The man remains adamant that Matt isn't going anywhere. Were they being held prisoner? Not moving an inch, the little super-strength guy keeps Matthew firmly in place like he had the power of multiple superheroes all at once. Was it that he didn't understand what Matthew was saying to him? Chris decides to chip in.

"Matt, what the hell are you doing?"

Matthew ignored his dad, his one-track mind overtaking everything else around him now. He was about to give birth to the mother of all shit babies and he was losing his patience. It was time to get a bit cunty with this guy who was clearly a bouncer of sorts.

"Cloakroom. Toilet. Toilette. The gents. Closet. Bathroom. Commode. Latrine. Lavatory. Lav. Loo. Can. Pan. Privy. Potty. Khazi. Chamber pot. John. Long drop. Johnny house. The dunny. Bog. Throne room. Pooper. Crapper. Craphouse. Thunderbox. Shithouse! I don't know how many other ways I can say it to you, but I need a fucking shit. Get out of my way now."

With that, Matthew grabbed the man's arm with every ounce of strength he could muster. He threw it aside with full force, breaking the man's hold on his chest. Triumphant and ready to blow, he gave the man a look that only a desperate human badly in need of a shit could be capable of. An unspoken conversation occurred, the man now comprehending what was happening, and Matt was shown to the hall. The bouncer pointed at a wooden door next to the boardroom. Finally, sweet relief awaited.

Chapter 20 – Catastrophe In The Can

Matt burst into the large toilet, six cubicles long, moaning and groaning. Why was it always so hard to keep it in when you enter the home stretch, he wondered? He ran towards the middle cubicle, desperately hoping that nobody had left the seat soiled. Ah, who was he kidding? Nothing was going to stop him now, even a dirty seat in this less than pristine bathroom. What was coming was an unstoppable force of nature.

To Matt's horror there may have been six cubicles, but not a single one of them had a door. What sort of place doesn't understand a man's need to take a shit in peace? This country, he thought, he'd absolutely had enough of it.

"Jesus fucking Christ," he shouted as he came to the realisation that, not only was there no door, but there was no actual toilet. "What the fuck is this?"

It was a squat toilet – an eighteen-inch wide hole in the floor basically.

"Where's the fucking bog? I can't shit standing up," he shouted again.

Time was almost out, though, and he started to pull his belt off frantically. He whipped his trousers and boxer shorts down as quick as you can shake a toilet brush, spun round and hovered over the little hole and let loose. Any intentions of aiming at the hole with a degree of accuracy went right down the shitter. Shit exploded everywhere, Matthew feeling like his bowels were exploding out of his anus.

Matthew looked down at the terrorist attack launching below him and then around him. The walls were splattered with shit like someone had shot a bar of chocolate with a sawn-off shotgun. He wasn't done though. It just kept on coming, firing out, soggy fart after soggy fart, the sounds bouncing around the cavernous room. All the while he was moaning and groaning with a confusing mixture of horror and relief. He was grimacing at the smell too, which was rank beyond human comprehension.

The runny shits wouldn't let up, coming in painful waves. It was difficult to maintain consciousness as he was close to swooning with wooziness. He grabbed the walls for some balance before he fell into his own shitty mess.

After some time things began to settle down, but all sense of time was now gone. He had no idea how long he'd been in the toilet. It felt like he'd released the entirety of his lower intestines by now and it was time to regain control of the situation.

He asked himself, "Right, what's the plan here, Matt?" He almost daren't look around for toilet paper, assuming that it would be like gold dust at a time like this, certainly knowing his luck thus far. Of course, there was none to be found anywhere, not even an empty cardboard tube to scrape away what he can before pulling his boxers and trousers back up. It transpired that this would be the least of his worries just then.

Matt could hear someone shouting in another part of the building. Thinking nothing of it, he continued his hunt for toilet paper. The sound of the shouting actually felt like it was really close to him. Was there someone in the same room who had heard what was going on? He hadn't checked the other cubicles before getting going. Then it hit him like a punch in the face. Looking down beneath his still squatted legs, he could see that, at the bottom of the hole in the ground, there was a little Chinese face staring up at him covered in shit. What the fuck? It suddenly dawned upon him that nothing separated the hole in the floor from the other toilet below and the ones below each floor. It was like a giant, vile tube to transport shit, to where?

The shit-covered man was rightly irate. Who wouldn't be after being showered in the excrement of another man? Matthew was totally hypnotised by this angry little man, unsure of what to do with himself. Looking around, he was so aware of the fact he was covered in shit. It had been bouncing right back up all over his arse. The little man downstairs would have to fuck off. Matthew had bigger fish to fry. He had no idea how he was going to get cleaned up, but it needed to happen.

As he tried to formulate a plan, he remembered what Arthur had said about richer people in China living higher up. That was bloody why. The higher you lived, the less shit you had to come pouring down upon you. Clearly, the same applied to business buildings as to residential buildings. Matthew had heard something similar on a trip to Edinburgh once. A tour guide told him that, in the old town, the richer you were the higher you lived because people threw shit in buckets out of the window. On the top floor, the wealthiest would be all good, but below? Nope. It put a whole new meaning to penthouse living.

With no firm plan in place yet, he shuffled out of the cubicle praying that nobody would walk in and disturb him. Even out in the main part of the toilet, he couldn't see anything he'd be able to use to clean things up. Not a single one of the toilet cubicles had any toilet paper in them. All he could see was a lone sink against the wall. Matthew stared at it, wondering if it would be possible to sit on it and use the tap to get things sparkling down there once again.

He backed up against the sink, sizing it up like a snake lying next to a human to see if it can manage to consume it. It was too tall, though, his arsehole only reaching the edge of the sink. He realised that he would need to try a different approach, but what would it be?

Matthew backed up to the sink again and lunged backwards and upwards. With a stroke of luck he landed right in the sink bowl. But he scratched his back on one of the taps.

"ARGH," he yelped in pain. "Come on, you can do this," he told himself out loud.

He yanked hard at one of the taps but it was completely stuck. Close to giving up, he looked to the god he didn't believe in and prayed the other would work. It did, but it sprayed out scorching hot water. From one steaming hot liquid to another, he thought. The sink was filling up rapidly, his arse still wedged firmly in there. He tried to stop it but the tap wouldn't budge a millimetre. Matthew wiggled his bum around in agony as it was scalded by the water, but even that was stuck. His arse cooking in boiling water, the sink held him there like a suction cup. He started to scream in agony, writhing. He tried to recall the same strength that had compelled the bouncer off him in the boardroom to pull himself off this cauldron.

Hot water splashing all over the floor of the toilet as Matt struggled, a man burst through the door. At first, Matthew thought that it might be someone wondering what all the commotion was about, but the brown substance all over him told a different story. It was the man from below – the poor bugger who had been in the very wrong place at the very wrong time. He went straight for Matthew who was vulnerable and unable to go anywhere, screaming and flailing his arms around. Out of nowhere, the man delivers a swift backhander across Matt's face.

"What the fuck is wrong with you?"

At this moment a saviour arrived. The very bouncer who had tried to stop Matthew getting to the toilet in this first place was now here to intervene. Lophead, we'll call him, said some stern words to the angry, shit-stained employee. Whatever it was that had been said it worked, as he stepped back, bowed and left.

"Please, mate. Help me," Matthew implored Lophead, holding his arms out like a sad little teddy bear looking for attention. This was not his most dignified moment.

The bouncer obliged taking Matt by the arms and yanking as hard as possible. He slipped on the water that was now all over the floor. The pair of them fell to the ground with a flood, Matt covering Lophead in water. He lay there looking down at the disaster zone he'd created, lying half-naked on top of the guy. Matt hadn't even noticed until now that he was still erect. Who'd have thought that a perpetual boner during a business meeting would become the least trouble of the day? As quick as you like Matt got himself off Lophead, stood up, and began grovelling.

"Jesus Christ, I'm so sorry. So, so sorry."

Without a word Lophead shook himself off, getting rid of excess water, and left the room without a word. Matthew was mortified, in pain, and smelly. He was mostly free from shit now, even if it had come at the cost of scalding his butt cheeks. It must have looked like they'd been spanked raw. Matthew shook off as much water as he could and reassembled himself. There were still flecks of shit on his trousers, but there wasn't much he could do about that right now.

Feeling like he'd been gone for the longest time, and wondering if Lophead had just gone right back to tell them all about the farcical scene he'd found in the toilet, Matt knew he needed to get back in that boardroom. He looked himself up and down and took a deep breath.

"Here we go," he said to himself, trying to get psyched up for returning looking like he'd just been through ten rounds with Mr. Hanky the Christmas poo himself. Lophead was waiting outside the door for him, and Matt realised he must have been there the entire time to make sure he wasn't doing a runner or something. That would mean he'd heard the lot, and why he was able to get to Matt's rescue so quick when the shit-covered employee had rocked up. Matt would just have to shelf his mortification for now. Lophead accompanied Matt back to the boardroom.

Chapter 21 – The Gift

Back in the boardroom all eyes were on Matt, including a pair of very confused ones that belonged to Chris. All he could do in response was shake his head, open his eyes widely, and distort his mouth. His dad needed no further explanation, nudging him as he sat down and motioning with his head at Hwong.

By now Hwong and his men had finished going over everything and went back to staring at Matthew.

He was about to open his mouth to say something, although he didn't know what, when Arthur interjected.

"While you were gone, they say that they can do the tooling easily, that the plans are good and that they can arrange the order within three weeks. They want you to type up the contract on your laptop now and they can print it for everyone to sign."

Matthew was relieved that it had all been approved, more relieved than when he'd finally made it to the shitter. He nodded and furiously typed the remaining details into the contract that were dictated by Arthur and his dad. It took twenty-five minutes all in, the room in total silence other than Matt's heavy breathing of concentration. Once complete, Chink printed off several copies and everyone signed it. Matthew found it very strange that Hwong and his men failed to read the contract before putting their names to it, but that wasn't his problem.

Chink spent a couple of minutes saying something in Mandarin to Arthur whose face dropped. He seemed to understand what she said perfectly, but it didn't seem like good news.

"They have thanked us for coming and signing the contract with them. It is customary in China to now go and buy Mr. Hwong a gift to show loyal friendship between us. We need to drive to a local shopping centre where Mr. Hwong will choose a gift that you and Chris must pay for. We will then drive for dinner at a local Chinese restaurant where we will party till the early hours of the morning to celebrate closing the deal."

Matthew and Chris looked at each other baffled, new to this form of business. Hadn't they already bought the fucker a gift? Wasn't it expensive enough?

Quietly, Chris whispered to Matthew, "Oh, let's go with it. He might just want a new pair of trousers."

Matthew nodded in approval, thinking that the only one who needed a new pair of trousers at this given time was him.

"How bad could it be?" he asked his dad rhetorically.

Feeling a lot better after his clear-out, but feeling less than fresh to say the least, Matt couldn't help but look forward to the end of the evening. It seemed that every day something terrible would happen that would make him keen to get the day over and done with.

Everyone stood up and Hwong left the room first. Arthur, Chris and Matthew followed, the others in tow, watching them like hawks. Once outside Matthew stood still for a second taking in a huge gulp of fresh air. Contract signed, sealed and delivered. Next.

Matt had taken in just about as much air as he needed to refresh himself after the events of the day, and what had felt like absolute fear inside him had now subsided to a mere desire to head into the home stretch of this shitshow. He looked around him as everybody appeared to be standing still for some reason. He caught a glance at Won who was signalling to Arthur in a way that appeared to mean they should be making tracks. Matt wanted to make sure everything went smooth from now on, although he was in no doubt that some other tragedy was lurking around the next corner for him to stumble his way through. What, pray tell, would that be?

He made for the vehicle as Won was stepping into the driver's seat, and as it came into Matt's sight he realised this wasn't going to be any old relaxed journey onwards to the restaurant for a celebration. No no, as he saw five black cars surrounding their own, all with blacked-out windows – which were also presumably bulletproof – he understood they were going to continue to be watched like hawks until they all parted ways. That is if they would be parting ways at all.

Matt gulped and looked at his dad who was motioning with his head at the cars. Matt mouthed, "I know," thinking they resembled the Sentinel from the *Grand Theft Auto 3* video game. It had been a while since Matt had played that game mind you, but there was no doubt this cluster of cars looked just like the mostly BMW-based cars featured in the game's universe. Not only did they all have tinted windows, but body kits and blinds over the rear windows, which presumably couldn't legally be tinted. Good solution, Matt thought, admiring their ingenuity while also wondering exactly what it was they needed to hide from the outside world. Another gulp clogged up his throat as he took in what was clearly nothing short of hang vehicles. Another look from Chris told him they had both come to the same realisation.

Matt and Chris both stepped into the car, their every move observed. Lophead came over to the driver's side window and knocked on it. Won stepped back out of the car and he and Lophead engaged in a hushed conversation that lasted for a short twenty seconds or so and then they seemed set to head off. Arthur sat down in the passenger seat as all the others outside got into their convoy of doom and the engine revved up. Looking around outside before he said anything, Arthur then turned to look back at Chris and Matt.

"They have said to me that we must follow the two cars there in a convey."

Matt knew what he meant and didn't feel the need to correct him and continued to listen.

"Now, that sound not bad, but what sound bad is they say to me that we must not pull any sudden wrong turns or drive too fast. We must stay behind those two cars at all times."

Christ, the calm Matt had been feeling exiting the building was now being taken over by a sense of dread that had become very commonplace on this trip.

Matt interrupted. "Did they say anything else? That doesn't sound too threatening, does it?"

Arthur went on. "Well, no. That doesn't sound too threatening, but they do say as well that if we do any of that, even if by innocent mistake, they crash into us on purpose. You see, the other three cars, they stay behind us."

Matt had already got that. He was more than aware of what a convoy was. In fact, he'd once seen a convoy in London; some fancy black car led and was followed by a series of police cars and motorbikes. He'd been on the pavement when he'd watched it pass, glanced into the back of the fancy car and made eye contact with its passenger. It had only been Queen Lizzy herself – the ultimate Don Corleone. Matt was sure she must have had a couple of enemies bumped here and there if they stepped out of line. A lot of people thought it was her behind the Princess Diana crash, but it was never confirmed. Anyway, Matt thought, if it's possible for the Queen to take out those who cross her, these guys certainly would.

Matt caught sight of Won's face in the rear-view mirror, and he looked worried. He'd managed to keep the car protected up until this point. There had been no damage. He'd looked after this thing like it had been his own kid.

They were deep in it now; the convoy formed. They pulled away slowly and in the opposite direction than they had arrived earlier in the day. The other direction was just as rough as the way they'd come in, full of rundown buildings and poor people going about their business. The shacks soon turned into shinier, newer buildings which alleviated some of Matt's concern. Just a little though.

"You alright with all of this, Dad?" Matt asked Chris, who didn't seem perturbed at all.

"Yeah, I'm sure this is all par for the course. You know how these things go. They're just swinging their dicks" he reassured his son. "Anyway, what the fuck happened to you in there? You stink like poo and your trousers have had better days!"

Matt looked down at himself. He had forgotten about his wet shitty pants and trousers and the smell in all the commotion of leaving. He shook his head.

"Oh god, sorry, Dad. It had to come out. I have never seen anything like it in that place. The toilet is not a toilet by any definition. It has nothing to sit on and just an eighteen-inch hole in the middle of the floor. I had to squat and I was in so much pain as I crouched my arse pebble dashed the walls, floor and me! I won't tell you the rest but there was a guy in the floor and I shit on his face."

Chris looked on in pity, shaking his head slowly, open-mouthed.

"Sorry, Matt, but that's pretty fucked up. How the fuck do you shit on someone's face? I think you're hallucinating from the tea Arthur gave you."

With that Arthur pipes up.

"No, no, no, not my tea. Mr. Matthew tells the truth. He probably excreted onto the people below. Here in China, sometimes toilet not finishes in buildings. He must shout down warning."

Well, that was it. Chris could not believe his ears. Matt had obviously just been through some properly bad shit. Chris howled with laughter, patting Matt on the back.

"Suck it up, son, suck it up. I have a feeling we're in more danger now than we have been since we got here."

Matt didn't respond, looking out of the window as the wonders of the city went by. He thought that one day in the future it would be amazing to come back to China, and even other Asian countries to really appreciate it all without stuff like this going on at the same time. He'd bring Sarah, that was if she hadn't divorced him by then. On second thoughts, nah. It's too fucked up in China. They'd swing by somewhere far more chilled out, like Bali for example, where they could lie on a nice beach knocking back cocktails without a worry in their minds. That sounded far superior to this Asian gangland shit.

They drove for what seemed like an age, but when Matt looked at his watch it had only been seven minutes. As the car slowed down and came to a standstill, he was comforted by the sight of a swanky-looking shopping centre with loads of well-heeled locals swarming in and out of it. The front of the huge building was pure white, and Matt wondered if they're only capable of keeping it that way by painting it all year round as they do with bridges – starting back at the beginning once they finally get to the end. What a thankless task that seemed like. Leading up to some grand glass doors were sweeping marble steps that looked terribly regal. It was a nice environment to be in for a change.

Matt saw the lackeys running from their black cars towards theirs, and a few of the crowd outside the shopping centre picked up their pace to move on elsewhere. That couldn't be a good sign. Won stepped out of the car as the men stood outside waiting, opening the back door as Matt and Chris shuffled onto the street. The lackeys formed a shell around them, leading them towards the big glass doors of the shopping centre where they'd clearly be picking up that gift for fatso Hwong to demonstrate the lasting bond of friendship between them. What a load of bollocks – greedy bastard. Matt looked around to see that Lophead and Chink were also behind them. Although the formation may have been stranger than anything he'd been in before, Matt couldn't help but feel an odd sensation. He felt important like he was the president of the United States, the leader of the free world and the most powerful man on the planet, surrounded by his secret service agents who would unflinchingly give up their lives for his own. Of course, he knew that wasn't the case with these guys, who would most likely give up their own grandmothers if it meant saving themselves from any kind of impending threat.

With the men huddled around them, Chris and Matt entered the shopping centre, locals jumping out of their way without question. They definitely knew these guys were not to be messed with. They made their way towards an escalator, which was just one of many in a vast network of them angled everywhere, stretching from one level to another. How many floors did this place have?

As they were carried upwards to the second floor, Matt let his head wander. Burberry, Gucci, Prada, Versace, Ralph Lauren, Louis Vuitton, Armani, Hermes, Chanel, they were all there, the priciest brands in the world. Even the brands that Matt didn't recognise were clearly bank-breaking too. There wasn't a single cheap shop in this joint, and whatever gift Hwong was going to request – if that's how this would go down – would not likely be an affordable one. A million quid, Matt, he told himself, keeping his eyes on the prize. What was it they say, "you need to speculate to accumulate?"

On arrival on the second floor, Chink pointed towards a magnificent jewellery shop. It wasn't a brand Matt had ever heard of before, but as they got closer it appeared to be one of these independent places that stock all sorts of different brand names. They stopped outside the shop and Matt wondered why they weren't going inside. The men in front of Matt and Chris moved out of the way, circling behind them and bringing the contents of the shop's window display into their line of vision. Chink took Chris's arm in her hand and led him forwards slightly, pointing at a specific item in the window.

"Here we go," Chris said discreetly. "The fucker doesn't want a nice pair of trousers. He wants a fucking gold bullion bar, and with a casual price tag of sixteen bloody grand."

Matt looked at Chink who was waiting for a response from Chris, but Chris wasn't quite finished with his little rant just yet.

"If that fat fuck thinks I'm going to buy him an actual bar of gold then he's absolutely got another thing coming."

Matt could feel the fear rising. He was imagining his dad flat out refusing to buy it, the two of them being shot dead and left in a pool of blood right there in the shopping centre as nobody dared to step in. What was Chris going to come out with? Please, Christ, let it be reasonable.

There was a silence before Chris eventually turned to Arthur and piped up. He'd obviously been pondering the best move.

"Tell them that we say yes, we will buy this for Mr. Hwong, but we don't have the money right now. Add that we will buy it for him tomorrow morning after we have all partied together, once I have had time to transfer some money from one account to another. This, unfortunately, can't be done immediately with the bank I'm with."

Matt was pleased that his dad's response was more reasonable than he imagined it might be. He was standing his ground, but without getting the two of them killed. Arthur makes the proposal to Chink, who then responds to Arthur.

Arthur says, "OK, they say this is good and that now we go see Mr. Hwong who will also be happy with this arrangement."

At this point in the game, Matt couldn't be more cognisant of the fact that this was the world's least normal deal even he imagined. What a strange way to do business, spoiling the people you're doing the deal with so that they feel important. It was utterly ridiculous. What the hell would they want next? A vial each of their blood and piss? Some skin scrapings to keep on file? That would come as no surprise after everything so far.

Chris whispered something to Arthur, who in turn took it to Chink. She nodded putting her hand up to tell the goons not to worry, and Chris started to slide away from the group. Matt had no clue what was going on here and why they were now letting one of their party wander off on his own. Chris looked back at Matt.

"Just off to the bog, son. They're all good with it. Meet you back at the car."

Matt hoped his dad would get on better in this toilet than Matt had back at the last one he'd visited. He shuddered at the memory and thought that he should probably pick up a new pair of pants at some point. He didn't want to push their luck right now though. They were already trusting Chris to go off alone which was very surprising. Matt first assumed it was because they'd managed to establish some degree of trust before it came to him that it could be they simply cared to avoid another lavatory fiasco. The idea that was behind their reasoning made Matt chuckle internally. Every cloud.

As the group walked on, making their way to the bottom of the escalator, Arthur turned to Matt.

"I think we might need some lucky money. The red parcel. We might need a way out if this goes wrong, and really I think Chris should have bought the gold bar."

Matt looked at Arthur, making moves to ask what he meant by this exactly. At that point Chink drew Arthur's attention away, posing a question about why Chris was taking so long. Matt thought to himself that his dad was taking a hot minute to get back. He could see in Chink's eyes that she was getting really concerned.

Chink turned to one of the goons, ordering him to go look for Chris. But as the guy made it to the top of the escalator on Chink's command, Chris appeared on the escalator. Phew, Matt thought. Thank Christ for that.

When they had reached the bottom of the escalator Chink and the pack of goons look completely relieved. Matt raised his eyebrows at his dad, obviously questioning why he had taken so long in the toilet. Chris leaned in and quietly said, "I was taking a pony, son. I was only ten minutes! Can't a man drop one in peace these days? Well, you certainly can't. We know that much for sure."

Matt smiled and responded, "Arthur thinks that we need what he called 'lucky money'. 'We need red parcel,' he said to me. What the fuck is a red parcel?"

"Oh, I know what he means. Or at least I think I do. Don't worry, I have a bit of cash if it's needed. I'm sure that's what he means by lucky money. The red parcel, so to speak."

After the very awkward wait for Chris the lot of them were dispatched back outside to the waiting convoy of cars. As they moved along the lackeys huddled around them once more, so any trust they thought might have been established was obviously in Matt's mind.

Once everyone had taken a seat in their respective vehicles the convoy set off. Nobody had said exactly where they were going now, but Matt thought it had to be the restaurant where they would go to celebrate the close of the deal. No other steps had been mentioned back at the business premises, so he hoped there were no other surprises along the road. Again, the time that it took to get to their next destination seemed much longer than it actually was. Matt's perception of time had become warped in China.

Chapter 22 – The Party

When they pulled up at the restaurant, Matt was thankful that they were still in a reasonably nice area of Tianjin and not back at the scabby one they'd come from earlier. Hopefully, this would mean the quality of food would be high, even if he wouldn't describe half of what he was probably about to have to eat as food as he knew it.

The detached building containing the restaurant had some similarities to the teahouse they'd been to that morning. However, whereas the teahouse had been traditional, this place was clearly a reproduction. There was a lot of red paint which Matt had come to understand was common in China in general, on old or new buildings. The roof of the restaurant was covered in green tiles which made for a striking contrast with the red.

Earlier, Matt had thought it ridiculous that Hwong needed such a large group of goons to keep an eye on Matt and Chris, but as he looked out of the window at the restaurant he realised that, clearly, Hwong didn't think that enough. Standing in front of the entrance to the building was another eight Chinese guys all dressed in black suits like the lot they were already with. By this time they were outnumbered by something like five to one, but Matt supposed that was the whole point.

They all stepped out of the cars simultaneously, facing the men in regimented lines like ninja warriors, only with their faces uncovered. The men in the cars didn't rush to huddle around them this time, probably aware that Chris and Matt would be too afraid to run even if they wanted to. Arthur and Won both looked nervous at the sight of all the goons. Matt considered that he might not need to be concerned with what they'd be eating for dinner because they would, in fact, be the dinner. Chris turned to Matt.

"Are you ready, boy? You got us into this shit, now you can get us out."

Matt gulped, nodded at his dad, and then looked on. He still wasn't feeling absolutely tiptop in the digestive department, but that was definitely no priority right then and there. He took on board his dad's words. It was true; he had got them into this shit, and there was nobody but him to make sure they navigated through the rest of this without any further farce or trouble.

Matt stayed silent for a short while, strategising in his head. He ran through a series of different potential scenarios of varying levels of danger, thinking about how he might kung fu his way out of them. Ah, if only he'd learned any form of martial arts in his younger years instead of spending all his time swimming. He certainly wouldn't be able to butterfly stroke his way out of danger here.

He might not be proficient in any form of martial arts, but what Matt had done when he was younger was learn how to effectively profile people of all sorts in London boozers. When they would enter the joints Matt would closely observe them, categorising each of them into groups of varying levels of threat. This had been something Chris had taught to him from a young age to keep him out of trouble, knowing exactly who to avoid, who you could square up to if needs be, who you had to knock out first in a fight, and so on. It had been foolproof throughout his life, so perhaps it could be useful at this moment.

As Matt and Chris looked at the entrance of the restaurant still flanked by Hwong's ever-increasing pack of hounds, Matt quickly put his old method into play.

"Dad, I've categorised them. I know you'll have done the same, so I just wanna check that mine match up with yours."

"Shoot," Chris said in response.

"Mr. Hwong is a ten." It was a pretty standard scale. Ten was the highest and one was the lowest. Matt went on.

"Lophead is a nine. All the guys at the table alongside Hwong – you know, his lackeys – they're all six. This crew in front of the restaurant are three in my estimation. Surprisingly, Chink pips them to a four."

"Yup, pretty spot on, Matt. Didn't have Chink down for a four, more a three. But now I think about it, she might be a bigger threat than I'd imagine," Chris replied.

Speaking a little quieter now, even if he was aware that nobody could really understand a word he was saying, Matt gave his dad instructions. He was really taking the reins here and he could tell his dad was impressed by that. Chris motioned for Arthur to come a little closer so that he could hear everything Matt was saying.

"Right then. I've got a plan of action if it all goes Pete Tong, Dad. You'll need to take out Mr. Hwong seeing as he is the biggest threat. I'm sorry, I know that's not the perfect solution for you, but you know you're a lot more capable of handling him than I would be. While you're dealing with that fat cunt, I'll go straight for the guys who were around the table earlier, as they look a lot tougher than this new crowd. Arthur – who I think could be a nice little secret weapon to have in our arsenal – will have to take on this new crowd, or at least keep them busy while we handle our guys. And if Won is as good with his hands as he is driving a car, then we can get him to help us out by covering Lophead and Chink."

Arthur piped up to ask a question.

"But who is Pete Tong?"

Won nods his head in agreement with Arthur, clearly not understanding the English and also wondering the same thing.

Matt chuckled. It made sense that they would have no idea what this meant. "Pete Tong, guys, is East London cockney slang for wrong. 'If it goes Pete Tong' means 'if it all goes wrong'."

Even after the explanation Arthur and Won still looked as confused as they could be. They didn't pursue their line of questioning though, giving up on trying to understand.

Matt knew that this was a big play by any definition, but if every one of them had a strong idea of the role they would be playing if the shit hit the fan, then things should work out fine and they'd have a better chance of coming out the other side alive, or at least with all of their limbs. Arthur seemed to understand the plan and regaled it to Won, who looked surprisingly cool about the prospect of getting into another movie scene. This would be the first time that Won joined them anywhere other than when he was driving them around. Matt wondered how the driver felt about the prospect of leaving the precious car unattended. Perhaps he knew there was more at stake here than a mere car. Arthur said something else to Won, and when they all started to make their way towards the entrance of the restaurant, Matt worked out that it must have been for Won to join them. He didn't argue.

As they approached the goons, Chris spoke up.

"Arthur, I just want you to know that the plan we just ran through is a total worst-case scenario. It's not something we should assume will happen, but we should definitely anticipate the possibility of that so that we can protect ourselves. Got it?"

"Understood," replied the little Chinese man affirmatively.

"Chances of it happening are one in six, tops," added Chris.

Matt had no idea where he was getting these odds from, but it was a guesstimate at best. So, the escape plan had been hatched successfully, but Matt was still obviously hoping that the rest of the evening would go down without any major hitches. He could just about handle eating whatever arsehole or knuckle that was stuffed in his face. He could just about handle shitting all over some unsuspecting toilet-goer. He could just about handle pretty much anything that had been thrown at him thus far. But what he couldn't handle in any shape or form was walking away from all of this without the completion of the deal and the prospect of that £1 million being pulled just that bit closer. Completing the deal was the ideal scenario. It would be the best solution all round, but Matt didn't hold much hope that the close of the deal would be as smooth as he'd like.

A few times across the trip, and not even the worst parts necessarily, Matt had contemplated the idea of putting pen to paper one day – or really finger to keyboard – to write a book about this almost completely inconceivable escapade him and his dad had been on. There was certainly enough material to work with, that was for sure. As they stepped through the front entrance, Matt thought, who knows, perhaps one day I will actually get around to that.

A popular quote popped into his head but he couldn't quite remember who it was by. Some really famous author beginning with E. Ah, yeah, that was it – Ernest Hemingway. He'd once said that, "A man's got to take a lot of punishment to write a really funny book."

Well, if Matt hadn't taken enough punishment to write at the very least a mildly amusing book, then he wondered what on earth the funniest authors in the world had endured. He couldn't imagine it had been the tiniest bit tolerable.

In the open expanse that was the restaurant, Matt looked around. He couldn't believe it but it could almost have been a direct replica of the one back in Beijing where he'd first had the delight of eating a donkey's cock, only on a much larger scale. They stood in silence for a while, all the King's men and all the King's horses standing right behind them.

Matt turned to Chink thinking that this time it would be a better idea for him to talk to someone who could speak a little English to ask permission to go to the toilet instead of just making his way there. He wasn't in the same state that he had been in before, mind you, but he certainly needed to finish off what he had started earlier. Now seemed like the best chance he would have to do that.

Chink understood and politely pointed at the toilet door at the back of the restaurant. It was right next to a bright red and green flickering neon sign that said something in Chinese.

Matt walked slowly towards the toilet, all eyes monitoring his every move as expected. One goon followed him there, setting up camp outside the toilet door as he went in.

Inside, Matt noticed that it was a huge room. All in there were six cubicles, all without doors, and six hand basins sitting opposite each cubicle. There was also a large mirror near the entrance. Each basin had hand soap. The whole room, which reeked of urine, was dark and seedy with flickering fluorescent tube light humming above.

Matt decided to head to the furthest cubicle from the door in order to get some privacy. Once again he was met not by real toilets, but just by holes in the floor. Matt peeped over the top of the hole he was about to shit in, just to make sure there were no prying eyes from below, and more importantly to make sure he didn't need to holler down a warning like, "Watch out below, English turd incoming!"

Matt thought twice, shouting it down anyway. He figured it was best to do that for luck before dropping his ruined trousers and pants and squatting over the hole.

This time he was able to exert a little more control over the situation and managed to aim his business a lot better. There would be no arse pebble dash on this occasion, thank the lord. Instead, he squeezed out something that could be compared to a chipolata sausage, a long and skinny one if you need any clarification.

Nobody in this world would be excited by the sight of a sausage-like poo, but when he saw this Matt thought he had won the lottery. Finally, his dark days were over.

The joy was sadly short-lived, as he felt warm water running down his legs. Despondency crept in as he realised he'd pissed himself. Matt had forgotten his giant erection, which had been hard for so long now – nearly twenty-four hours altogether – that it was now totally numb. He wasn't entirely sure how he could have forgotten Erectiongate, but he was merely distracted by the fact that he could now take a crap in peace. His concentration had been on pooping and nothing else. Peeing hadn't even entered his mind

Matt's already damp underwear and trousers were now drenched by urine, which would no doubt add to the delightful scent in the already stinking room. Wonderful, he thought. It was a strange feeling having part of his body feel completely numb. He made a sad attempt at angling his penis down towards the hole in the ground, but to achieve this, he was forced to bend his face towards the disgusting, dirty floor, while now kneeling and using one arm to prop himself up. It was quite a sight.

Despite his best efforts, Matt was unable to accomplish the angle he so desperately needed to pee into the hole. His penis was dead set on staying vertical, pointing upwards towards his face.

He pressed himself further towards the floor now, with his face touching the badly mopped excretion of the cubicle's previous occupant.

His arse facing the ceiling, his penis was angled towards the hole. Success at a terrible cost. Once again, he tried to urinate. Matt's bladder was having none of it, the position obviously blocking the tube his piss should be coming out of. He stood up, cursing his penis.

"The number of times I have desperately wanted you hard and you have let me down. Now I don't fucking need you and you won't go down. Unbelievable."

He slapped his cock before pinching it, but he felt nothing on both occasions. He exited the cubicle, shuffling with his trousers round his ankles and looking for the mirror. He wanted to get a better view of his cock.

As he shuffled along the toilet floor, of course, the entrance door swung open. One of the goons walked in and stared at Matt and his bulbous erection.

Matt was caught by surprise, even though he shouldn't have been at this stage in the game and apologised.

"It's not what it looks like," he shouted as he waved his hands around. "I am not a pervert, honest."

The goon left the toilet quickly without comment.

"Pervert? Honest? Really, Matt?" he questioned himself while shaking his head and continuing to shuffle towards the mirror. He was determined to get there to check himself more closely.

Once he'd arrived at his destination, he looked into the mirror and examined his penis. He was horrified at what he found. The helmet had warped in shape and looked more like a golf ball. It was the longest and most swollen he had ever seen it, with the sides bursting out like a beer belly – his beer belly more to the point – and the colour was far from normal.

Fuck, he thought, things are not good down there. Matt stared in the mirror, looking himself in the eyes. Am I sane? Really though, am I? Why on earth would I trust my own mad decision to come to China? What is going on here?

He continued to stare into the mirror and began to shout at himself. A pep talk was just what he needed right at this moment.

"TRUST YOUR OWN MADNESS, MATT."

He tried to turn a very negative situation into something positive, convincing himself that he's not mad. The thing is he just couldn't believe himself, no matter how much he was encouraging himself to believe in Matt.

The door flew open. Clearly the goon who'd come in had gone and blabbed to Chink as she was now standing right there in the doorway, flanked by Arthur and Chris. Matt didn't know where to look.

"Guys, please. Can I have some privacy?"

Too tired, both physically and mentally, to bend over and pull up his trousers, he just stood there like a nugget. Chris opened his mouth.

"Matt, son. Your cock. Have you seen it? It looks worse than that time I got kicked in the goolies by that donkey at the circus thirty years ago."

Matt nodded. He had, of course, seen it. It was a mess. Chris was right. If they'd been back at home he would be at the hospital without delay, but that wasn't bound to happen here in China.

Matt remembered the day his dad was talking about. Chris had been flat out on the circus floor with his trousers and underwear pulled down to his knees, his tackle out for all the audience to see, blood and all. It was like a day out in the butcher's back room.

Arthur turned to Chink, who was standing mesmerized by the giant, throbbing penis. She was either distressed or absolutely loving it. Matt couldn't tell which of the two it was. Probably the former, he told himself. It was more likely.

"Chink, do you have a sharp object? Anything. A pin? A cocktail stick?"

Matt looked horrified.

"No, no, no, no, no, no, no, no. No more bloody cocktail sticks. I mean it."

He was holding his hands over the top of his bulb-shaped helmet for protection.

Chink opened her mouth to speak, closed it, and then opened it again.

"Wow, it be so big!"

All the while she was demonstrating a length with both of her hands like it made a difference or like anybody cared. It was then that Matt realised that she wasn't distressed by the state of it, just purely taken aback at the size of it. Perhaps she was used to seeing smaller penises if she was used to seeing them at all. Perhaps the Chinese weren't as promiscuous as the Brits.

"We need a doctor, Chink. You know what I mean by a doctor?" Arthur said.

Chink now looked up and tried to break her concentration on the monster cock, saying something to Arthur in Chinese and then leaving the toilet.

Matt looked at his dad.

"Well, this isn't embarrassing much, is it?"

His sarcasm was thick. He could see in Chris's face that his dad was starting to get concerned for his health and probably his future libido too. Chris wanted more grandchildren at some point after all.

Arthur shouted out into the restaurant.

"Chink, check with Hwong to see if they can take Matthew to a doctor."

Then he turned to Chris and Matt.

"But we must stay here until they return. It the only way they will agree. I am sure of it."

Chris nodded in agreement with that plan, and Matt too. There was no other viable option on the table.

"Matt, can't you feel that fucking stonker? It looks so bloody painful. Ain't it absolutely throbbing?"

Matt responded.

"No, Dad, it's as numb as a prostitute's cunt. What do you think?"

Matt was now starting to get very angry at all the questions being fired his way in such a vulnerable position.

Chris could see that his son's patience was pushed to its limit. He ushered Arthur out of the toilet leaving Matt to sort himself out. He knew that it would be safer for everyone involved to give Matt some time to himself.

Once he'd got his shit together – well at least to the best of his ability in the circumstances – Matt exited the toilet with a huge bulge in his trousers. Everyone in the restaurant obviously now knew about it and all eyes were now on Matt's crotch area.

Chink and three of the goons walked forward, pointing Matt towards the exit and then left, Chris, Arthur and Won remaining behind.

Chapter 23 – The "Operation"

Once outside of the restaurant the lot of them jumped into one of the black mafioso sentinel cars. One of the goons drove. It was odd to be in a different car surrounded by this bunch rather than being with his dad and the rest of them.

Matt sat in the middle of the back seats, with Chink on one side and a goon on the other. He hadn't thought to look at the car from the outside, but it was strangely small on the inside. It could just about fit two and a half people, so Matt, who wasn't the smallest guy as you know, was forced to sit sideways with his bum pressed against the goon and his bulge hard against Chink. It was an uncomfortable situation to be in and Matt felt very awkward.

The whole time Chink was smiling and staring at Matt with glee. She was obviously still fixated on the idea of his enormous penis.

He had no idea where to look, so he stared out the window past her head so as not to make eye contact. It seemed like Chink was moving purposely so she could feel the bulging crotch rub up against her, even placing her hand right next to it. Jesus, Matt thought, she's really fucking getting off on all this. She must be sex starved.

Luckily, it was a short journey to the hospital. Matt had started to sweat profusely, and the awkwardness had now ramped up to the max. Not to mention the pong coming off of him.

Matt, the goons and Chink all clambered out of the car, Chink making it seem harder than it was just so that she could get a few cheeky gropes in. She even jokingly fell back onto Matthew and giggled, which was infuriating because he was so close to the help he needed. She was far from subtle about it, let's just say that.

Matt couldn't understand her and what she was up to; she was so forward. It was just the same as the "girls" back in the massage parlour. Maybe it was down to the fact he was a gentleman from far-flung shores. Perhaps that carried some warped sense of excitement, or it could simply be that Chinese girls were just as horny as they come.

Matt took in his surroundings once out of the car. It looked like they were in a very rundown back street of the city. It was nearly dark and it all felt eerie as hell.

Matt thought, hang on a minute. This is no bloody hospital. They were standing outside a shop with an alley down the side of it. On the front was a sign in Chinese. There was also an English translation underneath, which was quite rare to see in his experience there so far.

"Shen Nong", it said above "Drug Store".

Right, so they weren't at a hospital, but he had been taken to a drug store so that should suffice. His panic subsided. Matt was so excited at the prospect of calming this monster down finally and potentially getting a bit of feeling back into the old boy. He muttered to himself quietly.

"For once some good fucking news. I'm sure they'll have a reversal pill or medicine in there."

He walked towards the shop door, the goons grabbing his arms and redirecting him into the alley.

"But…" Matt whimpered, pointing to the drug store.

"But look, it's a drug store!"

Unfortunately, his message fell on deaf ears. It seemed that they were going around to the back of the shop. He was right, that's exactly what was happening.

Once at the back of the drug store they plodded down a dark stairwell to a dimly lit door. One of the goons raised his hand, which had a large ring on one finger. Bang, bang, bang, as the ring hit the door. No answer. Bang, bang, bang, once again.

After a short while a small peep slider popped open and Matt heard a voice talking through it in Chinese. A long conversation ensued between Chink and whoever was on the other side of the door. Matt stood patiently looking around him at the dank alleyway, starting to get the shivers while standing there. He wondered if the person behind the door was a doctor, or at the very least a pharmacist. Likelihood? Zero, he thought.

All of a sudden the door opened and a man of very similar size to Matthew stood there. He was Chinese, about six foot two, very stocky, and wearing a long, dirty apron that looked like it might once have been white. Clearly, health and safety cleanliness standards weren't in operation in this particular joint, whatever it may really be.

The big guy ushered all of them in hastily, all the while looking around and up the stairs making sure they had not been followed. What was this place?

The door slammed shut behind them and five large metal sliding bolts were secured in place. Matt hoped that the aim of those was to stop people from coming in rather than preventing people from trying to escape. He gulped.

They were led along a corridor with lots of doors on either side of it. He could hear the strangest of noises coming from behind each of the doors. To Matt the noises sounded like scratching, but they didn't stop beside any door for him to properly assess them.

Scratching or not, he didn't care. He was there for one thing, and one thing only: Viagra reversal tablets. Once they reached the end of the corridor, which must have been at least forty feet long, they entered a square room.

The walls and an examination table in the middle of the room were all clad in stainless steel, and a light hung above it. Dotted around the room was a variety of medical utensils and machines that looked like they had medical purposes. Matt suddenly felt at ease, realising that this was a medical practice of some kind, legal or otherwise. Why the dodgy back street entrance? he wondered. Yeah, it must be illegal.

Matt started to thank Chink and the goons for taking him there, shaking their hands vigorously as they retracted from the handshakes. The big man who had let them in talked to Matt in broken English.

"Please, can you lie on examination table and loose trouser."

As he said this he signalled with his hands for Matt to drop the trousers to his knees. Matt did so before shuffling across to the examination table, everyone watching him. There was going to be no dignity here then, not that there had been much up until now.

The doctor, or whoever he was, spoke again once Matt got to the table and was laying down on it.

"Please, you put your arm out above head."

Before Matt could get a chance to obey the instruction and put his arms – he assumed both arms even though the guy just said "arm" –

above his head, two of the goons launched towards him, taking an arm each and slowly guiding them towards some handles that seemed to randomly pop out from underneath the table.

"Spread legs please," the guy said to him, and the goons strapped his hands to the handles.

The goons then moved down towards his legs and strapped his ankles to another two handles that had popped out at the bottom of the table. Matt was now lying on the table like a starfish as if he was in a mental institution or something. He was unable to move. As he looked at the faces around him, wondering why this was necessary, the goons then restricted his movement even further by attaching a wide leather strap across his chest.

Then the big man spoke in English to Chink with amusement in his voice.

"OK, do you want to play doctor and nurse?"

Chink, all excited, nodded her head.

"Yes, I want. Yes, me nurse, you doctor," she said while giggling.

Matt was terrified.

"Erm, OK. So, let's go with no on this one. I want to get up now, please. I don't want to play your doctors and nurses game."

Chink continued to giggle as the big man stared at Matt.

"I mean it. This is not a fucking game. What are you doing here? Who are you? Please tell me…are you a doctor?"

The big man responded with a resounding negative.

"No, I am not. But we play doctor and nurse. You patient. Don't worry, I work in a pet shop. Don't worry, I very good."

A fucking pet shop? He was in a fucking pet shop? It may have been stuffed with medical equipment, but it was designed for use on animals. Jesus, Matt thought. Human bodies were a little bit bloody different from animal bodies.

With that announcement, Matt went crazy.

"I do not give you permission to do anything to me. You can't do anything to me without my permission. Stop this now. Stop this immediately."

Chink was still going nuts with the giggling and the big man was now smirking. Matt got louder and more assertive.

"I DON'T WANT TO PLAY DOCTORS AND NURSES!"

One of the goons reached over to a side table, pulling over a dirty piece of cloth and using it to gag Matt. His complaints turned to mumbles and he realised that all he could do now was surrender to whatever was about to happen to him. Was he going to be tortured? Is that what prisoners of war feel like?

Matt looked directly at Chink, hoping that the fear in his eyes would appeal to her humanity. She was now at his side, her wandering hands within inches of his bursting penis, ready to take hold of the prize she'd been eyeing up since they left the restaurant.

Matt thought to himself, who says men can't be raped? Not in the traditional sense where a penis enters a vagina without consent, but surely this must count as some form of personal violation akin to rape?

His attention was then yanked over to the big aproned man, who was grasping a huge syringe full to the brim with a brownish, watery substance. Holding it up, he squirted a little of the vile-looking liquid from the needle, and Matt felt this land on his thigh. It wasn't the first watery substance he'd felt trickle down his leg within the space of an hour.

The syringe was the biggest Matt had ever set eyes on. He was pretty sure it was designed for use on one of the bigger animals this vet might have to work with, like an elephant or something that size. There was no way that much of any medicine should be injected into a human in one go. No way. He shouted, but all that came out of his mouth were muffles. The situation was totally out of his bound hands now.

And then it hit Matt that this probably wasn't even a legitimate vet surgery, but probably something like an ivory dealer or some other shady shit.

It was now Chink's moment. She threw her hands out, joy written across her face, taking hold of the giant penis as the big aproned man moved in for the kill. He shoved the needle straight into the side of Matt's penis where it had bulged out like a beer belly.

Matt didn't feel a thing though. It was the oddest thing seeing that happening but not feeling it. He thought that must be what it's like in a hospital when a doctor asks someone after an accident if they can feel pain in one of their arms or legs but they can't. They can see instruments touching the limb, but nothing.

The needle in his penis, the liquid drained millimetre by millimetre, every bit of the brown substance entering his bloodstream. Quickly, he started to feel a burning sensation all over his body as the stuff coursed through his veins. And then it was over.

Matt dropped his head in relief, one of the goons removing the gag and allowing Matt to breathe properly. The big aproned man took the syringe away and started to do something with it. Matt couldn't see what though.

Matt looked up at Chink who was still holding his penis in her hands.

"Erm, you can let go now. It's finished. It's over."

Then it suddenly occurred to him that perhaps it wasn't quite over yet. He looked over to see what was being done with the syringe, but the big man's back was blocking his view.

Chink was reluctant to let go of his dick, and even if there was more to come Matt would rather she'd let go of it in the interim. His hands and legs were still tied so he couldn't push her away.

"Yes, that's it. Let it go. Let it go free. Come on now."

Chink slowly and reluctantly let go of the now limp but still swollen penis, placing it into Matt's untamed bed of pubic hair. She looked absolutely gutted like it had died and that she was in mourning. Christ, this chick was mental.

Matt was so relieved, hoping that his penis had been saved and that no permanent damage had been done. No penis funeral would be needed today.

As he lay there on the table he imagined his penis in a little cardboard box being buried in his back garden like people do when they bury a budgie or some other small pet that's passed away. Then his thoughts got darker as he called into mind the 1983 horror film *Pet Sematary*, imagining that same buried penis coming back to life to fuck him up. He shuddered.

The goons unstrapped Matt and he was able to sit up. Chink and the goons left the room giving Matt some space while he got himself together. Was this now over? He thought so.

"Hey, apron guy."

The big man turned around. Matt was in need of a favour before he left.

"Before I go, I'll do you a trade. My shitty trousers for your nice, clean ones?"

The guy's trousers weren't totally clean, but he was about the same size as Matt and they looked like some cheap beige chinos that he wouldn't miss.

The guy sized up Matt's trousers, walking behind him to check the label. He saw that they were indeed expensive trousers even if they were in a bit of a state.

"Yes, nice trade. They are dirty, but I clean."

Matt couldn't believe his luck. He had undoubtedly been chancing it, but the guy was actually keen. Sweet.

The guy whipped off his trousers passing them to Matt, and vice versa. Matt nodded in thanks as he started to put on the guy's trousers.

"Ohh, hang on. Here, I need to do this."

He grabbed Matt's dick and slapped a plaster on the side where he'd stuck the needle in. A little stream of blood had run out of the needle prick.

"There, all finished. Have a nice day."

Matt didn't flinch as the guy grabbed his penis to apply the plaster. His dick was free for all here in China. It had become everyone's, but that was OK because it was now cured of Arthur's magic powder and that was all that mattered right now. He pulled the trousers up and went to meet Chink and the goons in the corridor.

As they left the building some random in a dirty apron Matt hadn't seen before was pulling the security bars open for them. He enjoyed this new sensation of not having a giant bulge in his trousers. As they made for the car he could feel some sensation returning and was also able to walk properly again. It was a miracle.

The drive back to the restaurant was more relaxed, Chink minding her own business and not trying to get in about his penis the whole time like a horny teenager.

Chapter 24 – Back At The Party

Once back at the restaurant Matt had a spring in his step once more. He felt a bit more himself now. Whatever that was he'd been injected with back there had given him a new lease of life and he felt on top – ish – of the world.

Arthur and Chris saw them come back in. Arthur was the first to approach Matt.

"Ah, you back. How are you feeling?"

Chris nodded as if to repeat Arthur's question. He smiled and winked at them both.

It seemed as if time had stood still while he had been gone. Nothing had happened, everyone sitting in silence waiting for them. Chris turned to Matt.

"Son, I'm so pleased you're OK. How did it go? Did you win?"

Matt replied, "Dad, let's just put it this way. It's better left in the 'let's not talk about it' box, just like the rest of this cursed country. Is that OK?"

Chris smiled and nodded. "Sounds like a plan."

At that they both turned towards Mr. Hwong.

Some instrumental music started to play. With a command from Mr. Hwong, the henchmen all scrambled to pull out red velvet chairs for Matt, Chris, Arthur and Won. All of a sudden these grim-faced bastards were all smiles and couldn't be more obliging to their guests. Three of them took the seats that had been pulled out for them. As he plonked his arse down, Matt noticing that his chair stank of a combo of stagnant water, mouldy cheese and dried out alcohol. Won hung back though. Arthur signalled for him to take a seat but he quietly said something and took a step back, standing there like a guard, arms behind his back.

Arthur turned to Chris and Matt. "He say that he not comfortable sitting down. It not honourable for him sit at the table next to his masters."

Matt didn't want to argue with the hierarchy in operation here, but he felt sorry that Won felt unworthy of sitting next to him at a table to eat. It made him feel like an elitist crumb as it had the night Won had refused to come into the hotel to sleep. He turned and smiled sympathetically at Won, winking. Won didn't react and Matt felt like a fool.

Even so, Matt turned and looked around the room, taken by a sense of calm. At least as much of a sense of calm as he'd been able to feel over the past few days. Now that it seemed as if the worst parts of the day and the entire trip had passed them by, and that this was one business deal back on the track it should be on, Matt was convinced that the only way was up from there. Thankfully, the only way was not up for his penis, which was now firmly soft, down, and tucked away where it can't cause any further trouble. Matt looked across the table at Arthur who must have been reading his thoughts. Arthur held up his index finger rigid and then folded it over, smiling and nodding. Clearly, he was indicating that he was pleased for Matt that his penis was fixed.

There was some awkward silence at the table. Matt and his dad both looked around the table at the henchmen, quickly diverting their glances once eyes met. Whenever Matt caught himself making eye contact with one of these guys, he felt like he was attacked with a death ray. It had been the same ever since they'd come into each other's lives, albeit temporarily.

Realising that things were feeling a bit strained, Matt posed some pleasantries to Hwong looking directly at him while speaking English. He had considered speaking to Chink who would obviously then translate, but he felt that it would be a mark of real respect to direct the question at Hwong. After they had gotten some polite chit chat out of the way – polite chit chat that Hwong had been entirely unresponsive to – there was a lull in the conversation that Chris took advantage of.

Turning to Matt, Chris said, "Right, my boy, you're up now. Close this down for us, make us some money, and get us the hell home." Chris had said this last part a little more hushed than the rest of it so as not to seem desperate to get out of there, which they of course were.

Matt was thankful that his dad had intervened at this point as his ability to make polite conversation was starting to dry up. In fact, Chris had fielded much of the speaking until now, but he was absolutely right. It was Matt's show now, and there were some finer details of the deal that still had to be discussed with Hwong.

Chris stood up. "Excuse me, gentlemen, I need to freshen up a little. Please allow my son to talk over things with you while I retire to the shithouse for some time."

His dad now gone, this was Matt's turn to shine and make his dad proud. He jumped into action, going through all of the logistics of the deal with Hwong. He and his dad had been through so much in such a short space of time he didn't care to risk any other disasters. For that reason Matt made sure not to glaze over any aspect of the deal whatsoever, covering the most minute details however insignificant they seemed. At the same time he was conscious of avoiding boring the man to death, so he used succinct language, careful not to ramble. He was totally numb by now, and there would be no more embarrassment. This deal would be closed within the next few hours.

Matt looked around at the surrounding tables.

"Have you lost something, Mr. Matt?" asked Chink.

"Do you have a pen and paper by any chance? I can't seem to find the notepad I had with me."

Chink said something to the closest goon in Chinese. In two seconds what he needed arrived in front of him. With this, he was able to sketch a crate and write down the relevant measurements: 3.2m x 1m x 1m. This was the size of the crate they'd be using.

"Now, Mr. Hwong, what needs to happen is that these steel parts have to go to Iran, and then they have to be delivered to Tehran. The plan is as follows. As you're well aware, we own a neon museum called God's Own Junkyard…"

Chink relayed this to Hwong, who smirked. Of course he bloody knew.

"So, I'm going to send you a crate containing a neon sign from there. What I need you to do is pack the steel parts in with the neon sign. It is absolutely crucial that you ensure all the parts are packed in that one crate. The reason for this is that it'll simply be easier to transport. The more crates there are, the more suspicion we're likely to raise. Thus, one it is."

As Chink translated Matt's instructions, Hwong nods in agreement, responding briefly. Plain sailing, Matt thought.

"Yes, he agrees with all of this. Excellent," Chink said as Hwong turned to one of his associates. They also nodded to show their agreement.

By the look on their faces and their positive tone of voice, Matt believed the men were impressed with his understanding of how to ship goods through customs. Perhaps he was even teaching them a thing or two.

"As you are all well aware, all of this must fly successfully under the radar. It cannot be intercepted, and it cannot be detected. If either happens we're all fucked up the proverbial arse."

The men stared at Matt once Chink had done what Matt imagined was her level best to describe "proverbial arse" to them.

"Pardon my French," Matt said. He figured that would confuse them even more. They continued to stare, so he took this to mean it had.

Arthur interjected. "It will be my job to arrange the certificates necessary for the goods to get through the Tianjin port."

"They trust you to do what needs to be done," said Chink. Hwong and the suits engaged in some conversation amongst themselves which didn't look too serious. Arthur was taking in his surroundings. He also had fear etched into his face. It appeared that even he was totally out of his depth here. Matt could see that he was trying to hide it though. At some point he'd told Matt never to let these men see his fear because it just gives something to take advantage of, but growing up in East London that was a concept with which Matt was very familiar. His dad had taught him the exact same thing when he was younger, and not just for situations where he'd be facing up to trouble, a bully, or the likes. He had taught him this to use in many different situations, even the swimming.

Matt followed Arthur's lead, looking around the room. He didn't really need to look anywhere to register the awful, damp stench that filled the air. It reminded him of a sweaty football boot, which is never a fun scent to have lingering in your nose. As he'd thought earlier, it was pretty similar to the first restaurant he and Chris had been to in Beijing with Arthur, only much larger. It was also a lot darker, which was likely a conscious effort to hide how grubby the place was. It hadn't been opened to the public that night. Whoever the hell it was that owned the place Matt never found out, but this lot certainly had the sway to keep it empty for the night. He wondered if it was actually company owned or if Hwong and his goons were simply the types not to be messed with, that whenever they entered a restaurant, the owners, management, and staff were forced to bend over backwards for them just to keep out of bother.

As the conversation between Hwong and his suits continued, as Arthur looked around vacantly, and as Chris continued his seemingly extended vacation at the bathroom, Matt felt increasingly uncomfortable. Everything seemed to be going their way, but it didn't negate the awkwardness of dealing with these folks. He sat there twiddling his thumbs, half hoping that somebody would speak to him to break the awkwardness, and half hoping that everyone would just leave him in peace. Matt wondered if the evening was going to be over quickly, or if it would be a long and drawn out affair. He prayed that it would be the former, but something told him that it might be otherwise. When would the food be arriving?

As if his mind was being read once more, a side door swung open and Matt turned around expecting to see trays of food being brought their way. It was just his dad though, returning from his extended adventure to the toilet. Matt looked at Chris questioningly, but he was just met with a little shake of the head. Obviously, his dad hadn't gone through the same as he had when he'd been in the same toilet earlier. As Chris took his seat, Matt turned to the sound of another door swinging open. This time, it was food. It wasn't that Matt was starving or looking forward to whatever delights were likely to be brought their way, it was more the case that he was looking forward to having something to do instead of sitting there while everyone talked among themselves.

Plate after plate of food was plonked down on the table, some of it recognisable based on the stuff they'd been eating thus far on the trip and some of it completely unfamiliar. Matt sighed internally, wondering why this so-called Chinese hospitality was required. The deal was closed, so why the fuck couldn't they just go? He was so keen to get out of dodge. Matt was about to dip into the least offensive looking dish on the table when a valuable nugget of information popped into his head. He looked around the table at the others who were all waiting for something.

Of course, Matt remembered. They could only begin eating after the host – Hwong on this occasion – had begun. Matt had learned the same respect and honour the night before, and even though it had been awful, he was pleased that he'd had that as a practice session. Because they weren't just with Arthur now, it was like being in a pressure cooker making sure not to go against the customs of this country. Matt thought this was mind before matter – or, in his case, mind before Matt. There always had to be a little time for humour in adverse circumstances.

Once they were permitted to eat Matt did so without complaint or question. He tucked into the spring rolls at first, and coming to the conclusion that they were OK a hunger was awakened in him that he hadn't realised had been lying dormant. It made sense because, despite everything that had been going on, it had actually been a while since he'd put any food in his belly. And he really went for it, not thinking about what he was shoving down his gob and not really caring to be honest. They were alive and the end was so close.

It did enter Matt's mind once or twice that the food or drinks could be poisoned, but then he convinced himself this was just paranoia talking. If the men wanted to kill them they'd have done it earlier instead of sitting through the rest of the night with them. Matt and Chris knocked back the drinks, given this was about the only thing getting them through. At first all they were drinking was some beer-like beverage which had a weaker but still hoppy taste to it. Perhaps it was just really shite beer, but it reminded Matt of something. Probably just the watered-down beer you used to get in some tight pubs in London back in the day.

As the food and libations were brought out, and as empty dishes and glasses were replaced by fuller ones, the room was filled with nothing other than the sounds of eating and drinking. Matt chowed down on all sorts of things served on dirty plates and using chopsticks that had clearly been used without being washed afterwards. It was vile. This time his hosts were less inclined to explain every dish as Arthur had done, but customs other than waiting for your host to eat first were apparent. Although Matt was keen to get out of there, observing these customs was a truly fascinating part of the night for him.

One had truly caught his attention more than any of the others. After about fifteen minutes of chowing down, a selection of small baskets with lids was brought out to the table. Matt was engaged in conversation with Chink who had got pissed as a fart insanely fast and was making little sense, so he was distracted. The sound of conversation, eating, and drinking had now turned into a rabble, but that rabble was soon replaced by the sound of intense clapping. At that Matt turned from Chink and towards Mr. Hwong. He'd put some of the contents of the baskets into his bowl, and when he lifted some to his mouth with his chopsticks people were clapping in celebration. Why on earth would they congratulate a man for eating something? It must have been donkey's balls or something equally gross. It surely couldn't be any more disgusting than that anyhow.

But oh how Matt couldn't be further from the truth. Once the clapping quietened down a little he was able to hear some sounds coming from the baskets. The sounds were very gentle but definitely distinguishable as little squeaks and chirps. Oh, good lord, Matt thought, this guy is eating something live. When Hwong next took the lid off one of the baskets Matt's fears were confirmed. Sat before him was a pile of live chicks and mice, He was horrified. As he looked closer, it became apparent that these animals were not only alive but looked as if they had just been born. The chicks were still wet as if they had just hatched minutes before, writhing around trying to get their legs. The mouse pups were so pink it looked as if they had been skinned, but Matt knew that's just how newborn mice looked. He had a scientist pal who operated on them as part of his research, and he'd shown Matt a couple of pictures of them once or twice.

So, there was Hwong, lifting these poor, defenceless little creatures to his mouth and then chewing away to his heart's content before gulping them down. When Hwong began to chew everyone began to clap once again, but while the sound of the clapping was just as loud as it had been before, Matt could hear it all. It was as if he couldn't help but drown out all of the other sounds around him, concentrating on the squelching and crunching of the animals being torn apart in the fat man's mouth. It took every ounce of his willpower not to hurl all over the table in front of him. This was next level repulsive.

Matt turned to his dad and whispered, "Oh my god, I'm not sure if I can sit and listen to much more of this."

"Listen to it? Son, I think we're gonna have to follow suit and eat one of these poor little fuckers."

"Are you shitting me? No, surely not. Do you think?"

"Son, I don't think it. I know it."

Chris motioned his head towards Hwong who was pointing Matt towards the baskets. Jesus, Matt thought, the whale was honouring his guest by offering him what was likely a real delicacy. You hear about this sort of stuff, especially in Asian countries, but you never think you're going to be faced with it; with the prospect of putting a live animal in your mouth. The idea of eating, say, a fried cockroach on a stick in Thailand was bad enough, but this? IT WAS ALIVE FOR CHRIST'S SAKE.

"Dad, no. No way, mate. I can't. I just can't, Dad."

"Matt, we're at the final hurdle now. The finish line is so close I can almost taste the white paint of the ground indicating that it's time to go home. Please do not fuck it up now. Just eat one of those little things."

Matt just stared into his dad's eyes like a sad puppy. Chris stared back at him with resolve, occasionally looking over at Hwong, smiling and nodding to show his offer will be accepted. Chris's voice, now less of a whisper, was getting stern.

"Son, come on. You got to do what he wants. He's the CEO. Plus, if you don't eat what he wants he might eat you."

Chris smirked, trying to make light of the situation. Matt thought that if he had to eat one then so would his dad. That made him feel marginally better about the whole thing. He gave himself a pep talk.

"I think I'll take one of the mice. They look like little chunks of cured meat. Yeah, cured meat. That's what it is, Matt," he convinced himself, as his hand hovered over the box, making sure that he was making the right choice. Oh, and what a choice this was. Of course, he was exaggerating, but he felt just like Meryl Streep's titular character in the film *Sophie's Choice*, selecting which of her children to live and which to be sent off to be gassed. He finally moved towards one of the mice, deciding that it looked like the lesser of two evils.

Matt picked up the little thing as it wriggled about, all eyes on him. Holding a full, cold beer in the other hand, he just went for it, dropping the creature in his mouth, but there was zero chance he was going to chew on it as Hwong had done. He kept it there in his mouth, feeling it moving around, and almost lifted his drink to wash it down in one. It suddenly occurred to him that, if he did that, the mouse would be in his stomach alive. The mere thought of a baby animal crawling around inside him was enough to make him reconsider. The most reasonable part of him knew that the animal would suffocate long before it got to Matt's stomach, but still. He knew what he was going to have to do. Using his tongue to feel about, he found the animal's head. Using his tongue again, he turned it around so that its head was wedged between his molars. Here goes, he thought. And crunch. No more movement. With a large gulp of beer, the mouse was gone, and the room was filled with applause. Matt downed the rest of the beer hoping that was the only one he'd be required to eat.

Next, it was Chris's turn, but Matt just couldn't bear to watch. He munched on some less offensive foods to remove the mousey taste from his mouth and produced the sound of screaming in his head to block out the much worse sound of chewing. His dad was doing as Hwong had done. What a trooper.

The food and drinks didn't stop coming for at least four hours after that. This was definitely no ordinary dinner going on here, by Chinese standards anyhow. This was nothing short of a celebratory feast, and it looked set to last the entire night. It got to a point in the night where everyone simultaneously needed to take a break from eating, but nobody seemed keen on taking a break from the boozing. Many a belly was being rubbed and many a libation knocked back.

Chink had begun to sing to herself throughout the festivities, amusing herself and annoying nobody it seemed. Matt was surprised by this, assuming that she wouldn't ordinarily be allowed to act like this being Hwong's subordinate, but perhaps the rules for employees were different when it came to celebratory occasions like this. It was no different in the UK really, at Christmas parties for instance, but usually, there was a level of drunkenness an employee wouldn't usually go past, and Chink had definitely gone past that.

All of a sudden the singing ceased as Chink slammed her hands down on the table and started squealing excitedly. The sound reminded Matt of the squeaking of the mice, which had now all incidentally been eaten. His stomach turned a little.

"I have very good idea, Matt. We play drinking game."

Chink turned around to one of the waitresses and ordered something. Soon, that same waitress brought back two bottles of Baijiu, a distilled Chinese liquor that was almost identical to vodka. Before Matt could even ask what the game involved, Chink produced a deck of cards from her handbag and he assessed it was undoubtedly to be some sort of card game. Well done, Sherlock, he congratulated himself. Matt shouldn't have even contemplated asking what the game involved anyhow because it wasn't like he was actually about to refuse to participate. A challenge had been put to him and that challenge would have to be accepted, as everything else that had been offered to him that night had to be accepted. Squeak, chirp.

Chink said something to Hwong and the goon who sat closest to her and they rallied around. Ah, Matt realised, this game wasn't just for him and Chink but for a small group.

"Right, then, what are we doing here?"

Chink started to explain the nature of the game to Matt. Chris listened intently to show respect even though he hadn't been asked to join in the game for some reason. She told him that it was a traditional Chinese drinking game known as card counting. Matt was amused by the name of the game given that the strategy of card counting used in blackjack was frowned upon in any casinos he'd been to. This sort of card counting wouldn't be the same though.

The rules of card counting were such that the dealer is tasked with counting between one and thirteen as he or she places shuffled cards one at a time face up on the table. If the dealer happens to say the same number as the one on the card being placed down at that moment, then every other player must rush to slap the deck of cards. The last player to slap the deck of cards must knock back their drink. Pretty standard drinking game to be fair, Matt thought. However, as Chink elaborated, it became clear that, as an added punishment for coming last, the loser must accept a dare decided upon by the rest of the players. Ah, so this was going to involve some pretty disgusting stuff, Matt assumed.

As Chink finished explaining the rules, she indicated to the goons to begin pouring drinks. One of them stood up and filled the glasses of all seven players full to the brim. Matt took a brief sip of the liquor to know what he was dealing with, but it didn't really matter as he was generally able to handle his booze. Anyway, he was already pretty wasted, so he could take whatever was coming his way. And this Baijiu didn't seem ridiculously strong. Matt felt confident, but then Chink called the waitress back and seemed annoyed as she pointed at the table.

Arthur then explained. "She didn't bring all the right drinks for the game. This is just plain Baijiu. We need special Baijiu and many other drinks."

"Oh," Matt exclaimed. "What else do we need, Chink?"

Chink ignored him, but the mysterious drinks soon arrived at the table and the game could begin. As the game went on, as cards were slammed down on the table, and as Matt's reactions were slow, he finally got to find out what it was that he was knocking back. Chink explained each drink to him with help from Arthur's translation before he was forced to down it.

The first was what they called "three penis wine". This was the same Baijiu drink that the waitress had brought out earlier, but this stuff was mixed with a number of curious ingredients. Some of these were derived from the penises of three different animals: dogs, deer, and rams. This was mixed with stuff that came from centipedes, and then the rest was fairly normal: rock sugar and a five-spice powder. Matt had come to distrust mysterious Chinese powders, especially when the word penis was bandied around at the same time. Bad memories, and ones that were still fresh. The second was "snake wine". In general with this stuff, live venomous snakes are placed into jars of rice alcohol (known as Huanjiu) and left to drown in there. Pretty dark but unsurprising, Matt thought. The poison from the snakes is then released into the alcohol and it gets broken down. The third and fourth drinks were variations of the second one, only instead of snake venom the booze was infused with snake blood, or it had been scorpions that had drowned in the alcohol and not snakes. The fifth drink was what Chink referred to as "three lizard liquor".

You can use your imagination for that one, but apparently the more lizards – or geckos for that matter – in one drink the better. Or at least that's what Chink said, claiming that it is traditionally believed to prevent evil spirits from causing a person harm. Matt wondered why he hadn't been introduced to this stuff the minute he and his dad had touched down in China, as some of the crap that had gone down might have been the work of evil spirits. And with the sixth drink, baby mice were making their second appearance of the night. This stuff was "baby mice wine", a rice wine product with baby mice drowned in it and fermented for at least one year. Yum yum. Finally, there was "giant centipede whisky", which was just as it sounds: whisky with giant centipedes in it.

Matt drank every single one of the concoctions, and most of them weren't as awful as a person might imagine. Chink's reactions were about as slow as Matt's so she didn't win many rounds, but Hwong's reactions were as fast as lightning. He'd been throwing back the alcohol just as much as the rest of them, but he was a much, much bigger guy after all, so he wasn't as sloshed as everyone else around him. Once Hwong had tired of the game, he waved his hand and one of the goons cleared the cards away. That was that. The master had spoken.

Hwong let out a twisted laugh, pointing at Chink, then to Matt, and then to the stage at the back of the restaurant. Chink grabbed Matt's hand, giggling, and pulled him, stumbling. The booby prize, Matt thought. This was it. Karaoke. He despised karaoke. So much worse than anything else Hwong could have concocted.

The stage was raised from the rest of the room, surrounded by blue and pink neon lighting. Matt noticed the shoddy quality of the neon signs and felt proud of the standards he and his dad operated by creating their pieces. As they neared the stage, a waiter rushed to flick on a switch and further neon lights came on. One sign was a huge microphone and the other was a smaller guitar.

Matt turned to his dad. "Save my soul."

"Oh son. Not my problem," Chris said with joy at not being in Matt's position.

Chris laughed hard as Matt reluctantly warbled away with Chink, bashing out a couple of karaoke classics. First, a dreadful rendition of "Purple Rain" by Prince, followed by a slightly better – but still screechy – rendition of Madonna's "Like a Prayer". Then came the worst of the three. "Islands in the Stream" by Kenny Rogers and Dolly Parton. With each song, Matt tried to edge away, but Chink wouldn't let go of his hand.

The music the two of them made together was far from beautiful, but for the first time on the trip Matt was letting loose. Despite his embarrassment, he couldn't help but feel good about that. They followed with a bit of "Up Where we Belong" by Joe Cocker and Jennifer Warner, which was a better effort than anything else they'd delivered. They never got to finish it though, as Chink had to run to the toilet to throw up. Matt was OK with that result and headed back to the table where Chris and Arthur patted him on the back for being a good sport. He took a long swig.

Matt noticed that one of the neon signs to the left of the stage was flickering; this messed with his professional inclinations towards repairing it. But he managed it. Nothing strange should happen at this point. Well, nothing stranger than the things that Matt had been witnessing until now.

Everyone was still drinking, and about six hours into the party more food and drinks came their way. Matt's guts began to turn again. He discreetly disappeared off to the loo halfway through the meal, praying to god the events of earlier wouldn't repeat themselves once again. Nobody followed this time, trust finally seemingly established between everyone. Thankfully, it turned out that this was a standard toilet visit. Although, after the amount of booze consumed, things were hardly solid down below. Yet, Matt managed to keep his new trousers free of stains before returning to the restaurant. He was now well versed in using these holes in the ground to do his business.

Chapter 25 – Who's The Boss

When Matt was back at the table things had fallen quiet and Chris was indicating towards a door at the side. Everyone seemed to be looking in the same direction. Out of a back room came a multicoloured creature. Unlike everyone else who were dressed in suits, this guy was flamboyantly clad in some fabulous silk gown that could not have been intended for a man to wear. It was bright orange with bats of all different sizes and colours all over it. Matt assumed that he was getting away with wearing something like that – whether he was gay or just really bloody confident in his sexuality to wear whatever the hell he wants – because nobody dares to cross him. It reminded Matt of the gay pirate played by Robert De Niro in that film *Stardust*, only he kept his penchant for dressing in ladies clothing from his crew. As if a brightly coloured silk gown wasn't quite enough, from the top of it stuck out a plume of peacock feathers. They pushed up around his neck making him look like a wonderfully campy Ming the Merciless of Flash Gordon fame. It might not have been up Matt's street, but it was quite something.

As the guy neared them Chink stepped forth and held her arm out towards the man speaking to him in English – as much as she could in her inebriated state.

"Mr. Henri."

Ahhhhhh, Matt thought, as he recalled the name. This was the guy that he had first communicated with by email, the only one that had got back to him to say his company was able to make the deal with him. He'd also been the one who'd dropped that terrible news that Matt would need to bring the tooling with him, but that had all worked out just fine in the end. Matt thought back to his email chats with this guy, whoever he was. The emails written from Henri had been in broken yet understandable English, so Matt thought perhaps this portion of the evening with this guy might go a bit more in their favour with the conversation conducted in English. Relying on Arthur had been a bit of a fuck up until this point, and Matt was glad that they might finally speak directly with their new business partners.

As Chris shook Henri's hand and nodded, he muttered to Matt under his breath. "This is the true boss, son."

"How'd you know that, Dad?"

"It just is, Matt. Who the fuck else would get away with wearing this shit?"

Matt observed that Henri was the only one who looked wealthy here, so much so that he actually had a healthy, colourful glow that complemented his outlandish robe. The others were pale and looked drawn out like they hadn't slept or like they were on drugs. They were all wearing cheap clothes, cheap suits, cheap shoes, and cheap watches – if they were even wearing one at all. Their hair was dishevelled and it felt like Matt and his dad were dealing with peasants. He hadn't really noticed the state of them before until there was this comparison.

Henri extended his hand to Matt too, again smiling. If this is the real boss, then what the hell had been going on the rest of this time? Who had they been running the gauntlet against thus far?

It suddenly came to Matt that his danger assessment earlier had been a little inaccurate. The scores he'd given Hwong and Lophead could perhaps be reduced by a digit or two because Mr. Henri was clearly the head honcho, the "Big Boss" as they call it in video games. Everything they'd gone through right up until the restaurant had been testing them, which again was so far from being a normal part of business deals it was utterly insane.

There was an excruciating silence, finally ended by Henri. It turned out that his English wasn't that broken after all. Matt now assumed he hadn't actually been communicating with Mr. Henri originally. Either he'd got someone else – an assistant or the like – to compose the emails on his behalf, or his spoken English was far better than his written English. The guy barely even had an accent as he addressed Chris.

"Mr. Chris Bracey, I have great admiration for you."

Chris smiled, clearly pleased at the compliment but surprised that Henri knew of him. Perhaps his reputation preceded him.

Henri went on. "In your country, I understand that you are a very well-connected man and a very powerful one at that. But may I say, you are no longer in Soho. You are now in my country, China."

Now Chris's mouth fell open at the same time as Matt's did. This had been his deal, and he'd barely mentioned a thing about his dad. How on earth did this Henri fella know about Chris's reputation back at home? Did they have some kind of file on the two of them? If so, man, do these people do their due diligence.

Chris was about to open his mouth to question Henri when the Big Boss put his hand up to silence him. "It is not your turn to speak, Mr. Chris."

Oh fuck, Matt thought. Where's this going? But, at that point, a twist in the tale that neither he or his dad had anticipated.

"CHINATOWN," Henri yelled loudly.

There was a connection between them. Fuck, fuck, fuckity fuck. This couldn't be good.

"Ah, yes. Did you think that I did not know who you were? Aye, you did, didn't you? Hmm?"

Chris raised his eyebrows, honestly clueless as to what Henri was on about. Chinatown? Matt thought about the business, and sure, his dad had been involved in some dealings in Chinatown. It was right next to Soho after all, so he'd done a lot of the neon signs there as well, but he couldn't think of any events that would get the pair of them in trouble.

"You look confused, Mr. Chris. Are you confused?"

"Well..."

Henri cut Chris off. "I said, it is not your turn to speak yet."

Matt couldn't help but think that it clearly was Chris's turn to speak given that Henri had posed him a question. Christ, this guy was a true psychopath. But it was hard to take a psychopath seriously when they're dripping in orange silk and when their plumage collar ruffles as they get all worked up. But take this guy seriously they must.

"Mr. Chris, do you remember the Crazy 5? Aye? Hmm?"

Chris looked to the side, scrunching his forehead, clearly thinking back to his business dealings in Chinatown. Matt ran through the ones he knew of too. He'd never heard of any organisation called the Crazy 5. Perhaps Henri was referring to this old Chinese family his dad had encountered years before. He was certain his dad had told him about this at some point. There were five guys, perhaps all brothers or some of them cousins, but all definitely members of the same family. They had been known for the fact there were five of them, yeah, and they were all pretty dangerous, but the Crazy 5? Matt just couldn't recall if that's what they'd been called. Anyhow, the family owned a Chinese restaurant there, and they'd commissioned neon signs for next to their door. They'd been very specific about it not going above the door which was suspicious.

Chris, no longer scrunching his forehead, seemed to know exactly what Henri was referring to. He opened his mouth to speak once again, but Henri raised a finger to his lips.

"Ah, aye. You know just who I'm talking about, don't you?"

Chris froze, daring not to attempt any further responses to questions Henri clearly didn't want answers to. Instead, he simply stood there in silence.

"They are my cousins. Aye, Mr. Chris, my cousins, and you know who they are."

Henri's clothes may have made it difficult to take him seriously, but the way he spoke really didn't help very much either. Every time he rounded off a sentence the last word would be drawn out, his long and winding voice making these words continue like echoes. It was all terribly theatrical. The silence from everyone else just made it all the more like this was a play and that they were audience members gripped by the drama.

"So, Mr. Chris. If you remember correctly, I think you did, in fact, shit on my cousins. Yes? Is it not true that you took their neon sign because you accused them of not paying? Aye, Mr. Chris? Aye?"

It was then that Matt recalled the remaining details his dad had told them about that lot and they most certainly had been called the Crazy 5. Chris had done exactly what Henri was suggesting that he'd done. They had failed to pay their bill for over two months for the latest work he'd done for them. A sign repair, Matt thought. Whatever it had been, the total bill had come to just over £1000, which would be about right for a sign repair. Chris, of course, wanted the money, but they got sick of him coming to try to collect and had threatened him with violence should he be stupid enough to re-enter Chinatown, even if not to chase them up. How mental was that, to expect him just to give up all his business there because they didn't want to pay a bill that wasn't even that expensive. Crazy was the right word for them.

One morning, some weeks later, they'd got to the restaurant and the sign had vanished in the night without a trace. Chris heard through the backburner that they'd replaced the sign with one bought from a Hungarian company undercutting Chris significantly. The only trouble is the Hungarian lot botched the sign, placing one word on it in English. Chris hadn't known this at the time, unaware of what the Chinese symbols on the sign meant, but it had indicated that the restaurant was upstairs. They had been so adamant that it shouldn't go above the door because they wanted to make it seem like it belonged to the shop next door. The council clocked on to the fact that there was a restaurant up there after some of their officers got a bit suspicious while out on foot patrol, and it came out the place was illegal and unlicensed. Of course, that meant they had been shut down immediately. The Crazy 5 had got into a brutal bust-up with the council guys who came around to close the place, the police were called and every one of them was arrested. The eventual outcome was the lot of them being deported back to China.

Mr. Henri stared at Chris. "Now it's your turn to speak. So, what do you have to say to me about this? It is your fault they were sent back to China. It is your fault they lost their home and their business in London. They knew it was you who stole the sign. I know it was you too. So speak."

Matt looked at his dad as he maintained eye contact with Henri, refusing to break it. There was absolutely no way this nutter would hesitate to kill every single one of them, Arthur and Won too even though they have nothing to do with any of that Crazy 5 business. Matt willed his dad to think fast on his feet or there would be real trouble. What was he going to say? Was it time to crack out the escape plan now? Matt really hoped this could be handled with words rather than fists.

"The Crazy 5? Yeah, I know exactly who they are, Mr. Henri. And yes, I stole the sign because not paying the money you owe is disgusting. With all due respect to you, they were – and I'm assuming still are – complete cunts. As a good businessman what would you do? Huh? Business was quiet at that point and I had counted on the money from their bill to pay for things. I wasn't able to feed my kids and I nearly lost my firm over them. The Crazy 5? Na, more like the five fucking shithouses. They don't even deserve a decent title. So, family connections aside, you tell me that you'd do any differently. Go on."

Matt was glued to the spot. What the hell had his dad just done? He'd practically just signed a death warrant for them all, and it wouldn't be long before a bullet or a knife came their way. Chris was heavy with breath as he awaited Henri's reaction. He'd made a big old bloody gamble playing the obstinate card and there wasn't a chance he didn't know that. Henri twiddled his thumbs for a few seconds before erupting into wild fits of laughter. It was the most hysterical thing Matt had ever heard, but he knew not to trust this as a sign everything was all good. He'd seen moments like this in movies before, you know, where someone is ballsy enough to stand up to the villain. The villain laughs uncontrollably in response, then the ballsy guy starts to laugh too. And BOOM, his head is lopped off quick as you like.

Henri managed to curb his laughter and looked at Chris.

"Oh, you cockney geezers fucking crack me up. Yes, shithouses."

He laughed a little more. Maybe a good sign? Then the solemn tone of voice returns.

"But, Chris, seriously. These guys are my cousins. What is it that you think I should do to avenge them? Aye? Hmm?"

Without thinking about it, Chris came right back at him with the best he could. "Absolutely nothing, that's what I think you should do. You, Mr. Henri, are a businessman. You aren't going to chance losing this deal – which is worth a hell of a lot of money for both you and me – over those wank stains. You're not though, are you? Not reasonably."

Henri looked on now, totally straight-faced and contemplative. He rubbed his chin – which was as smooth as a baby's bum – with his fingers. Matt could see that the apple might not fall far from the tree with Henri, but that he was obviously far more successful than any of his cousins had ever been. They were mere louts while he had some sense about him, so surely he wasn't going to let this deal slip through his chin-stroking fingers.

With all the luck of every casino across the world, Henri began to nod. Cautious of counting their chickens too fast, Matt still expected the worst until the little bundle of silk and feathers slammed his hand on the table smiling.

"OK, the deal must go ahead. You are right, are you not? Aye, I think you are right."

Matt and Chris looked around at all the goons surrounding them. Every one of them was fully prepared to get the gloves out at the drop of a peacock feather and the tension still hadn't lifted.

Henri threw his hands up and shouted something in Mandarin. This was the first time that Matt had noticed Henri had a long gold nail on the little finger of his right hand. It had curled over but it looked about three to four inches in length. Matt was a little repulsed by this but completely unsurprised based on the rest of his outfit. Arthur told them, "The longer the gold nail, the higher up a mafia boss is in China."

Arthur understood the gist of what was said and sighed in relief. This made it clear he'd ordered the goons to stand down. Arthur turned to Matt.

"Mr. Henri, he tell the men to show his guests some respect and that it ridiculous they all still ready to fight. He make them know that all good now."

Mr. Henri stared at Chris for an extended period of time before saying, "Chris, how about you teach me some of this famous cockney rhyming slang of yours from London?"

Matt was taken aback that Henri knew what it was, but then again he had said that he liked cockney geezers after all. He must have picked it up from the Crazy 5 after their spell in London.

He went on, "I have heard a few of the phrases but remind me of some more."

The others around the table were all eyes on Chris, even though they had no idea what he was saying. That's their obedience for you.

"Well, Mr. Henri, why don't you tell me what you know and then we can go from there?" said Chris.

"Ah, good idea, Mr. Chris. It has been good to do business with you because we will both make some bees and honey."

Chris laughed. "Very nice. Very nice indeed. We certainly will make some money."

Henri laughed too. "Yes. And when we make some bees and honey together, perhaps it will come in the form of a goose's neck?"

They both laughed together, as did Matt.

"Yeah, it might very well come as a cheque, Mr. Henri."

The flamboyant Chinese man was getting very excited by this time. "Oh, oh. I know another. Hmm. Yes. Perhaps to let you know the deal has gone well, I will have an associate call you over the dog and bone?"

"Well done. They would probably call me using the phone, yeah."

Matt thought it would be a good idea to get involved in the conversation at this point. "I think we're all a bit elephant's trunk right now, eh?"

Everyone stared at him as he explained. "It means drunk. We're all a bit drunk."

Henri looked blank before bursting out into hysterical laughter. Every goon in the room laughed along maniacally with him, as if they didn't laugh when he found something funny it was a sign of disrespect.

"Well, our Chinese drinks, they are so good that you cannot help but getting a little, how do you say, elephant's drunk?"

"That's the one, Mr. Henri," Chris said as Matt was about to correct him.

"Not a good idea, son," Chris said quietly to Matt smiling.

"Now," Henri practically shouted, clapping his hands together. "I bring the night to a close."

The night? It was almost morning. They had been in the restaurant stuffing their faces, getting pissed, playing games, and singing almost the whole night. The restaurant staff had waited around patiently, and it was clear that they would be leaving when Mr. Henri decided they would be leaving.

"Yeah, I think we all need a little bit of bo-beep...sleep," said Chris.

Henri let out a semblance of a laugh, looking back and forth between Chris and Matt. "But more importantly my new china plates. You know that? My new mates?"

Chris and Matt nodded. Henri continued to speak. "Yes, of course, you do. But more importantly, I need to have a dicky bird with you about the meal. Yes, I need to have a word with you. Well, three dicky birds. Three words. You are paying."

Henri laughed mentally again as Chris and Matt looked at each other. They had to pay for every single person? There were about twenty of the fuckers altogether. It would cost an absolute fortune. All of a sudden the pleasant atmosphere that had developed across the night fell away. Matt was keen not to argue and just to pay as requested, but Chris was more inclined to stand his ground as he had done earlier with regards to the Crazy 5.

"Now, Mr. Henri. We've had a very lovely evening. We settled our differences and we've made a great deal together. I think it would be a tiny bit fairer if we came to some sort of arrangement to split the bill seeing as all of these men here had very little – if anything – to do with the negotiations. What do you say to that?"

At that point a waiter brought the bill. Henri pushed it towards Chris.

"No, no, Mr. Chris. It is much more customary for the guest to pick up the bill when a deal has been closed. That is how it always works and that is how it is going to work tonight too. Understand me?"

As Chris opened the bill, Matt glanced over and saw that it was 7000 Chinese Yuan. Pissed as a parrot and not thinking about the exchange rate, Matt assumed it was $7000.

Arthur finally chimed in. "Chris, I think you should just pay the lucky money."

Chris made moves to stand up for whatever reason.

"Dad, I think we should just…"

Before Matt could finish his sentence, two of the men at the table had jumped up and grabbed Chris's arms.

Chris said, "Hang about, lads, I wasn't…"

Won jumped into action from the side lines thinking there was about to be real trouble. Henri sat there watching with glee the whole time. Sadistic little weirdo, thought Matt. As Won stepped forwards to stand up for Chris, another two men got up from the table to stand in his way. Then the floor screeched with any number of chairs with people getting up to get involved. By now many hands were holding people back, many arms were extended to let people not to make any further advances, and many tempers were frayed. It all seemed just about under control without the need for violence to make its way into the situation until Matt raised his hand to wipe the sweat from his brow. The events had caused a flare-up in his digestive situation and he was feeling as rough as a camel's scrotum once more.

Seeing the raise of the hand as a threat, four of the men with free hands launched at Matt, pinning him against the wall. He almost vomited in their faces, and in a way he wished he had. Chris tried to pull away from the two guys holding him back, but they were as strong as oxen. He couldn't get out of their grip even though he was a beefy guy himself.

While Matt was a big guy too, the four Chinese guys – who were all pretty tiny compared to him – had a good technique and kept him pinned there. Their faces were shaking with anger, which almost made Matt laugh. He didn't have the chance, a hand coming out of nowhere to slap his face so hard that it felt like a million bees stinging his cheek at once. One time wasn't enough for the bastard slapping him like a little girl, and the slaps came in hard and fast. Then, when he stopped, Matt saw his face wasn't filled with anger like the men holding him back. This guy was smiling. This was amusing him. The twisted little fucker was getting off on it. Matt certainly wasn't getting off on any part of it. Never had he found himself pinned against a wall by several Chinese men, being slapped by another, all the while in a river of sweat feeling like he's about to shat.

"Get your fucking hands off my son," Chris shouted.

The men holding both Chris and Matt loosened their grip when Mr. Henri nodded at them to do so. Lophead then decided that he was going to kick Won's head with a loud "hayaaaaaa." The pair of them entered into a full-on kung fu fight, both seemingly as skilled as each other. Legs and arms flailed, both speedy as hell, and both managing to trick each other when you'd least expect it. They were throwing all of the moves Matt had ever seen and then some; all the punches, blocks, and kicks. They were all there: the horse stance, the cat stance, the twist stance, the punch-block-punch, the front kick, the side kick, the roundhouse kick, and all the rest.

Everyone watched the fight unfold like it was planned, like it was a show put on for them. Matt found it really thrilling even if there was the possibility that Won could be fed to the pigs or that all of them could be fed to the pigs for that matter. A drunk Chink sang throughout, swaying back and forth and giggling intermittently. It was absurd.

From the corner of his eye Matt saw Chris drop his hands into his suit jacket pocket. For a short, ridiculous second, Matt envisioned his dad pulling out a 9mm handgun he'd picked up somewhere along the line, but his head was in fantasy land. Out of the pocket Chris pulled a gold bar. Matt was aghast. It looked just like the gold bar they'd all been looking at in the shop window earlier, but it couldn't be the same one because they'd been standing beside the shop the whole time Chris had supposedly gone to the bathroom. It didn't make sense until Matt considered that gold bars were likely standardised. Whatever his intentions had been, Chris had picked up a gold bar from the jewellers on the way back to regroup with them. Had that been his plan from the beginning?

Chris slammed the gold bar down on a table just to his side, stood back, and looked at Mr. Henri smiling. He motioned towards the bar with his hand and waited to see what happened next. The room was filled with silence and stillness, as everyone waited to find out the exact same thing.

Matt, desperate for the silence to break, wondered why nobody was saying anything. Henri remained quiet before beginning to walk towards the table and the gold ceremoniously like a pigeon, his gown dragging across the wooden floor behind them. Hwong stepped out in front of Henri, and he stopped, raising his hand to his ear mysteriously in silence. Without a verbal command Hwong bowed his head to Chris and Matt, stepped to one side and remained there at a half bow. Henri, still continuing with his ceremonious pigeon walk, approached the table and stood before the shiny, gold offering.

Matt and Chris both stood there transfixed by everything that was happening in front of them, wondering if they had accidentally dropped some acid before they'd arrived. But nope, they hadn't. This was one splendid Chinese transvestite putting on quite the show for them whether they wanted it or not. Matt wondered if this was what people meant when they talk about exhibitionism.

Matt flinched for a second as a bright red spot of light from the ceiling bounced off the gold bar. It was one of the brightest things he'd ever seen when the light hit it, almost as bright as the million quid soon to be in their pockets it represented. Matt tried to edge slightly to the left to prevent the gold blinding him, looking at one of the goons as he did so. His grimace told Matt that he should remain just where he was, so he stuck to that spot thinking that he was firmly in his dad's hands now.

The tension in the room was high which was the oddest thing given that nothing had happened. It was definitely palpable though, so Matt could feel himself preparing for the fight to kick off again. He looked to his right and Won looked set for battle, one leg forward as if he was ready to pounce at any minute. Arthur had his head raised, war face on, and Chris's hands were at his sides, tensed, and ready to go should this tension erupt into violence.

The silence in the room wasn't just ordinary silence, it was the sort of silence that unquestionably spelled trouble. Matt could even hear that the henchmen remained dead still, frightened to breathe audibly. Perhaps that was why it was such an eerie silence, so many bodies in the room but not a single breath to be heard. It was really as if they were unconscious or even dead, and that was a terrifying thought to Matt who considered he and his dad may very well soon be in either one of those states. There was no way that silence like that was caused by anything other than a paralysing fear of death at the hands of the brightly coloured Big Boss. Was he so incredibly dangerous and evil that nobody dares to carry out the most basic of human functions like breathing? It was like some freaky circus act. It made Matt realise that fear was how these big shots like Henri controlled their minions.

The glinting gold was the least of Matt's problems at this moment in time, as the flickering neon over by the karaoke machine grabbed his attention again. It was agitating him more than it should have done under such tense circumstances, but he knew that if he was to head over to fix it he might end up with a knife in his back. He considered it one more time, but as he was about to step forwards one of the henchmen gently shook his head and Matt saw this in the mirror ahead of them. Right, he told himself, enough of your OCD nonsense, Matt.

Chris finally broke the silence as he also threw down cash on the table. "Mr. Henri, we'll pay, and this gold bar is for you. Put a stop to this."

Raising his arm, Lophead backed off and Won stood down too. Everyone was dripping, beads of sweat rolling down their foreheads and onto the floor beneath them.

Henri started to giggle like a child. This was all a bit of a game to him and his henchmen.

"Well done, Mr. Chris," he said as Chris smirked and shook his head. Standing his ground was never going to cut it on this occasion, and he'd predicted a situation like this might arise. Chris looked at Matt and they both laughed with exasperation because that was all they could do in response to the total slapstick that had unfurled that night and throughout the entire trip.

As Matt and Chris gathered themselves, Henri made his way towards the door without saying "thank you" followed by Chink, Hwong and his goons. Henri threw his hand up in the air, pushing his feathers from his face, and looked back at them briefly.

"Speak soon. So long, bitcheeeeees."

"Fuck me, son. That is one unhinged psycho."

Matt, Chris, Arthur and Won waited until they could hear all the cars pull away outside.

"Jesus fucking Christ, son. What a fucking night."

"Dad, I can't even…Is it over? Is it really over now?"

"I think so."

"Arthur, Won, you both OK?" Chris asked.

They both nodded, Won understanding what Chris meant. Chris and Matt laughed again because it was all there was left to do.

"Should we talk about Henri's outfit?" said Matt as they made their way out of the door.

"Fuck me, son. He looked like a tart's window box."

Matt had heard that from his dad before, but it was usually in reference to how someone smelled: "He smelled like a tart's window box."

They made their way back to the hotel in silence, everyone other than Won taking the chance to close their eyes. Back at the hotel Won was back to his usual, overprotective self and refused to leave the car. Chris and Matt thanked him wholeheartedly for his efforts that night, said their goodnights with Arthur, and then found their way to the room.

Finally, Matt was finally able to tear off his clothes and get into something totally fresh that actually belonged to him. He thought for a few seconds about what to do with the random trousers before he instinctively stuffed them into the bin. Even though they had been useful at the time, he'd happily never see them ever again, plus Sarah would notice an odd pair of chinos when unpacking his suitcase. Shower, shit, and shuteye, that was all he could think of by this time. Luckily, the curtains let in very little light, so they'd have a decent kip even if it was already light outside. After a long shower his dad was giving it big Z's already and Matt collapsed onto the bed. As he drifted off into a deep slumber, he thought about Sarah. Must call Sarah first thing in the morning, he told himself.

Chapter 26 – The Last Days In China

When Matt finally woke up at two pm, his dad was still in full sleeping beauty mode and he didn't want to disturb him. Chris deserved as much sleep as he wanted.

Matt made his way into the toilet to freshen up, his trouser snake catching his eye. The plaster that Mr. Doctors and Nurses had slapped on his cock was now hanging off it, stained with blood. Matt thought that it was absolutely amazing how a good night's sleep can make something awful seem like a distant memory. Even though it had just happened less than twelve hours before, it felt like nothing more than a dream. But, my oh my, was he aware that this had been no dream. His penis was a bit bruised with a needle prick in the side, but it seemed to be in a decent state. The head was now back to its usual Darth Vader helmet shape, which was a pleasing outcome. He could feel some sensation in it once again and even pee standing up, which was a relative triumph at the end of the day.

Matt was more than relieved that he felt better now, his body finally accustomed to the Chinese diet. He stared at himself in the mirror.

"SHIT!" he yelled as he heard his dad turn over in bed. He looked out into the room, but he hadn't woken him up with his shriek.

The cocktail stick was still stuck in his ear. He'd completely forgotten about that little adornment. He muttered to himself as he poked at it.

"Ah well, Matt. It's all mind over matter, isn't it? If I can take a needle to the dick, then pulling a wooden cocktail stick from my ear should be a cinch, huh?"

Matt tugged at the cocktail stick and realised that he had suddenly turned into a big wuss. It was a lot sorer than he had imagined it would be and it took him a good ten minutes – on top of a hefty amount of screeching in a high-pitched voice – to extract it. With some perseverance it finally popped out. Surely that was the last thing he had to do to end what felt like an eternity of punishment? Ah, not quite.

Matt poked around the room a little more like he'd done the day before, but he still couldn't find where the hell his phone had disappeared to. Chris's phone was sitting on the bedside table charging though, so he swiped that, threw on some clothes, and made his way to a small terrace at the end of the floor below for some privacy.

Matt stepped into the lift, angling himself slightly as an old lady walked in after him. He didn't want her to spy his boner. It was reflexive now, that sort of response to being around other people even though he was no longer faced with the problem. He relaxed, comfortable he didn't have to worry about that any longer. As he and the old lady both stood there waiting for the lift door to close, Matt noticed she was wearing a hideous but brightly coloured silk blouse. It reminded him of Henri's outfit. He chuckled thinking of his dad's "tart's window box" comment just as he caught sight of the buttons on the shirt. They were disgusting. The thing was obviously as ancient as she was and had never been washed. The buttons were caked in dirt that looked like shit, and Matt would know because he'd definitely seen enough of that. It made him gag but he didn't vomit. After everything that he'd been through since coming to China, he still had a phobia of buttons and he realised he was not feeling quite as healthy as he would have hoped.

Matt eventually got to the terrace and plonked himself down. He was alone. As he sat in the stifling afternoon heat shaded by a small palm tree and listening to all the noise of the city in the background, he dreaded speaking to his wife. What the hell was he going to say to her? What the hell was she going to say to him? She would undoubtedly eat him alive.

He unlocked his dad's phone seeing a barrage of missed calls and text messages from Sarah, Chris P and his mum. Should he read those first? Hmm, maybe just a couple to get a flavour of what I'm in for, he thought.

He first opened one from Sarah. It read: *You tell him that he's done for. If he doesn't call me soon, I'll take the kids and fuck off.* Shit. It was bad.

He then opened one from Chris P. It read: *Chris, man, I don't know where you guys are at now or what you're up to, but you really need to call Linda or Sarah to let them know what's going on. I'm really getting it here. CALL THEM.*

He felt bad that Chris P had been forced to bear the brunt of his wife's anger. He'd been there and it wasn't fun. And he was about to go there again.

Matt was too scared to read any of the texts from his mum, so he just went for the kill. Here goes.

He dialled her number and there was a single ring before she answered.

"Matthew, what the fuck? Where the fuck have you been?"

"Babe, I'm so sorry. You would not believe everything that's been going on here. Really. It's been a nightmare. The worst of my life."

"Fuck me, Matt. You had me so worried. What the hell's been going on with you two? Why haven't you been in touch?"

"Well, first of all, I've lost my phone. I know I could have used my dad's phone, which I'm clearly doing now, but it's been insane. I've barely had a minute for anything."

"Because of what?"

"We got into a bit of trouble, darlin', which is a total understatement."

Matt spent the best part of half an hour fabricating everything that had been going on, making up lies about losing phones and getting lost. He refused to tell her about all of it; that the two of them had been swimming around in a big bathtub full of shit and piss, that they had been acting like stuntmen in a real-life action thriller film starring Arnie Schwarzenegger, that they had been followed by a bunch of gangsters with Christ knows what agenda in their heads, that they had been chowing down on a veritable feast of animal dicks and brains, that he'd got into a diarrhoea-covered mess shitting all over some angry Chinese dude's head, that they'd practically been held prisoner by gangster businessmen, and that they'd got into a huge restaurant fight, kung fu and all.

Matt told her about none of it, especially the fact that he'd had a close encounter with a few ladyboys and that he'd had a boner the size of Big Ben for the past few days after being drugged with some

Chinese herbal penis enhancer. He was back to safety, he no longer smelled like excrement, and his aching hard-on had finally calmed its tits down. All of that and his wife was also shockingly understanding now she'd finally heard from him. He couldn't believe his luck.

The whole way through the chat Sarah gasped, exclaiming shock at their bad luck getting lost and losing their phones. She went through the full range of emotions and reactions you'd expect of someone hearing from their partner they thought might be dead. She might have been sympathetic, but she certainly didn't hold back on letting him know how panicked she'd been.

Matt was utterly unsurprised. He had, after all, promised that he'd keep in touch regularly, so there was no wonder she was curious why he wasn't sticking to his word. He usually did.

Sarah also wasn't keen on holding back on what she thought of Chris P, the poor bugger that he was.

"Your best mate," she said. "He needs to seek medical help."

Matt laughed.

"It's not funny, Matt. Some of the stuff he told me was so fucked up it's unreal. Did he know what was going on?"

Chris P had been oblivious as to Matthew's whereabouts up until the frenzied phone call they had when he and his dad were barraged by a pile of furniture in their room, hiding from a bunch of gangsters that turned out to merely be the weird little Chinese man trying to get them to come out for dinner. After he'd received the call, he had not the slightest clue what to do. What could he have done from so far away, anyhow? Nothing, that's what. What he could do, though, once he knew about everything that had been going on with Matt and Chris in China, even if it was the briefest versions of the story Matt could pass on in the short time they had on the phone, was to cover for his pal. God knows, Matthew had covered for Chris P so many times in the time they'd known each other.

Matt laughed. "Not really, but he would have just been making sure you weren't worried."

"It's so not funny, Matt. Not at all. I'd rather have known what was going on than the things he came out with."

"Like what?"

"Well, first of all he just kept making excuses about why he couldn't talk to me, then he'd hang up for no reason. It was a farce. Then he'd lie to me saying he couldn't get hold of you."

"Ah, well, that was true mostly. He was only able to get in touch once, at the halfway point of all our misery."

"Right, well. Then he fed me stuff about your phone battery, blah blah."

"Again, mostly true."

Sarah then spent the best part of another half an hour ranting about all the crap Chris P had thrown at her, every lie and excuse more ridiculous than the last. Matt did his best not to laugh because that would not have been a wise plan.

There was voodoo magic of some sort preventing calls coming through; an old woman who had collapsed in the street and a subsequent rush to get her to the hospital; a lack of anyone understanding Chris and Matt's English; the fact that Chris P couldn't talk because he had to shave his arse and generally indulge in manscaping; an old guy in their hotel who'd somehow managed to sever his toe in the escalator and another subsequent rush to the hospital; Chris P faking white noise or pretending that he was going under a tunnel and the reception was cutting out; an episode of *South Park* he absolutely couldn't miss; an unpaid phone bill rendering Chris P unable to use his phone; Arthur having a violent allergic reaction to pizza and then puking over Matt's phone; Chris P breaking his fingers at work making him unable to answer the phone, even when he got out of hospital; excuses that he was drunk and/or high; Chris and Matt had got stuck in a lift and had to be rescued by emergency services. And what would any series of lies be without the trusty old helping a cute little puppy that had got itself stuck up a tree? You guessed it, the puppy also chewed on his already vomit filled phone, making it even more difficult to use now that the screen was all scratched and chipped.

"OK, so you weren't exaggerating in any shape or form when you said he needed mental help," Matt told her in response to all of this. But he couldn't help but think it's probably himself who was not quite the ticket. At this point in the game, was anyone more fucked up than him? Unlikely.

Even he couldn't quite comprehend some of the stuff his best buddy had come up with though. Next time he had to go on a trip like this – he shuddered at the thought – Matt would enlist a far more talented actor to cover for him. Give him his dues though, the guy had done a passable job under the circumstances.

"Your mum, by the way, is raging at you both."

That, Matt knew, was irrefutable. In some ways, he was more worried about facing her wrath on returning to the UK. Linda had been very insistent on not worrying Sarah. She was hooked on *The Sopranos*, obviously all about mobsters, and she had convinced herself that the pair had got themselves involved in some heavy stuff. The truth is they had, and it had all been pretty bad. Just not as bad as Linda had imagined, the two of them chained to a radiator with their faces smashed in or buried alive with no means of escape, or something like that.

"Now, THAT, I will deal with once I'm home. Babe, any chance you can fill her in before then? Although I'm sure my dad will give her a holler today once he's woken up. We finally got to have a decent kip last night. Glorious."

Sarah promised that she'd give Linda the – false – details and then had to rush off with a bit of pregnancy sickness.

Matt sat there relieved that the call was finally over and that Sarah wasn't even that mad with him. He thought it was funny how concern can quickly turn into anger.

Matt went back to the room where Chris was getting dressed after a shower. They were to meet Arthur for some lunch. Chris insisted they went to a pizza place he'd seen nearby. For that decision Matt would be eternally grateful. As he was gathering up his stuff to pack, Matt never found the lost phone. That would be another expense, he supposed. Never mind though, he told himself, with all that wonga coming his way soon the cost of a new mobile would be nothing at all.

Down in the lobby Arthur was there to greet them. He was looking fresh and revived too.

"You can say thank you later," he said with a grin on his face.

"Thank you. What do you mean?" Chris replied.

"For paying for an extra day this morning so you could sleep late."

"Christ, Arthur. I hadn't even thought about the fact we were supposed to check out today. Had you, Matt?"

"Nope. What time is it now? What time was check-out?" Matt said.

"It's 3.45pm. Check out at 11am. I wake up at 10.30am and ask to keep rooms for longer so we can sleep. We needed it, yes?"

"Ohhh yes," Chris and Matt sang in unison.

They went on to the restaurant where they ate pizza that didn't taste like the pizza back home, but more like a soggy omelette. They reminisced about all the craziness of the trip and Chris thanked Arthur for everything he'd done for them. Matt was sure they might have been better with someone else, but considering the situation at times he'd done OK, the strange little Chinese man.

They packed their bags into the car and Won drove them back to Beijing. The journey was thankfully uneventful. He took them straight to the airport first as Arthur was returning to Hong Kong that day. Chris and Matt weren't due to return home for another three days, three days they had factored in for sightseeing. To be honest neither of them could see it far enough, but it would have been too pricey to change the flights at such short notice. Besides, Won had been hired to stay with them for the rest of the trip.

As they dropped Arthur at the airport Matt was fairly surprised that it was actually quite an emotional send-off. Even though Arthur had been a pain in the dick for the most part, Matt had oddly grown to respect the fucked up little guy. He thought back to the movie *Big Trouble in Little China* and wondered if this business trip had been much different. Arthur shook their hands, thanking them both for an interesting business meeting.

"I have never been to Beijing before. This is my first visit to the home city of my homeland, and this gave me a reason to visit. I now have to return to Hong Kong and once again take up my role as Chief Buddhist monk at the temple."

Chris held Matt's shoulder and squeezed hard, reminding his son to bite his lip. Matt stood still on the spot, shocked to hear that Arthur had never been to Beijing and that he can actually cure people. Matt thought to himself, he has a fucking strange way of going about it. He then ironically assured himself that everyone in

Hong Kong must be running around with raging boners and cocktail sticks hanging out of their ears. Right, that all seems very probable.

As much as Matt was hoping for an apology from Arthur about the way events had unfolded, he knew this wasn't going to happen. Arthur was unable to see any wrongdoing on his part. Although he couldn't guess Arthur's age accurately, Matt estimated that he was a lot older and that this probably wasn't his first rodeo. He also guessed that there must be plenty of situations and places in China where these things go down on a regular basis. Was the story that Arthur was a Buddhist monk some kind of cover-up for his daily shenanigans? Was this guy really a well-respected member of the community? It was all so unclear.

Arthur turned to Matthew and Chris.

"I hope that you will visit me in Hong Kong and stay with me at my home. It would be my pleasure to show you around Hong Kong and the mainland manufacture industry of Shenzhen. In Shenzhen, they give excellent massage."

With that Chris stepped in front of Matthew to shut the conversation down. There was no doubt that, at the mention of massage, Matt was going to open his gob and blurt out something that Chris knew would be far from subtle.

"Thanks, Arthur. We will see you very soon. Be lucky."

Arthur nodded and made his way towards check-in. Won uttered something in Chinese and smiled, Arthur giving him the OK sign with his hand. As they drove away from the airport, Matt and Chris looked at each other, smirking in the back seat.

"There's something about him, isn't there? I think he's one of those people who grows on you, Matt. I've known him for twenty or so years, and he has never knocked me for a penny. Once I had to pay him $10,000 for something in advance, and I got exactly what I paid for. If he has anything to do with this deal, which he has had, it will be completed successfully. I am absolutely, one hundred percent sure of that."

His dad's words put Matt's mind at ease. Maybe Arthur's honesty and loyalty would rub off on this deal. Then again, putting a Buddhist monk in a situation where he's helping export unknown steel parts to a sanctioned country could be somewhat of a jinx.

During the rest of their time in China, Chris and Matt checked into a pleasant, problem-free hotel in Beijing. They did eat more Chinese food but in more touristy places with menus in English, so they were able to be a little – or a lot – more selective about what they put down their throats.

Arthur had preorganised a tour guide to help them check a few sights off their bucket list. She was pretty, a young Chinese lady called Fei Hong who was very polite and friendly towards them. Her English was decent too. The only problem was that she would end up arguing with Won in the car. As is the case with a lot of tour guides in Asian countries, they want to take the tourists to places that they've made deals with. How it works is that they take customers to these places, such as restaurants and small attractions like silk factories, and in return they get a commission. Won, who was more than aware of what Matt and Chris had been through in the past few days, wanted to let them have it their own way. He communicated this in broken English, but the guys got the gist of it.

All in they managed to take in the majority of the sights they'd dreamed about seeing before leaving the UK. These included: The Great Wall of China, The Forbidden City, The Summer Palace, Tiananmen Square, and The Temple of Heaven.

Matt was done in after recent events and really struggled around all the tourist destinations. There were so many steps everywhere they went, loads more steps than he could ever imagine. But Chris, who was older and done in too, loved it. Matt didn't complain. Well, not much anyway. After everything his dad had been forced to endure because of him, the man deserved to enjoy the sights.

In the evenings Won would remain with his precious vehicle as he'd done the whole time. Matt and Chris would spend their time having drinks in the packed hotel lobby. Every evening they saw Fei Hong there. The first time they noticed her, Matt offered to buy her a drink, but she pretended she didn't know them. It was really strange, and neither Matt not Chris had a clue what her game was. Then the next day, she pretended to have no idea what they were talking about as if claiming it hadn't been her at the bar. It definitely had been even if she was done up like a dish of fish compared to what she was wearing during the day. They eventually got it out of Won that she was a prostitute. So, that's what her game was. Now that was something they hadn't expected and a detail that Matt would be keeping from his wife along with the ladyboys and boner stories.

All of the sightseeing out of the way, Matt and Chris finally came to their final day in China. For Matt, this was undoubtedly the best day of the trip. He knew that this hell was finally over. They'd got through the worst time of their lives and everything would soon return to normal when they got back to their family, their business, and soon a huge cash injection. Never, and he meant absolutely never, would he plan to return to this godforsaken country again. It had been their own personal – but much more nightmarish – version of the film *Lost in Translation*, and they were finished being lost in it. Time for home. Time for steaks. Time for good wine. Time for a kiss from Sarah. Time to hug his kids. Time to give Chris P a clip around the ear. Time for home. Home, home, sweet bloody home. It was going to be wonderful.

When Won dropped them at the airport for the flight home, Chris awarded him a $500 tip. It was a lot but Chris was so grateful for everything that Won had done for them, and so was Matt. The driver was over the moon explaining that this was a month's wages. He also gave them his phone number to call if they ever found themselves back in China. Chris laughed at the suggestion.

"I don't think so, my friend, but it won't hurt to take your number just in case. Here's our number too," he said handing him Matt's mobile number. In retrospect, it was probably a bit daft to give Won Matt's mobile number seeing as he'd lost his phone, but no doubt Matt would be able to keep his old number once he managed to sort out a new phone once he'd returned back to the UK. "And if you ever want a holiday in England, Won, you let us know."

Won thanked them, deciding it was time to break the news that his name is actually pronounced, "Whon, not Won." Chris and Matt were both a little embarrassed that they'd been pronouncing it wrong the whole time, and Matt wondered why Won hadn't said anything until that point. In general, Matt thought, it was nuts that he and his dad were learning more about their driver in the last fifteen minutes of their trip than they had the entire time there.

It took him a while to get it all out, but he told them a fair few details about himself. He let them know that he was getting married next year and that the $500 tip would go a long way in paying for everything. Just before they said their goodbyes, Won told Chris and Matt that his boss was a very powerful man known as Ugg Lee who owned a huge fleet of cars – hundreds in fact – and had a significant property portfolio. At some point in this final story Matt stopped paying attention to Won's words, trying his best not to laugh at the name Ugg Lee. Once Won had gone Matt had to say, "I bet he's a good-looking bugger."

Chapter 27 – Homecoming

Chris and Matt landed at Heathrow Airport just after 3.30pm, a little over twenty minutes earlier than expected due to good tailwinds. Being back on British soil was so much more exciting to Matt than it had ever been after returning from any holiday. In fact, coming back from most trips abroad had always been a bit depressing, but not this time.

There was a long delay getting the bags out on the carousel and then the queue through passport control and customs was insanely large as it seemed a billion flights had landed at exactly the same time. Matt wanted to stop off in duty free to pick up a few bits and bobs too. In all the commotion he hadn't even thought about picking up gifts for anyone, and he was scared that if he turned up empty handed those hands might be lopped off.

Sarah had sent a text the day before to say that she and Linda had organised a nice welcome back dinner for him and his dad. Even though they'd been bad with their communication, they were assured they'd be welcomed home with open arms. Everyone was simply happy that they were still alive. Matt was sure he'd still get a bit of a rollicking from his mum, but he was prepared for that anyway.

It was now 6pm and they were to head to Nino's in South Woodford by 7.30, a restaurant that everyone was a huge fan of. It was a fancy place, a silver service sort of affair. There, they'd get treated to those juicy fillet steaks Matt had been dreaming of, with all the trimmings you could ask for. He couldn't wait. They eventually managed to secure a taxi after waiting in a long line.

On arrival at Nino's the place was closed.

Matt looked at Chris, confused. "Eh? Is it a joke or something?"

They got out of the cab and went to have a peek through the window. There was nobody in sight, all the lights were off, and there was a sign on the door stating the restaurant was closed for a few days due to refurbishment.

"Check your phone, Dad. There must be some sort of mistake."

Matt was gutted. No steaks for him. He guessed his streak of bad luck wasn't quite finished messing him over just yet.

Chris looked at his phone which he'd left on silent, and they'd missed a couple of calls and a few text messages.

"Ah, your mum's saying that the restaurant had to close unexpectedly for some repairs."

Well, they'd worked that much out. There was now a big catered welcome party at God's Own Junkyard. Now, that sounds more like it, Matt thought.

Chris and Matt had a laugh about the balls up and hailed another taxi to head to God's Own Junkyard. When they pulled up there was no doubt that this place was open. All the spectacular neon signs were turned on, there was music pouring out the doors, and Matt could hear the rumble of voices from inside. They were mere metres away from their family now, the people they'd gone on this trip to make money for.

As they walked through the door everyone was there, all the family and friends they loved. Even Chris P was there, standing right next to Sarah. Somehow, she'd managed not to kill him.

"BABE," she screamed at Matt, throwing her arms around him. "You're back, you big shit."

It felt good to be in Sarah's arms finally. She drowned him in kisses as Chris received a similar welcome from Linda.

Chris P jumped in. "Can I steal your hubby for a hug?"

"Can you fuck, you nut job. He's mine."

Everyone burst out laughing and that set the tone for the rest of the night. It was full of fun, good nosh (even if it wasn't steak), booze, and laughter. Chris and Matt regaled their made up Chinese experiences to an audience with open ears. Matt would get around to talking to Chris P about the missing details another time – if ever. Nobody could believe what they'd heard about China, and that was the completely watered-down version. Linda told them that they were as mental as Matt's Uncle Kirk.

It was amazing to be back. A couple of times during the party, Matt sat outside alone looking up at the sky. They were in the winter months and the air was cold, fresh and crisp. He was overcome by a real sense of guilt about not telling his wife and mum the full truth about the trip.

"Some things are better not spoken about, Matt," said a voice coming from a dark corner of the junkyard. It was Chris P.

"How long have you been watching me?"

"Oh, not long, mate. I was just having a quick snooze. I've been drinking all day."

Matt wasn't shocked in the slightest as this wasn't unusual for Chris P. If he wasn't working, then he was somewhere drinking. Matt wasn't bothered about this though as Chris P was what Matt called "a happy pisshead". Matt had always been a firm believer of the saying that "everybody likes a drink, but nobody likes a drunk", and Chris P fell into the former category. He certainly didn't have a drinking problem. Well, maybe by medical definitions, but it wasn't problematic by any practical definition, and he never got mean when he was drinking.

"Chris, you fucker. I think you got me in more shit than I would have been if you'd said nothing at all."

Chris P burst out laughing. "Oh, come on. I had to say something, and she kept catching me at bad times. She just wouldn't leave off. One of the times she called me I was in the shower shaving my arse. Of course, she didn't believe me, but you know me. I like a bit of manscaping from time to time. Keep it all tidy and all that jizz."

Matt laughed, nodding.

"I promised you that I wouldn't let you down. Mate, though, you try shaving your arse with one hand while trying to talk on the phone with the other. It's quite a challenge. I'll tell you that for nothing."

Matt arrived at the decision that Chris P was, without a shadow of a doubt, a complete lunatic. He had nothing against a guy looking after himself and keeping it all trim down below, but only Chris P would try to shave his own arse.

They both erupted with laughter together. Even though they were both so different they had the same sense of humour in some respects, and Matt considered if he should tell his best pal the full truth about what had happened in China. He thought about what he had been through and wondered if he'd think any less of him. He chose not to say anything at that time though.

"How about the next time you go there you take me, Matt? You never know, we might have some fun."

Matt vigorously shook his head, fear in his eyes.

"No. A resounding no. Mate, we've had some adventures in our time, haven't we?"

"Oh, yeah. We have indeed," Chris P said without thinking about it.

"And we've also had our fair share of problems, but China is one place I do not belong, and it is no place for you either."

Matt was sure that this might be Chris P's cue to probe further into what went on, but he obviously decided to stick to his own advice that some things are better left unsaid. He took a long swig of his beer and lifted Matt up under his arm.

"Come on, mate. Let's get you back to your homecoming party so you can enjoy it instead of sitting out here looking morose. Whatever it is that you're not saying, no good has ever come of dwelling on the past. Look to the future, and it's all right there in that room." With that the pair returned inside.

The party went into the small hours, and after Linda had had one glass of wine too many she pulled Matt aside. Oh, here we go, thought Matt. The wrath has finally arrived.

"Listen, son, I know there's more to what you and your dad are telling us. I don't even want to know what went on out there. I really don't."

Matt tried to interrupt to assure her what she'd been told about was really all that happened, although it was a lie.

"No, no. Don't interrupt me," she said as she puffed away on a fag. "Whatever happened, I need you to know that if you ever leave your pregnant wife in a panicked state like that ever again, you'll have me to answer to. You hear me?"

"Yeah, Mum, I hear you. It's just that…"

"I told you not to interrupt. All the while I was convinced that you'd met some grizzly fate at the hands of some awful gangsters out there, I had to keep my shit together for her. Do you know how hard that was?"

Matt nodded, keeping his mouth shut.

"I needed to keep my concerns from her because that sort of worry can cause a woman to miscarry. That's all I'm going to say now. Next time do better."

The bollocking over, they returned to the festivities, and no more was said about it. That had always been Linda's style; firm but fair.

She'd have a go at Matt, or anyone for that matter, for doing something shitty, but she'd let it go after she'd said her piece instead of hanging on to anger for ages afterwards. Before, he'd even heard her screaming with rage one minute and whistling away another. It was quite a trait.

With everyone sufficiently fed and watered, and much merriment had, they all called it a night. Matt and Chris were both desperate to get back to their own beds.

As Matt and Sarah hit the hay she conked out much faster than him, at peace knowing her hubby was next to her once more. Matt was exhausted but he lay wondering about whether he should go into work the next day or just take a day to himself before getting back to it. Sarah had a busy day the next day, so he figured he might as well head in for a bit just to make sure everything was ticking over OK. Linda and Sarah had both been in every day while he and his dad were in China, so he was sure nothing disastrous could have happened. Anyhow, it was always nice to see for yourself, he thought, as he allowed the sleep to take him with all its might.

The next morning Matt woke up at midday, which was a lot later than he'd usually kip for. Although he'd decided the night before that he'd go into the office that day, he couldn't be arsed setting an alarm and getting up early. Sarah had already gone out leaving a note that she'd see him just before dinner time.

After a quick cup of coffee, a couple of bits of toast, and a hot shower, Matt headed to Electro Signs. He wasn't sure if his dad would be around that day or not, but when he got there his dad was in his office.

"Oh, I thought you might be taking the day off, son."

"I was thinking the same thing. Does this make us workaholics?"

"Na, just idiots who like what they do too much."

They both laughed.

"Fancy heading out for a bit of lunch in a couple of hours?" Chris asked.

"I'm in, as long as it's not Chinese food," Matt said as he made a retching sound.

They both laughed but he was deadly serious.

"Mum not in today?"

"Na, she's working on the accounts from home. She can concentrate better there."

"Oh, I've no doubt about it," Matt said as he popped through to his own office.

He threw himself down in his large exec chair, swivelling around a little as his computer powered up. His first course of action was to order a new mobile phone online. He didn't take too long picking one, opting for a mid-range Samsung flip phone with the intention of ordering something a bit flashier when the cash from the deal comes through. He pressed the order button on eBay and turned to his emails next. Matt assumed that, because he'd been gone for almost a full week, his email inbox would be inundated with important stuff to address, but there were oddly just a few bumph emails that he was uninterested in. However, there was one in particular that he needed to prioritise.

A new customer had been in touch. In his email the guy said that he was in the middle of opening up a new shoe shop in Soho. Like his dad, Matt had managed to make quite a name for himself on the neon scene in his own right, and not just as the son of Chris Bracey. This particular customer had heard of Matt and the work he was doing over at God's Own Junkyard, rather than the work of Electro Signs as a company itself. He said that he wanted something that nobody else had ever done before, something totally fresh that would impress customers and other businesses alike. And he was very complimentary, stating that he could think of nobody better than Matt to be tasked with the challenge.

After reading the email Matt sat back in his chair, flattered. He chewed the fat for a bit, mulling over some ideas for something that nobody in Soho had ever done before. Matt's mind worked fast, and it didn't take long before he came up with his idea, which was essentially a polished mirror box with a letter-sized hole allowing customers to peep through to see the new glam shoe of the week. He'd seen something similar at the Tate Modern before, but he couldn't recall what had been inside. It wasn't expensive high-heel shoes, of that he was sure. On the front of the box would be a powerful neon sign made from rare flamingo pink glass reading: "Peep shoe". It was genius, even if he did say so himself. It combined the guy's business – a shoe shop – and everything that Soho used to stand for.

Matt mentally patted himself on the back and regaled the idea to the customer who replied quickly to say that he loved the proposal and to go ahead as soon as possible. Matt was back doing what he did best, which was coming up with the most innovative ideas money could buy and ones that clients went mad for. The idea had been inspired by the film *Scarface*, which is what Matt always did; he used the things he'd come across in life to shape his neon artworks – just like his dad had always done. He'd use good experience and bad experiences for this purpose, and he could even conceive of taking what happened in China and transforming that into a creative vision.

As he sat there at his desk, Matt thought about what Chris P had told him outside of the homecoming party at God's Own Junkyard. Yeah, Matt, he said to himself, don't dwell on the past but think about the future.

His emails done and his phone ordered, what was next? Matt considered contacting Iran right there and then to say that everything was set after the trip to China, then hesitated. He went through to Chris's office.

"Dad, is it too soon to email Kuwait to tell them that the goods are en route?"

Chris still unaware the steel was going to Iran.

"Erm, I don't think so. I mean, it's all signed, sealed and delivered now. So, I guess there's no reason why we should hold off on that. I thought about it this morning when I got in but figured it was best just to leave it all to you. This was your deal, son, remember that. I was just along for the ride. And what a hell of a ride it was. Especially with Won – sorry, Whhhhooooon – at the wheel of the car."

"Thanks, Dad. I'll go ahead and get in touch now."

Back in his own office he did just that, drafting a brief email letting Iran know that the goods will be en route very soon, with an anticipated arrival date of four to six weeks. Afterwards, as he flicked through the huge pile of mail left on his desk – again, without much of real interest to him – his email server pinged as a reply from Iran came through within ten minutes.

Their response, strangely all in caps, couldn't have been any more favourable:

THAT'S GREAT. THANK YOU SO MUCH FOR THE UPDATE. WE WILL BE IN TOUCH VERY SOON ONCE WE HAVE INITIATED THE BANK TRANSFER TO WIRE YOU THE AGREED PAYMENT.

Sweet, Matt thought, again swivelling around in his chair. He shouted through to Chris. "Dad, they got back to me already. They seem happy and said they'd give us a holler when they had transferred the money."

Matt heard quick footsteps as his dad came through. He sounded as excited as Matt was. "Already? Blimey, that was a quick reply."

"Yeah, I know right? Perhaps they're just as happy as we are everything is working out."

"Yeah, maybe. Listen, so how about we head off in a bit and get lunch earlier. And, you know, celebrate?"

Matt looked at his email inbox and the pile of mail on his desk. "Yeah, let's do it, it won't hurt to have one or two. I guess we deserve it."

As Matt stood up Chris launched towards him, embracing Matt in a hug so tight that it could have crushed his internal organs.

"Nice one, Matt. Job well done. SO fucking proud of you. You did it. You pulled the impossible off."

Matt was chuffed at the way his dad was reacting.

"Give me about an hour and I'm good to go," Chris said as he went back to his desk.

Matt sat down until his dad was ready, closing his eyes. All these years things had been good. Business had been great. But not always. Sometimes it had been a real bloody struggle. And now? Well, things were about to change for the better.

He sat there – his head tilted back and eyes still closed – daydreaming about what he'd be able to do with all of that money. Finally, he and Sarah would be able to give the kids a bigger house to grow up in. Maybe they could even have more kids to fill it.

Matt had always hoped and prayed that one day he'd manage to find a situation that would allow him to make enough money so that he was truly comfortable. He didn't necessarily want to be absolutely loaded, although he would obviously never argue with that. However, what he did really want was to have enough money behind him so that he felt secure. He wanted to feel safe in the knowledge that, if anything was ever to happen to him and he'd no longer be around, Sarah and the kids would be looked after. It wasn't an unreasonable thought given what an unlucky shit Matt was, China's events being a testament to that.

Matt thought about the weather in the UK. His big wish, apart from the financial security of his family, was to have an outdoor pool. He wasn't totally sure the weather was conducive to that, but it could be nice on occasion. In fact, fuck it, he thought, with that kind of money maybe I can get an indoor pool – even better. And a new car; he wanted a new car. Although, if they had more kids, it might have to be something sensible. Nah, he thought, there are plenty of nice motors that can ferry a tonne of kids around just fine. Maybe a new Land Rover? Or a Range Rover? He was getting carried away, but why not?

But one thing Matt refused to do was become an arsehole who made it big and then just jacked in his work. That wasn't his style in the slightest. Even once he'd made his first million – which, of course would be split with his dad – he'd still want to come into work every day. He liked the idea of that, having a real purpose in life. He enjoyed what he did, partially because he was good at it, but also because he got to work with his family. It was the ideal set up, every day a bigger adventure than the last and never a dull moment to be had.

Neon was a big part of Matt's life. Not only was it beautiful, but every day that he worked with it he was able to see someone else attain a great deal of pleasure from it too. That was something that made him incredibly happy; to watch other people smile, filled with joy, especially knowing that he'd contributed to that in some way. Matt called into mind some of his favourite neon pieces, the ones he'd designed over the years. They all meant something different to him, each inspired by different moments and periods of his life. Now that he came to think about it, a few of them had been wholly applicable throughout this deal: "HOLY FUCK", "THE ONLY

WAY OUT IS THROUGH", "DIRTY BITCH", "TRUST YOUR OWN MADNESS", and "FAITH IS THE LIGHT THAT GUIDES YOU THROUGH THE DARKNESS".

Matt couldn't believe just how apt these were given the past week, and it might be that he didn't need to use his experiences in China to inspire new pieces because many of his older pieces summed it all up. He also considered how he'd come up with something that captured everything he felt about that business trip without raising any questions as to where the inspiration came from. After all, Sarah knew that his work was based on his own experiences. She'd definitely want to know what it meant. His thoughts were interrupted by the sudden realisation that he had something to do before he could leave the office for the day. He shouted through to Chris.
"Damn, Dad. I totally forgot. Can you pick a sign to send to Tianjin from the junkyard?"
"Yeah, good shout, Matt. That had slipped my mind too."
Matt heard Chris make a call to one of the lads at their factory, telling them to go grab sign number 127 from row 9 out of God's Own Junkyard and then box it up with everything. By "everything" his dad had meant all of the power supplies, the cable, and any relevant accessories.
"And make sure you don't bloody break it. It's very, very important," Chris said loudly and assertively to whoever he was speaking to at the factory.
The lads at the factory were usually pretty good at following instructions, particularly when those instructions came down from Chris. Matt was a bit of a softer touch with the factory lot, but Chris meant business. Nobody wanted to upset him, and he especially hated having to ask for something to be done twice. He was a busy guy, and this was a waste of his precious time.
Matt heard Chris hang up, but before he could shout through the call was over. Matt had forgotten to tell Chris something important. He called the factory and asked who it was that his dad had just spoken to. Pete, the worker who Matt was on with, said it was him.
"Your dad let me know what to do. Is there anything else?"

"Yeah, mate. Forgot to let my dad know that I've left detailed instructions for packaging up the crate at the office reception."

"No worries. I haven't done anything yet, so I'll head out there now and pick them up."

"Pete, listen to me. I know my dad said to make sure it's all done right, but I just need to reiterate that it is absolutely vital that you follow that plan to the millimetre. Not a single mistake to be made. You get me? Any mistake here and we could potentially lose a shit tonne of money."

"Gotcha, boss. Noted."

"Any problems, you let me know. OK? I'm in the office for a bit longer and then you can get me on my dad's mobile number. I've lost my phone and haven't got a new one yet."

Matt hung up and then thought that he should have asked which sign it was that his dad had picked. He considered calling back to check, but then he decided not to bother. His dad was an artist with impeccable taste and a strong awareness of the importance of this deal, so there was no chance in hell that he would have selected anything other than one of the best signs they had to send. Matt was confident his dad would have picked something classy. Chris was many things and one of those was a perfectionist.

He left his dad to finish whatever work he needed to bash on with for the next hour while he browsed the internet, making sure that he'd made a decent choice regarding his phone. After looking at about thirty of them he felt like he could have made a better selection, but it was all swings and roundabouts really. He'd just leave the order as it was.

An hour later the phone rang, and Chris answered before Matt could get to it. Matt listened through to his dad's office, curious as to who it was.

He heard Chris say, "Good job, mate. Yup, that's the one. Mhm, OK, perfect. Good stuff."

Matt heard his dad hang up the phone before there were heavy footsteps through to his own office. Chris popped his head around the door.

"That's it. It's done. They're finished packaging it up now and they're gonna arrange the shipping as soon as possible. Pete said you called to let him know about instructions, but that there's no address for shipping on there?"

"Ah, fuck. I'll call them now with the address."

"I'd send them an email if I was you. That way you can be sure that they don't fuck it up. And ask them to take a picture of the address once it's on the box and then send it to you. You know, so you can double, triple check."

"Good idea."

As Matt started to type the email, his dad carried on chatting.

"Have you organised shipping yet?"

"I'll do that after this email is sent off."

"So, the box will be collected and dispatched by airfreight before the end of the day tomorrow. Is that right?"

"Yeah, spot on. I'll use our usual shippers to get it to Tianjin, shall I?"

"Don't see why not, son."

"Yeah, thought so. They've never let us down before. Still feels a bit strange to be shipping to China. We usually only receive from China, eh?"

"Very true. But nothing about any of this has felt anything less than strange."

They both laughed as Chris handed Matt a piece of paper.

"Here, two things. That's the address. Just check it before you email the factory to make sure it's right. It probably is, but just so I can shelf that in my mind and we can go grab lunch without me worrying."

Matt scanned over it. "Yup, all gravy, Dad. Speaking of gravy, pie and mash for lunch?"

"Just what I had in mind, the other thing I need to say is what happened in China, stays in China, got it?"

Matt waited for a few seconds before answering, his Dad was deadly serious.

Matt gave a firm but then cheeky response "Affirmative Gov, Why what happened in China?"

Chris gave Matt a wink and left to finish up.

As Matt prepared to leave, he threw the enormous pile of junk mail in the bin. All was well, it was business as usual, and everybody was pleased that he and his dad were back where they belong behind the company's reins.

"Finish doing that and then let's head off. I'll be outside in the car waiting for you, son."

"Nice one. Won't be much longer."

Matt sent the email to Pete, double-checking everything. Then, while he was on the phone speaking to Sheila over at the shipping company they had been using for almost a decade now, he got a reply back from Pete. He'd taken a picture of the address label as requested and everything was good to go.

Everything was handled and it was time to eat. Matt pulled on his jacket, thinking that it felt weird wearing one after the warm weather in China. He'd take jackets over that place any day, but luckily he wouldn't be returning any time soon – or ever for that matter.

Just as Matt stepped out of his office the phone rang. He paused for a second, wondering if he should ignore it, but then thought better of – just in case it was something to do with this sign being sent off.

"Hello, Electro Signs. Matt speaking," he said picking up the phone. His face dropped as disappointment crept across it. Matt listened intently, mouthing the words "fuck", "shit" and "bugger" repeatedly. Once the call, which had lasted no more than a few minutes, was terminated, Matt stood for a minute, palms down on his desk and looking out of the window. Now he was able to do more than mouth the profanities. He slammed his hands down on the desk, and out of his mouth fell a loud "FUCK!"

Chris, who had just been leaning against the car door until Matt came down, heard his son raise his voice and ran up the stairs to the office.

"What? What's going on?"

Matt simply stared at Chris for about ten seconds before he could get past his frustration and let his dad know what the call was about.

"Matt, what is it? Is it Sarah? Is it the baby?"

"No, no. Shit, nothing like that, Dad."

"Then what? Tell me."

"You're not gonna like this, but I just got off a quick call from China. I mean, they called me."

"And?"

"Well, it turns out that it's not all going to be plain sailing like we thought. As they say in one of my favourite films, 'Houston, we have a problem'!"

"Oh, for fuck's sake. Here we go."

The End

Printed in Great Britain
by Amazon